**Invisible
Management**

C000120934

010220

To Julie

Very best regret

[signature]

■ SMART STRATEGIES SERIES ■

Invisible Management

The Social Construction of Leadership

Edited by

Sven-Erik Sjöstrand,
Jörgen Sandberg and
Mats Tyrstrup

THOMSON
——*——™
LEARNING   Australia • Canada • Mexico • Singapore • Spain • United Kingdom • United States

Invisible Management

Copyright © 2001 Sven-Erik Sjöstrand, Jörgen Sandberg and Mats Tyrstrup

Thomson Learning is a trademark used herein under licence.

For more information, contact Thomson Learning, Berkshire House, 168–173 High Holborn, London, WC1V 7AA or visit us on the World Wide Web at: http://www.thomsonlearning.co.uk

British Library Cataloguing-in-Publication Data
A catalogue record for this book is available from the British Library

ISBN 1-86152-767-5

First edition published 2001 Thomson Learning

Typeset by LaserScript Limited, Mitcham, Surrey
Printed in the UK by TJ International, Padstow, Cornwall

Contents

About the editors and authors

Lena Andersson, MSc in Economics and Business Administration at the University of Uppsala (Sweden), is a researcher at the Centre for Management and Organization attached to the Economic Research Institute at the Stockholm School fo Economics (SSE). Andersson has also studied rhetoric at the University of Iowa and the College of Alameda in the United States, and at the universities of Örebro and Uppsala in Sweden. Her research focuses on the ways in which leaders communicate, and how they use verbal and non-verbal communication strategies in different situations.

Gunnar Ekman, PhD and assistant professor in Business Administration at the SSE, is doing research at the Centre for Management and Organization attached to the Economic Research Institute at the SSE. He is also responsible for several of SSE's executive programmes. His writings include his thesis (in Swedish) *From Text to Truncheon* (Från text till batong, 1999). His current research interests include the management of large organizations, where he challenges the traditional view of leadership as a hierarchical phenomenon.

Daniel Ericsson, MSc in Economics and Business Administration at the SSE, is a researcher at the Centre for Management and Organization attached to the Economic Research Institute at the SSE. He is also a lecturer at the SSE. His current research and teaching are both concerned with organization and management, and his doctoral thesis deals with the problems surrounding the construction and organization of creativity. In a recent publication in Swedish, *A Pedagogy for Working Life* (Pedagogik för arbetslivet, 2000), he draws attention to how conceptions of creativity can represent an obstacle to organizational learning.

Charlotte Holgersson, MSc in Economics and Business Administration at the SSE, is a researcher at the Centre for Management and Organization attached to the Economic Research Institute at the SSE. She is also a lecturer at the same school. Holgersson is active in a research programme called *Organization and Gender*, where she is conducting a project on the recruitment of managing directors. Her published works (in Swedish) include chapters in *Leaders, Power and Gender* (Ledare, makt och kön, 1997) and in *Irony and Sexuality* (Ironi och sexualitet, 1998), and a book, *Chairmen on the recruitment of CEOs* (Styrelseordförandes utsagor om vd-rekrytering, 1998).

Pia Höök, MSc in Economics and Business Administration at the SSE, is a researcher at the Centre for Management and Organization attached to the Economic Research Institute at the SSE. She also teaches students in SSE's Master's programme. Within the framework of an ongoing research programme on *Organization and Gender,* she is conducting a research project on executive development programmes that target gender-equality issues. She has co-authored two (Swedish) books *Leaders, Power and Gender* (Ledare, makt och kön, 1997) and *Irony and Sexuality* (Ironi och sexualitet, 1998).

Markus Kallifatides, MSc in Economics and Business Administration at the SSE, is a researcher at the Centre for Management and Organization attached to the Economic Research Institute at the SSE. He also teaches students in the Master's programme at the same school. He is currently working on a project addressing the issue of responsibility in business organizations. His published works include the report *Leadership and the Ethics of Late Modernity* (1998).

Annelie Karlsson Stider, PhD and assistant professor in Business Administration at the SSE, is a researcher at the Centre for Management and Organization attached to the Economic Research Institute at the SSE. She is studying the management of large, established family businesses and has published *The Family Business as an Heirloom* (1996) and (in Swedish) *The Family and the Firm* (Familjen & Firman 2000). She is a member of the board of the *Family Business Network* – a network of family-business owners and associated researchers in Sweden.

Jörgen Sandberg, PhD and associate professor in Business Administration at the SSE, is doing research at the Centre for Management and Organization attached to the Economic Research Institute at the SSE. His teaching and research both focus on management issues, in particular learning and competence in organizations, and on research methods. In addition to several articles in international scientific journals, Sandberg's published works include *Human Competence at Work – An interpretative approach* (1994), and as co-author (in Swedish) *Management and Understanding* (Ledning och förståelse, 1998).

Sven-Erik Sjöstrand has been Professor of Management at the Stockholm School of Economics (SSE) since 1978, and is the current holder of the Matts Carlgren Chair in Management. He is also a member of the SSE board, chairman of the board of SSE's Economic Research Institute, and Director of the Institute's Centre for Management and Organization, which employs more than 20 full-time researchers working in the fields of management, leadership and organization theory. Sjöstrand also serves on the board of a number of research foundations and corporations. His published books in Swedish, Finnish and German amount to over 25, most of them relating to (strategic) management and organizational theory. In addition to a number of articles published in international scientific journals, Sjöstrand's publications in English include several books, among them *Organization Myths* (1979; together with Westerlund), *Institutional Change* (1993), *On Economic Institutions* (1996; together with Groenewegen and Pitelis) and *The Two Faces of Management. The Janus Factor* (1997).

Birgitta Södergren, PhD and assistant professor in Business Administration at the SSE, is a researcher at the Centre for Management and Organization attached to the Economic Research Institute at the SSE. She is also a teacher in both the Master's and the Executive programmes at the same school. Her areas of interest are organizational change and learning in organizations. Södergren's publications (in Swedish) include *When the Pyramids Have Fallen* (När Pyramiderna Rivits, 1988), *Decentralization* (Decentralisering, 1992), *Leadership for Learning* (Lärandets Ledarskap, 1996) and *Towards a Horizontal Organization?* (På väg mot en horisontell organisation? 1997). Her current research focuses on occupational conditions in knowledge-intensive organizations.

Johan Söderholm, *Econ Lic* in Business Administration at the SSE, is carrying out research on management control in an organizational perspective. His licentiate thesis, *Control in Decentralized Organizations* (Målstyrning av decentraliserade organisationer, 1998), focused on both financial and non-financial aspects in governing decentralized businesses. He is also engaged in management training at SSE's subsidiary for executive education.

Johan Stein, PhD and associate professor in Business Administration at the SSE, is a researcher at the Centre for Management and Organization attached to the Economic Research Institute at the SSE. He is also a teacher in both the Master's and the Executive programmes at the SSE. His publications in Swedish include *Learning in and between Organizations* (Lärande inom och mellan organisationer, 1996) and *Leadership Rhetoric*

(Övertygandets ledarskap, 1999), and in English, *Strategy Formation and Managerial Agency* (1993). Stein has also published several articles in international scientific journals.

Mats Tyrstrup, PhD and assistant professor in Business Administration at the SSE, is a researcher at the Centre for Management and Organization attached to the Economic Research Institute at the SSE. He is also a teacher in the Master's and Executive programmes at the same school. In addition, Tyrstrup is affiliated with the Centre for Advanced Studies in Leadership, which is associated with the SSE group. His publications (in Swedish) include his dissertation *Managerial Work* (Företagsledares arbete, 1993) and chapters in two anthologies focusing on managerial leadership. At present he is exploring ways in which conceptions of time are expressed in corporate organizing and leadership. Tyrstrup is also engaged in consultancy work and is a member of boards of several organizations.

Anna Wahl, PhD and associate professor in Business Administration, has been conducting research since 1985 at the Centre for Management and Organization attached to the Economic Research Institute at the SSE. During the same period she has been teaching students of management at the same school. She is currently involved in an ongoing research programme, *Organization and Gender,* which comprises a series of subprojects addressing gender issues in management and leadership. Her own research focuses on the way in which constructions of leadership and gender vary in different types of organization. Wahl's most recent (co-authored) book in Swedish is *Irony and Sexuality* (Ironi och sexualitet, 1998). She has previously published (in Swedish) *Organization and Gender* (Könsstrukturer i organisationer, 1990) and (in English) *Leaders, Power and Gender* (1997).

Acknowledgements

This book would not have been possible without the intellectual inspiration and support provided by the environment and the researchers of the Economic Research Institute (EFI) at the Stockholm School of Economics (SSE).

The empirical research that provides the platform for all thirteen chapters has been conducted at the Centre for Management and Organization – a centre that was established at SSE/EFI as long ago as 1951 by a pioneer[1] of empirical management studies, Professor Sune Carlsson (1909–99).

Economic support for the research projects reported in this book has been provided by several Swedish research foundations, both public and private, including Riksbankens Jubileumsfond, Rådet för Arbetslivsfrågor, Humanistiskt Samhällsvetenskapliga forskningsrådet, Tom Hedelius och Jan Wallanders forskningsstiftelse, the Volvo Foundation and the Family Business Network of Sweden. We are deeply grateful to them all.

We have also had continuous backing from several large Scandinavian and German firms, where most of the empirical studies have been carried out. Access to these business organizations, to their leading actors and to a great variety of corporate documentation has been a necessary condition for conducting the kind of research reported in this book. We thank all those who have been involved in our various research projects for their support.

We are also grateful to our language advisers Nancy Adler and Kelly Olsson for their patient help at all stages in the production of the different chapters of this volume.

Finally, our thanks go to Ingrid Kollberg for her excellent, persistent and thorough work in preparation of the final manuscript.

Stockholm 1 November 2000

Sven-Erik Sjöstrand
Jörgen Sandberg
Mats Tyrstrup

Note

1 Professor Carlsson's internationally best known book is *Executive Behavior* (Stockholm: Strömbergs, 1951).

To the reader

This book on invisible management is the result of several years of empirical and theoretical research carried out at the Centre for Management and Organization Studies at the Economic Research Institute at the Stockholm School of Economics.

In this volume, we seek to revise the agenda for the discourse on management and leadership as currently conducted among academics and practitioners. We do so from a distinct angle of approach, namely the idea that what managerial leadership 'is' and how it is 'conducted' are both determined by the social constructions of the phenomenon as these emerge in human interactions. Thus, we approach managerial leadership as a relational, ongoing process of social construction.

Our assumption implies a shift in perspective, away from viewing managers as the exclusive helmsmen of organizations and towards regarding them as one of several important constructors and practitioners of organizational leadership. This view may differ somewhat from that which most people have in mind when they refer to specific people as 'managers'. However, it is just this discord that motivates and defines the theme of this volume: that managerial leadership is an interactional phenomenon.

The basis for the present book is thus constructional (see Chapter 2) and, starting in Chapter 3, we will describe this approach as practised in eleven empirical investigations of management and leadership that have recently been completed in some large Scandinavian and German companies. Our strategy is to present theoretical conclusions founded on various empirical inquiries in which social constructionism has provided a common frame of reference.

To describe management and managerial leadership in a reality comprising a number of variously organized relations, rather than picturing it in the more usual way as operating in a world of relatively well-defined entities or units, presents us with a challenging task. It is our purpose here to accept this challenge. In doing so we have added three ingredients to the picture of the construction, reproduction and execution of managerial leadership – ingredients that have not hitherto been widely recognized in existing research. These are:

- small talk,

- a set of 'invisible' or unrecognized arenas, and

- institutional dynamics, interpreted here as the mutual influence of co-existing global and local understandings.

All eleven empirical chapters, i.e. Chapters 3 to 13, address in various ways the three themes described above. One or two of these themes have also been noted in other recent scientific publications in the field of organization and management theory, but they have rarely (if ever) been treated empirically, and have certainly not been brought together as part of a deliberate attempt to rethink and reformulate managerial leadership theory.

Chapter 1 provides the reader with an introduction, a summary, and an overview of the following chapters. Chapter 2 is also a kind of opener, in that it introduces the reader to the many faces of social construction-ism, and particularly the kind of approaches adopted in this volume. Both these chapters represent important platforms for all those that follow, from which the readers can then choose the topics (chapters) that are of especial interest to them.

It must be added, however, that although many authors have contributed to this book, it has been our ambition to maintain a rather more integrated approach (including the theoretical design) than is usual in edited volumes. Thus each chapter starting from its own unique empirical material, clearly contributes to the general theoretical proposi-tions that are presented in brief in the first chapter. The empirical and theoretical findings that emerge in the course of the book disclose a range of previously concealed aspects of management and leadership. Taken together these findings suggest that there is a need for a revised theory of management and leadership, framed in a social constructionist perspective.

Finally, it is our hope that this volume will serve as a source of inspiration for practitioners, who might pick up a few ideas that challenge their current way of thinking and acting, and for theoreticians, who might reconsider to some extent the paths to follow in any future research venture in the fields of management and leadership.

Sven-Erik Sjöstrand, Jörgen Sandberg and Mats Tyrstrup

CHAPTER ONE

Recognized and unrecognized managerial leadership

Sven-Erik Sjöstrand and Mats Tyrstrup

Introduction

In this book, we seek to revise the agenda for the discussion of management and leadership as currently conducted among academics and practitioners. We do so from a distinct angle of approach, namely the idea that what (managerial) leadership is and how it is enacted are both determined by the social constructions of the leadership phenomenon that emerge in human interactions. Thus, we approach managerial leadership as a relational, ongoing social construction process rather than as a single clear-cut phenomenon.

This assumption implies a shift in perspective, from viewing managers as the exclusive helmsmen of organizations to regarding them as one of many important constructors and executants of organizational leadership. This view may differ somewhat from what most people have in mind when they refer to specific people as 'managers'. However, it is just this discord that motivates and defines the theme of this volume: that managerial leadership is an interactional phenomenon.

The basis for the present book is thus constructional (on social constructionism, see Chapter 2) and, starting in Chapter 3, this approach will be described as practised in eleven empirical investigations of management and leadership that have recently been completed in a number of large Scandinavian and German companies. The strategy is to present theoretical conclusions founded on empirical inquiries in which social constructionism has provided a common frame of reference.

To describe management and managerial leadership in a reality comprising a number of variously organized relations, rather than picturing it in the more usual way as operating in a world of relatively well-defined entities or units, presents a challenging task. In accepting this challenge we have added three ingredients to the picture of the (re)production[1] and execution of managerial leadership – ingredients that have not hitherto been widely recognized in existing research, namely small talk, a set of invisible arenas, and institutional dynamics, interpreted here as the mutual influence of co-existing global and local understandings.

In this chapter we first discuss, in very condensed form, some of the important milestones in the abundant and lively 20th century history of leadership studies. The focus then switches to social constructivism perspectives, and we add the essentials of our own position. In the third part of the chapter we address a classic issue, namely organization failure, and argue that managers and managerial leadership to a certain extent emanate from the presence of this problem. We then suggest three ways of rethinking managerial leadership by adding, in turn, three main ingredients – small talk, unrecognized (invisible) arenas, and institutional dynamics. Finally, we summarize this introductory chapter and offer a (brief) structured overview of the following twelve chapters of the book.

Scientific understandings of managerial leadership

Existing theory on managerial leadership provides a vast and confusing body of arguments and concepts. Simply to review most of the theories would be an extensive task, certainly calling for a book of its own. However, we have already pointed out that this is not our purpose. Our theoretical approach, like many modern theories about management, leadership and organization, is concerned mainly with the limitations of managerial influence, that is to say the boundary conditions for assuming a hierarchical imperative. Contemporary theory includes many critical essays on the lines of 'does management matter?', how it matters and why, as well as when, where and to what extent. Researchers who are seeking for answers to these classic questions today often discuss managerial leadership in terms differing from those provided by the classic writers of the 20th century.

Earlier works on managerial leadership[2] emphasize its assumed contribution to efficient production (Taylor, 1911) and rational administration (Fayol, 1916). Leadership was regarded very much as an individual undertaking. The pioneers of the 20th century described leadership as 'managerial action' based on analysis, decision-making and planning; that is to say, they suggested an explanatory model based on a hierarchical imperative. At that time hierarchy was seen as a crucial concept, useful in many contexts such as the division of work, specialization and other systematic approaches to improving the management of organizations.

The social features of managing were soon recognized, however (cf. Roethlisberger and Dickson, 1939), and so too was the systemic nature of co-operative action (cf. Barnard, 1938). The workplace, even though it represented a particular context and/or purpose, did not eliminate human characteristics of thinking and feeling, developing interpersonal relations, fostering personal interest or wavering as regards motivation, and so forth. Although understandings of leadership and the exercise of authority did not change immediately (both still represented an executive privilege and responsibility), the environment in which these things occurred was perceived in a different light. A process manifested as a particular way of thinking about organizations had begun and took shape in the human relations school of organization theory.

Towards the middle of the century attention began to focus on the effectiveness of managerial efforts that were based on human relations thinking of this kind. Leadership research then came to address the different traits, behaviour and styles of leadership, and suggested a variety of ideas as to why some leaders might be more efficient than others (see overviews in Stogdill, 1948, 1974; Yukl, 1989; Wright, 1996). Although the results were confusing and sometimes even contradictory, many scholars soon gained confidence in solving the problems within a framework of situational or 'contingency' thinking (e.g. Hemphill, 1949; Fiedler, 1967; Hersey and Blanchard, 1969; House, 1971; Kerr and Jermier, 1978). Although the manager was still thought of as essentially the sole actor capable of dealing with managerial issues, it now became obvious that context and conditions imposed limitations on how this could be done.

By that time, however, researchers had also started to address the topic from a different angle, which came to be labelled 'the nature of managerial work' (Carlson, 1951; Hemphill, 1959, 1960; Mintzberg, 1973; Stewart, 1976, 1982; Forsblad, 1980; Kanter, 1982; Kotter, 1982; Luthans et al., 1985; Holmberg, 1986; Gabarro, 1987; Tyrstrup, 1993). Common themes in these studies were the fuzzy, fragmented and unpredictable patterns in managerial work, and the instant and improvisational approach used by managers to cope with various issues. Progress in organization theory fell in with these ideas, suggesting that the understanding of the manager as somebody smoothly and resolutely controlling co-operative endeavours did not qualify as a fruitful model for describing what was actually going on (e.g. Simon, 1947; March and Simon, 1958; Lindblom, 1959; Cyert and March, 1963; Cohen et al., 1972).

Several researchers further explored the possibility that certain factors beyond managerial control imposed limitations on the powers of management. First of all, of course, the concept of (managerial) power itself came into focus and was problematized (e.g. Pettigrew, 1973; Crozier and Friedberg, 1977; Pfeffer, 1992). But other ideas, too, were introduced to settle the discretion issue. 'External dependency' was an early suggestion (see e.g. Thompson, 1967; Lawrence and Lorsch, 1969; Child, 1972; Norman, 1976; Pfeffer and Salanzick, 1978). For similar reasons the two concepts of 'institution' and 'culture' were re-introduced in organization theory (on the former see e.g. Williamson, 1975, 1985; Meyer and Rowan, 1983; Sjöstrand, 1985, 1993a, 1993b; Powell and DiMaggio, 1991; Scott, 1995; and on the latter see e.g. Wilkins, 1983; Pondy et al., 1983; Berg, 1986; Gagliardi, 1990; Alvesson, 1991). Some researchers even referred to 'the evolving nature of organizations' (e.g. Nelson and Winter, 1982; and Pettigrew, 1985), when seeking to explain this lack of managerial control in organizations. From most of these studies it is evident that the influence of managers on organizations is severely restricted. These restrictions imply that managerial leadership has to be understood in terms other than those that have been dominant since the beginning of the 20th century.

Under the impact of other scholars, who suggested that leadership was about 'charisma' (e.g. House, 1977; Conger and Kanungo, 1987) and 'transformation' (e.g. Burns, 1978; Bass, 1985), the contours of a new kind of manager/leader surfaced. The content of managerial leadership was redefined as fostering a corporate culture (e.g. Deal and Kennedy, 1982; Frost et al., 1985; Sathe, 1985; Schein, 1985), or as providing visions (e.g. Bennis, 1989; Bennis and Nanus, 1992) or meaning (Weick, 1995). Other suggestions were empowering the workforce (e.g. Braverman, 1977; Clegg and Dunkerley, 1980; Kanter, 1984), or creating learning opportunities (e.g. Argyris and Schön, 1978; Björkegren, 1989; Senge, 1990).

In another influential contribution to the emerging picture of managerial leadership it was proposed that strategies rather than operative planning and decision-making were the bearers of managerial influence (e.g. Chandler, 1962; Ansoff, 1965; Andrews, 1971). Strategic management became a theme for a new generation of researchers in the field of managerial leadership. A second wave of strategy analysts further advanced these new ideas concerning the means of managerial influence, suggesting in turn that processes were more important than structure (e.g. Quinn, 1980; Pettigrew, 1985; Mintzberg and Waters, 1985; Tyrstrup, 1993; Stein, 1993; Sjöstrand, 1997).

Although personal frames of reference were introduced at an early stage into the field of managerial leadership (e.g. McGregor, 1960), a growing interest in subjectivism now found its way into theorizing on the subject (e.g. Calder, 1977; Pfeffer, 1977). Something surfaced – beyond individual subjectivity – which certainly mattered, namely socially developed understandings of what was to be considered 'reality'. The project of establishing a leadership theory based on some kind of social constructionism had been launched (e.g. Smircich and Morgan, 1982; Knights and Willmott, 1992; Bresnen, 1995; Sjöstrand, 1997).

A social constructionist perspective on managerial leadership

Rethinking managerial leadership, for example by adding a social constructionist point of view (see Ch. 2) is difficult, due to the solid impact still being made by classical writings on the subject. However, as has been noted, important developments have occurred in the theory in recent years. Contemporary research on organization and management provides enough theoretical and empirical progress to encourage further efforts towards a shift in the understanding of managerial leadership. In our own arguments we thus comply with those who suggest that the basic assumptions in use in mainstream research ought to be challenged (e.g. Westerlund and Sjöstrand, 1979/75; Meindl et al., 1985; Meindl, 1990; Knights and Willmott, 1992; Alvesson, 1996; Sjöstrand, 1997).

Our point of departure, and the assumption guiding the research endeavours presented in this volume, is very simple. Social constructionism provides a promising and less explored path for theory development in the field of managerial leadership (e.g. Smircich and Morgan, 1982; Bresnen, 1995). Social constructionism, as interpreted here, implies that various institutions (re)produce constructions of leadership that coincide with concurrent episodes and processes at the actor level (e.g. Hosking, 1988; Zucker, 1988; Chen and Meindl, 1991; Knights and Willmott, 1992; Sjöstrand, 1997). Institutions such as business schools, management education institutes and business journals all represent recognized grounds for such construction and diffusion processes.

Most theories on managerial leadership emphasize work contexts as representing the sole (or primary) location of management. Managerial leadership is thus expected to occur *within* organizations, and more precisely in the shape of actions in formal or informal episodes taking place in the everyday life of organizations. Our position is nonetheless different, since we claim that interactions extending into places more remote from those that are usually considered typical work situations also constitute important, albeit less widely recognized, media for the construction and exercise of managerial leadership.

According to the ontological position underpinning our research, the defining of what is to be considered organizational membership and a relevant organizing arena is neither an absolute nor a trivial matter. Rather, these are empirical issues and are part of the understanding of any organized context. Thus, theoretically speaking, there are no solid boundaries that prevent points of view, information, attitudes and so forth from dispersing in more or less unpredictable patterns, unless they are socially (re)produced and maintained by actions. This means that, regardless of moral judgements, visiting a nightclub, for example, is an organizational activity if it complies with – or alters – the normative expectations guiding people when they are enacting their organizational affiliation. As such, this and other similar arenas represent not only legitimate but also important research fields – important because they take the analysis beyond the espoused and publicly acceptable forms of running a business or a public institution.

Theories addressing socially established definitions of management regard communication between people as a crucial issue (e.g. Durkheim, 1933; Mead, 1934; Weber, 1947; Berger and Luckmann, 1966; Blumer, 1969; Giddens, 1984). Communication processes in the context of managerial leadership are certainly a well-investigated area (e.g. Barnard, 1938; Carlson, 1951; Garfinkel, 1967; Galbraith, 1973; Argyris and Schön, 1978; Kotter, 1982), and the relevance of constructionist thinking to such leadership studies has been advocated for more than a decade (e.g. Shotter, 1993; Watson, 1994). However, rather less attention is paid to the relevance of what can be called social conversation (e.g. small talk, chatting, and gossip). The empirical data presented in this volume indicates good reasons for believing that this kind of communication is also of great importance to the construction and the (re)production of managerial leadership, as well as to its execution in practice. The private or even confidential nature of many of these conversations easily inspires a sense of urgency, thus attributing importance to the communicative activity itself.

In trying to understand managerial leadership, a focus on small talk highlights a number of somewhat unexpected arenas such as lunch and rest rooms, coffee and smoking areas, elevators, stairs, corridors, etc. that are inside the work context, and others such as private dinners, night-clubs, saunas, tennis courts, golf clubs, hotel lounges, etc. that are traditionally regarded as being outside it. Leadership thus appears to be constructed, (re)produced and exercised in many unrecognized arenas in addition to the ones that are usually acknowledged. Consequently, theorizing on managerial leadership should include a variety of recognized and unrecognized, formal and informal, internal and external arenas, which all in various ways impose, restrict and shape the conditions relevant to the social (re)production and exercising of management.

Social constructionism implies further that interpretations may be shared by individuals, and not necessarily only by a few, which means that they vary in their extent; that is to say, they are more or less global (cf. Berger and Luckmann, 1966). This book emphasizes the co-existence of local and global understandings in empirical cases. The tension thus generated then renders the outcome of organizational processes highly unpredictable. More generally accepted norms or points of view, i.e. those that are institutionalized, may strengthen or erode a particular local understanding, for example in terms of what constitutes legitimate and effective managerial leadership. We also found some indications of the opposite, i.e. of local and sometimes temporal understandings being disseminated more generally as 'educational examples'. However, examples are also provided of co-existence in harmony, cases in which globally dispersed frames of reference are applied to aspects of organizational processes other than the local ones, thus representing a complement rather than a potential substitute.

To sum up: social constructionism provides a different and less rigid view of how relations between occurrences, perceptions and expectations emerge in processes and places. It encourages us not only to understand what appear to be the actions of those occupying managerial positions, but also to recognize various preconditions in terms of local understandings of the specific circumstances. It is particularly interesting to see how managerial leadership itself is interpreted and understood, and to grasp the dynamics of the creation and (re)production of such frames of understanding and how they are changed. Social constructionism offers opportunities for theory development when it comes to the ways in which managerial influence is either promoted or inhibited by the diffusion of beliefs in a complex time-space context. Social constructionism accordingly supports advanced theorizing on the dynamics of managerial leadership.

Organizational failure and the emergence of managerial leadership

Since managerial leadership is the focus of this volume, organizing and organizations are its self-evident background. It thus seems sensible to say something about the shared understanding of these phenomena among the book's contributors.

Apart from its general social constructionist frame, certain more specific aspects of organization have inspired the essays in this volume. Most important is probably our assumption that the social construction of uncertainty, as opposed to ideas about efficiency, power or ownership agency, provides the fundamental *raison d'être* of management (Sjöstrand, 1997). The presence of uncertainty in an organization implies the recognition that unexpected situations will arise and that they will continue to do so time and time again (Tyrstrup, 1993).

If co-operative efforts were to occur in a context of complete certainty, then work and activities in general could theoretically be dealt with according to procedures established in advance. That is to say, they could be managed once and for all at a particular point in time. Under uncertainty, however, unexpected events must be dealt with as and when they arise, and dealt with in ways, shapes and forms that are highly improvisational. In a sense, uncertainty provides a problem of co-operation: organized contexts must maintain some means of handling exceptions and unforeseen situations. Managerial positions (and conse-quently managerial leadership), it is argued, serve to some extent the purpose of solving this problem (Tyrstrup, 1993).

Managers are generally provided with opportunities to influence patterns of interaction and to assign responsibility to particular individuals. Since their responsibilities are relatively broad and unspeci-fied, managers have a right and an obligation to cope with any upsets or ambiguities caused by unexpected incidents. Such managerial discretion reflects a general understanding that allows and encourages managers to develop the specific settings of a particular organization. It also provides managers with an intrinsic, albeit not omnipotent, position from which to act. While chaos may be avoided in this way, it seems that managers must confine themselves to contributing what could be termed 'quasi-co-ordination' (Sjöstrand, 1997). But for many managers, with perhaps tens of thousands of employees, even this more limited managerial ambition seems almost unattainable.

Managers, as the ones who have to handle the unexpected, also have the task of deciding whether or not a situation is likely to reoccur in the future, and therefore should be the trigger for some reorganization. Thus – and this may appear paradoxical – managers not only participate in organizing activities, which makes them part of the organizational constructs themselves, but at the same time they also constitute the cover-up for their own and others' organizing failures. This resembles a kind of continuous programming and reprogramming of various organizational issues, ranging from routine operational procedures to long-term priority-setting among tasks and actions (e.g. Cyert and March, 1963; Mintzberg, 1973; Quinn, 1980; Tyrstrup, 1993).

From a social constructionist perspective, a very relevant source of uncertainty is the heterogeneous character of human beings. All these people occupy a great variety of jobs and positions, which provides them with unique experiences, interests, resources and outlooks. Further, they personify different ethnic groups, religious beliefs, genders, educational backgrounds, personalities, ambitions, ages, etc. Added to which, people usually enjoy a multiplicity of memberships or organizational affiliations, featuring different kinds of involvement (such as owners, employees, contractors, members, etc.) and implying varying levels of commitment (such as discussions of emotional ties). The actual time spent in (or acting for) an organization also varies from one individual to another. All this means that organizations are inevitably fragile constructions, and legal institutions offer no more than limited stability. Evidence of this state of affairs can be seen in the number of 'borderline' cases that arise, such as franchising, networks, alliances, cartels, federations and virtual organizations (Sjöstrand, 1997).

Thus, the members of an organized context do not base their actions solely, sometimes not even primarily, on any common or organizational interest. Instead they act to a large extent from what they consider to be important from a private or a local standpoint. This should not be confused with simply acting within a frame of self-interest. Rather, it is one of the circumstances that account for ongoing sense-making processes, and thus for what appears as, and of course sometimes does actually represent, a political element in organized endeavours (Weick, 1995).

In dealing with this human heterogeneity, management is expected to provide some organization, structure or order, thereby bridging various distances – personal, spatial or time-related – between individuals (Sjöstrand, 1993a, 1993b, 1995). In other words, managers are expected to contribute to the structuring and maintenance of collective action. However, the assumption that managers are able to influence the development trajectories of organizations carries particular implications in social constructionist theory: managerial leadership can then be interpreted as the involvement of managers in creating, encouraging and supporting particular expectations, perspectives and activities present in an organization populated by interacting, dissimilar individuals (Tyrstrup, 1993; Sjöstrand, 1997).

For several reasons managers are recognized as holding an advantageous position in these construction processes. They have been furnished with outstanding resources for creating and communicating suggestions, opinions and directives. Empowered with legitimate means for applying sanctions (e.g. through legislation), they are able to intervene in what they regard as dysfunctional action. However, since managers are attributed with the ability to govern in the formal sense, they also face demands with regard to handling issues and situations. This is particularly true for those involving ambiguity (e.g. decision-making), where a need for clarification is recognized (Tyrstrup, 1993; Sjöstrand, 1997).

In sum, uncertainty suggests that organizational failure is a recurring state of affairs in organizations. Individual understandings of reality promote differences in expectations and ambitions, making it difficult to mobilize co-ordinated responses towards such failures. Due to the way people perceive, (re)produce and enact organizations, individuals with managerial responsibilities are encouraged to become involved in such processes as serve to mould expectations (e.g. planning, budgeting, policy-making, etc.) particularly in situations where expectations are disproved or appear to conflict with one another. The specific features of these processes are certainly influenced by individual understandings of managerial work and responsibilities, which in turn are embedded in more general frames for the understanding of managerial leadership in a broader social context.

Rethinking managerial leadership: adding small talk

We have suggested three ways of rethinking managerial leadership. The first meant adding human small talk to the more visible public texts, conversations and speeches that occur in organizations. There are several reasons why talk can plausibly be regarded as a valuable source for inquiries into the construction and exercise of managerial leadership. Firstly, empirical studies of managers at work repeatedly confirm that talking (and listening?) is a main occupation of managers (e.g. Carlson, 1951; Burns, 1957; Stewart, 1967, 1976, 1982; Forsblad, 1980; Kotter, 1982; Hales, 1986, 1994; Tyrstrup, 1993; Watson, 1994; Sjöstrand, 1997). Secondly, the emphasis on human talk is neutral relative to the type of talk, i.e. whether it concerns decision-making, planning, directing or almost any other category of classification schemata regarding managerial leadership or organizational work. Nor does it matter whether the settings are formal or informal, whether or not the talk occurs across organizational or other borders either in time and space, and so on.

The connection between talk and cognition is a straightforward one, thus connecting managerial leadership to modern models of the human being. As it is a deliberate human action occurring between actors in a certain context/network, 'talk' is a social activity (e.g. Giddens, 1981, 1984; Harré, 1982; Harré and Secord, 1976; Sabini and Silver, 1982). Talk links perceptions of reality with symbols. It makes common understanding (awareness) possible (Czarniawska-Joerges, 1988). Talk is 'talk action' when it (e.g. an utterance) creates activity (Searle, 1969; Allwood, 1976). Talk can also be seen as 'work' (Garfinkel et al.; 1967; Silverman and Jones, 1976; Gronn, 1983; Rombach, 1986); for example consultants, teachers, priests, etc. Talk may also be seen as a 'meta-action' or as 'governance' when other people's actions are being structured in important ways (Czarniawska-Joerges, 1988).

The focus here, however, is small talk, which basically consists of narratives significantly laced with evaluations regarding the actions and qualities of people. Very often the activities (appearance, talk and action) of those not present are in focus. Judgements are also frequent, and may be about incidents, events, things (products, tools, machinery, etc.), services, procedures (budgeting, recruitment, payment, etc.) or situations (crises, conflicts, success, etc.). What might appear to be endless informal conversation is in reality small talk that shapes the lives of people, making them organizational (or other types of) members, or denying them such membership. Small talk carries people's emotions, shapes their ambitions and promotes or disparages them (Silverman and Jones, 1976). Like Broms and Gahmberg (1983) and Gustafsson (1994) we claim that it is here, in these conversations, that most ideals, norms and rules emerge and are then circulated in organizations. And obviously managers are often the targets of these more or less normative construction and (re)production processes (Sjöstrand, 1973, 1997).

Small talk stabilizes the expectations of people in organizations regarding management issues, for example. Through these innumerable, fragmented, episodical but continuous conversations, an intersubjective construction emerges about what has happened, what is happening and what will happen in the future in the organization (Shotter, 1993; Watson 1994; Ekman, 1999).

Managerial leadership then emerges in the wake of this interaction in the shape of hierarchic or asymmetric historical grooves with agreed-upon but continuously changing twists and turns. A shared past evolves as a kind of descriptive sediment, which hardens over time to form intersubjective texts, buildings or other material/immaterial structures (Sjöstrand, 1997). In some cases small talk becomes public talk, such as a formal discourse or text that may either support and/or undermine these types of structure. Sometimes the opposite is true.

Sederberg (1984) claims that in organizations the power belongs to those who can define or describe circumstances in ways that convince others that things are as they say they are. People in power positions then have a right to talk and produce texts that provide shared meanings. To a large extent managerial leaders thus govern by directing meaning through talk, that is to say through ordering, explaining, colouring and making accessible. Those who decide what to talk about and who set the agenda also possess this power.

Rethinking managerial leadership: adding unrecognized arenas

Recognizing the general significance of small talk encourages us to explore the problem of where – in which arenas – managerial leadership is socially constructed, (re)produced and exercised.

Having considered private and other less visible arenas and included them as part of the organizational framework, it seems by no means certain that scholars and practitioners have really comprehended the broad overall context of managerial leadership. Our research indicates that managerial leadership is constructed and accomplished in many places apart from those that have been focused in scientific writings. Indeed, it embraces places that have no spontaneous connotation connecting them with work or systematic problem-solving, decision-making and similar activities. Although these additional unrecognized arenas might recall certain earlier approaches, for example the discussion about informal organization and organizational politics, it can be claimed that this approach extends the (managerial) leadership field a bit further.

Thus here we focus on arenas outside that which is usually considered part of an organization. But it also includes less noticed internal arenas and others crossing between the two. In other words it suggests the existence of many disregarded or invisible arenas both inside and outside the organization, where it is tacitly understood that what is going on is related to leadership. In initiated business circles, for example, it is well known that a weekend of shooting, anniversary celebrations, garden parties, a day at the races, sailing, etc., like other seemingly social events, are crucial to the framing of important managerial decisions (such as who is getting that important position or assignment – and why). Thus we stress that these arenas offer room for mixed processes, usually combining relaxation and social intercourse with important management activities. The existence of such invisible arenas is fairly well known – to judge from (auto)biographies and gossip at least – although the associated rationalities have not been adequately explored (and thus not fully recognized). In fact they make the very identification of an organized context a hazardous undertaking.

On the basis of the collection of examples presented in this book we suggest that private (or closed), disregarded and invisible arenas represent an organizational construct that is more widespread and diversified than well-known concepts such as informal organization imply. They also often acquire significance on a stand-alone basis – they do not arise merely in reaction to dominating formal constructs.

Small talk in such arenas may be the most common form of organizational activity, since it is part of almost every individual's actions and nobody – in principle – is excluded from any one of the arenas mentioned. Rather, everyone is likely to participate in at least one or more contexts that fall within the frames of our concept. Likewise, people who are not managers also construct and (re)produce their own private arenas (offices, stairs, toilets, trains, sports grounds, galleries, etc.), where important issues are dealt with – important because they represent processes that could be placed alongside the leadership of managers as a way of directly and continuously influencing what is going on in an organization. The construction, (re)production and execution of leadership thus flow back and forth in all the kinds of arenas suggested here, namely the formal/informal, public/private, recognized/unrecognized, visible/invisible, focused/hidden and open/closed. Although the activity in these arenas primarily concerns those who are present there and then, it is far from rare for small talk to be circulated well beyond the local context. Sometimes it even has global effects.

Apart from the fact that ideas about leadership are cultivated in all these places, and that managerial activities are simultaneously being carried out there, two factors in particular explain why these overlooked arenas are genuinely important to the strategic functioning of organizations as well. First, these invisible arenas are characterized by subtle boundaries that let in some people while excluding others. It is thus important to understand how such 'arena memberships' are created and preserved. Descriptions of such situations are to be found in several of the following chapters. Second, the emergence of these arenas is beyond the control of single individuals, irrespective of their position or standing. But the possibility cannot be excluded that the construction of some invisible arenas of this kind can be encouraged or hampered, governed or manipulated by powerful actors, such as managers

(Sjöstrand, 1997). This point will also be discussed further in several chapters in this book.

To summarize: a private or hidden arena is a place where small talk is a significant part of what is going on. In other words, almost any place can qualify. The disregarded or invisible arena is not unrecognized because its existence is rare, but it is underestimated in terms of its importance. Characterizing some organizational arenas as hidden, private or invisible has encouraged us to ask questions about the location and spatial dynamics of social construction and the exercise of managerial leadership within the context of small talk. It also provides a new point of view in analysing the establishment of organizational boundaries: arenas are created when people start to talk or when they stop talking. Silence and selective attention become strategic ingredients in the shaping of organizational context, reflecting a process that is usually outside everyone's control. This analysis supplies some examples of the mechanisms and procedures whereby this process unfolds, and some examples of the consequences that are likely to ensue.

Rethinking managerial leadership: adding institutional dynamics

During our attempt to complete this research mission we began to note the significance of the global as well as the local constructions of managerial leadership. According to contemporary social science this is what is to be expected. Coherent systems of affirmed and sanctioned norms (i.e. institutions) have long been the subject of scientific interest. In organization theory the tension between local and global institutions has been a topic of major interest since the mid 1990s. According to the institutional approach to organization, institutions are subject to local interpretations, even though they may shape cultures and whole societies (Sjöstrand, 1985, 1993, 1995).

When institutional research is applied to leadership and management it is usually concerned with either global homogeneity or local variety. Our position, however, is that global and local understandings co-exist: a purely and exclusively local understanding is not possible, since it would have to be regarded as the global understanding within a context of its own. Global and local constructions generally compete, creating a kind of institutional dynamic. Consequently the focus should be on the (potential) tension and interaction between local and global frames of reference.

Some of the empirical cases presented in this book illustrate how managerial leadership is institutionalized on a global (or societal) level. To some extent managerial leadership is thus provided by the societal discourse on management and other related topics such as power, gender and rationality. But some indications have also been found of the opposite, namely of local understandings being dispersed more generally as illustrative or educational examples within organizations and beyond them. Thus the position is that more or less institutionalized frames of reference continuously interact, implicitly as well as explicitly, and that the study of such processes and patterns can offer a fruitful basis for more ambitious and dynamic theory-building regarding management and leadership.

Much of what we consider to be related to managerial leadership seems to have an institutional character (e.g. the [legal] position as managing director or president of an organization). Some global constructions thus provide the necessary framework or preconditions for the evolution of local features. The importance of the individual actor, for example in terms of how he or she conducts the mission of being president of the organization, cannot be personal or local without also implying the presence of an understanding of how presidents in general conduct their missions. A common understanding of this latter construct does exist, at least regarding its main features.

In this book we provide some examples of how the (re)productions of managerial leadership emerge as interactions between institutions, thus challenging the classical answers as to why and how managerial leadership arises in organizations (Sjöstrand, 1995). Such an interactive approach alters the traditional interpretation of why and how leadership comes about in an organization. One obvious consequence of this is that historical processes become crucial to our understanding of the development of social constructions of management and leadership. To concentrate on present circumstances and future expectations, as is common in management studies, thus means overlooking important information (cf. Mintzberg and Waters, 1985; Pettigrew, 1985; Tyrstrup, 1993; Sjöstrand, 1997).

A few conclusions

Management and leadership can be discussed from several perspectives. Historically these areas have been dominated by approaches which assume axiomatically that leadership refers essentially to understanding the ways in which certain individuals (e.g. managers), or groups or organizations exert influence over other individuals (e.g. employees). The distinction between leaders and followers has thus been emphasized in these writings.

An alternative view, which is advocated in this volume, is to regard leadership as a kind of flow or flux in people's variously patterned relations and interactions. The character and content of a relation is thus given pride of place, while classifications and categorizations (e.g. leader/ follower) are given a more subordinate position. The relation is granted status in its own right, and as such can be developed, altered or dissolved.

For several reasons social constructionism is well qualified to offer a meaningful gateway to the development of institutionally flavoured leadership theory. First, it relies on relations as the medium for creating and recreating understandings, which makes both leaders and followers (to use the commonly accepted terminology) part of the preconditions for the emergence of managerial leadership. Second, it makes no fundamental distinction between the performance of managerial leadership and its social construction. The understanding, performance and perceived consequences of managerial leadership are assumed to influence each other, with no particular direction of causality *a priori* being implied.

From this platform, and in opposition to much current writings, we try to show that talk, and small talk in particular, is important to management and leadership. In conversations of this kind crucial ideas about managerial leadership are raised, as well as opinions about such things as issues, situations, incidents, processes, and individuals. Small talk shapes organizational politics and alliances as well as fostering opinions.

In studying small talk we become aware of an important but previously less exploited source of information regarding management and organization. By mapping such conversations it becomes possible to penetrate behind the usual rationalized, adjusted descriptions of occurrences and processes. In small talk people tell stories that differ, partially at least, from those that are told in written documents, at formal meetings, in official declarations, and the like. Moreover, small talk involves almost everybody, albeit in many different arenas and with varying impact.

Closely related to the significance of small talk is the idea that private, informal, hidden and invisible arenas are important to managerial leadership. Here, boundaries become crucial, particularly those border-lines that people informally and continuously (re)construct in their (inter)actions, or when they fall silent or start talking due to the presence of others. Such 'primitive' organizing constitutes the landscape of emerging as well as of maturing arenas, thus including some people and excluding others. Many of these places become important because questions about the who, what, why, how and when often include an aspect that is delicate, although not always conspiratorial or political.

Thus, leadership is also constructed and exercised in subtle but comprehensible settings, in which some individuals have a say while others are more or less ignored, settings in which some topics and conversations are promoted while others are labelled inappropriate or inconvenient. In this way the likelihood of certain ideas, suggestions and opinions being met with sympathy is regulated. Often, however, this does not occur, because the content itself is not evaluated, but only the legitimacy of the promoter and the suitability of the act of promoting in a particular context.

Several competing systems of norms usually exist in organizations simultaneously. They become visible in the differentiation of the arenas as such, and in the ongoing small talk in the various groupings or crowds. In most management and leadership research, however, one such normative system has been particularly emphasized; namely the one that refers to the more formal (e.g. legal), official and therefore visible circles and arenas (such as the board of directors and its board room, or the executive group and its meeting room, and so on). This lack of differentiation cannot be explained only in terms of the problems associated with obtaining high-quality empirical data. It also belongs to the rationalistic tradition that still dominates management and organization research (Gustafsson, 1994; Sjöstrand, 1997).

Whether or not these customarily unrecognized aspects of managerial leadership contribute to performance and efficiency is not the crucial issue here. In our opinion, the fact that they are part of interpretations of what is considered managerial leadership is enough to make them interesting. Such aspects clearly qualify as empirical understandings relevant to the territory of managerial leadership, and thus to theorizing on the subject.

The classical issue as to whether leadership is independent of time and space or whether it represents something of a situational character also appears in a rather different interpretative light when a social constructionist approach is adopted. The seemingly trivial answer is that it represents something general in as far as it is possible to identify globally prevalent perceptions and understandings of leadership. However, the empirical cases presented in this book show that local constructs are very likely to develop. Thus, the global/local dichotomy becomes a crucial factor in itself, and its particular mix will be specific in every separate context or study. It is thus very important to theory-building around the construction, (re)production and institutionalization of leadership in organizations as well as in society at large, that such particularities – and how they arise – are investigated.

In sum, the empirical research presented and analysed in this volume suggests that small talk, a number of less widely recognized arenas, and the reciprocal influence between global and local constructs are all crucial aspects of managerial leadership – crucial, that is, to the social construction, (re)production and execution of managerial leadership. To what extent this is the case we do not know for certain. The same applies to the more specific implications of our findings on, for example, organization theory. These have yet to be determined. We are convinced, however, that the research areas highlighted in this book represent a promising path for the study of managerial leadership in the future. It would be surprising if the three basic aspects mentioned above, and which will also be explored in the following chapters, should prove to be of no more than minor importance to managerial leadership theory.

Chapter presentations

There are two introductory chapters, this one and Chapter 2, *The constructions of social constructionism*. The eleven subsequent chapters all explore in various perspectives the three themes described above, namely small talk, unrecognized areas and local/global understandings. One or two of the topics addressed here have also been taken up in other recent scientific publications in the field of organization and management theory, but they have seldom, if ever, been treated empirically, and have certainly not been brought together as part of a deliberate attempt to rethink and reformulate managerial leadership theory.

In the second introductory chapter, *The constructions of social constructionism*, Jörgen Sandberg describes the basic attributes of social constructionism. He begins by identifying and describing the features that are common to the social constructionist approaches as well as those that are different. He then provides a more extensive account of an approach to social constructionism that will be used in most of the following eleven chapters, namely one that adopts a phenomenological perspective. One of the main assumptions here is that human beings reproduce existing realities rather than constantly producing new ones. It is possible to break this ongoing reproduction, but to do so requires knowledge of the way a specific aspect of reality is constructed.

In Chapter 3, *The tough ones,* Markus Kallifatides introduces the theme of enacting managerial leadership by way of conversation and bases his argument on observations from an in-house trainee programme in the Swedish subsidiary of a large European industrial company. The particular occasion was a one-day meeting attended by the CEO and financial director. Although various management issues are the explicit subject of the meeting, the jokes, remarks and judgements expressed by the two executives reveal a special understanding of what managerial leadership is all about in this particular company. Interactions between the executives and the other participants reproduce what is considered to be legitimate managerial behaviour and the appropriate responses, which constitute one of the more important lessons to be learned by the chosen managers-to-be.

The theme of externalizing managerial leadership also comes up in Chapter 4, *The rhetorical dimension,* where Johan Stein and Lena Andersson analyse the performance of a CEO in a series of video films aimed at alerting employees to upcoming strategic changes. Taking rhetoric as their frame of reference, the authors argue that the primary message concerns the CEO's qualities as a leader and the appropriateness of his personality in the specific situation confronting the company. Although the videos reflect an attempt to influence organizational sense-making in terms of meaning, Stein and Andersson conclude on a basis of their rhetorical analysis that a sense of reliance on the CEO's ability, rather than any behavioural guidelines, is the most likely outcome of viewing the videos.

In Chapter 5, *The home – a disregarded managerial Arena,* home environments are analysed as arenas for managerial leadership. Adopting a historical perspective, Annelie Karlsson Stider studies the (re)production of leadership and organization in family gatherings and social incidents and events in a large private Swedish publishing company. A patriarchal managerial leadership model provides the contours for the interactions of family members and relatives. It appears, however, that interwoven with all this, female members of the clan perform important tasks in terms of managerial leadership. The fostering of new generations for executive duties and obligations is revealed as one example. Further, a deep involvement on the part of the women in the development and maintenance of networks of business associates accounts for an influence on strategic policy-making.

The interaction between local and global understandings of managerial leadership is the theme of Chapter 6, *The social construction of top executives.* Here Charlotte Holgersson analyses the co-existence of two rather contradictory aspects of top management recruitment: we expect to discover a careful matching of top executives and specific jobs, and yet we find a striking homogeneity among CEOs in terms of gender, background, education and experience. Holgersson identifies a difference between being recruited as a CEO and being accepted as a candidate at all. Through 'co-option', which is based on more global constructs of CEO-ship, individuals are selected for the candidate population. This is where homogenization works. The selection of a particular person for a specific position, however, occurs in interactions among board members, stakeholders, 'head hunters', and other individuals involved, including the retiring incumbent. Here, the specific understandings of particular jobs, persons and circumstances are developed in terms of a local construction underpinning the final choice.

In Chapter 7, *From lack to surplus,* Anna Wahl returns to a classical managerial arena – the top management group in a company – and addresses a situation in which women constitute a majority in the management team. Again the theme of local versus global understandings of managerial leadership and gender is unveiled. Although the case provides many particulars in terms of understanding and the exercise of managerial leadership, the implied presence of male-dominated settings serves as the frame of reference for the executives concerned. It is suggested that specific constellations of women and men do make a difference to the representation of a local, and thus a particular, understanding of managerial leadership, despite the constant influence of global gender orders that guide the more prevalent understanding.

The institutional theme is also present in Chapter 8, *Management as uncontrollable sexuality,* where Pia Höök addresses constructions of managerial leadership, masculinity and sexuality. Höök starts by discussing different perceptions (constructions) of sexuality within organizations. She then moves on to discuss how these constructions are (re)produced, and how they provide boundaries that include heterosexual men, but exclude women and homosexual men, from arenas where managerial leadership is performed and (re)produced.

In Chapter 9, *Educational rhetoric or leadership practice?* Jörgen Sandberg looks at global understandings of managerial leadership by investigating the constructions of managerial leadership produced at the leading Swedish institute for management education. The identified constructions all contain a strong humanistic element. Due to the unique historical importance of this institute in the Swedish management community, Sandberg expected to find that the humanistic orientation in its teaching would have had a powerful impact on the way managerial leadership is practised in Swedish organizations. He concludes, however, that this is not the case. Rather, the prevalent construction of managerial leadership is identified as being saturated with a strong vein of 'toughness orientation'. One explanation for the meagre impact of the humanistic construct is that the actors at the institute understand managerial leadership as a phenomenon attaching to the individual, rather than as something socially constructed. This means that the actors are unable to identify, describe or influence the crucial processes whereby managerial leadership is (re)produced and exercised.

Providing a similar example, albeit in an ordinary work setting, Daniel Ericsson analyses the social construction of creativity management in Chapter 10, *Creative leaders – or prisoners of the past?* The editorial boards of two Swedish newspapers provide the empirical base. Although the editors-in-chief of both newspapers perceive creative leadership as 'giving room' for creativity, their understandings of that particular task differ significantly. Ericsson argues that local culture and personal orientation account for these differences, and suggests that describing the efforts of the editors-in-chief as (re)producing routine editorial procedures is just as valid as sustaining the idea that their leadership is all about managing creativity. In a sense, what are being (re)produced are 'newspaper jargon' and the structural relations between reporters, in a context of modern management thinking and vocabularies.

The construction theme is further analysed in Chapter 11, *Professional norms and managerial leadership.* Here, Johan Stein studies the ways in which professional recognition and networks provide employed experts with organizational authority. This community of experts serves as an arena for the exchange of knowledge and information, in some respects undermining the hierarchical authority in the organization concerned. Thus, processes of establishing professional norms for action and reasoning limit the influence of the managerial leadership, including that exercised by those in top executive positions. Depending on the situation, the social construction of expertise occasionally seems to override the social construction of managerial leadership and authority.

By analysing small talk among policemen in Chapter 12, *Constructing leadership in small talk,* Gunnar Ekman introduces employee conversation as a substitute for managerial leadership. The focus is again on immediate on-the-job situations and it is expected, in accordance with most management theories, that guidance and instructions from higher levels in the hierarchy (i.e. from managers) will govern actions. Instead, however, Ekman finds other explanations for what happens. Norms about what is considered to be rational or sensible police action, emerge in informal peer discussions among the policemen themselves. These norms serve as sanctioned guidelines among colleagues about how to uphold justice and order, and when they conflict with instructions provided by superiors, it is the former that take precedence. These guidelines also concern the decision-making authority and task assignments among the policemen.

In the final chapter of the book, *Managing positions or people?* Birgitta Södergren and Johan Söderholm address a topic that is much discussed at the present time, namely the significance and consequences of a growing volume of 'knowledge-intensive work'. This chapter explores what happens when the constructions of managing-by-numbers clash with the constructions of knowledge-intensive work. The authors focus on three aspects of knowledge-intensive work that may *not* fit in with the increasing popularity of numerical measurements in organizations and the requirements attached to them. Firstly, knowledge-intensive work is loaded with tacit knowledge, and this dimension is often neglected or even destroyed by a narrowing focus on numerical measurements. Secondly, this kind of work requires flexible professional roles, continuous interaction between individual people and groups, and a network spanning across many organizational boundaries, whereas numerical measurements often focus on the individual or the work unit. Thirdly, knowledge-intensive work requires constant and informal learning, while most measurement systems are based on a control rationale.

The authors ask themselves whether there is a risk that the constructions of 'management-by-numbers' may not come to replace a more genuine dialogue within organizations, redirecting the managerial focus away from the intricate development of qualitative, professional competence, and towards more formal, explicit and measurable action. Thus, the language of management-by-numbers does not seem to be in accord with the language of competence.

Notes

1 (Re)production is written thus, with parentheses around 're', to emphasize the reference to what is 'produced' (created) at any given moment, and to what is 'reproduced' from previously established constructions.
2 The term 'leadership' itself is in fact a relatively recent addition to the English language. It has been in use for about two hundred years, although 'leader' appeared as early as AD 1300 (Yukl, 1989).

References

Alvesson, M. (1991). *Kommunikation, makt och organisation*. Norstedts, Stockholm.

Alvesson, M. (1996). *Communication, Power and Organization*. De Gruyter, Berlin.

Allwood, J. (1976). *Linguistic Communication as Action and Co-operation: A Study in Pragmatics*. Gothenburg University, Gothenburg.

Andrews, K. R. (1971). *The Concept of Corporate Strategy*. Dow Jones-Irwing, Homewood, Illinois.

Ansoff, H. I. (1965). *Corporate Strategy*. McGraw-Hill, New York.

Argyris, D., and Schön, D. (1978). *Organizational Learning: A Theory of Action Perspective*. Addison-Wesley, Reading, Mass.

Barnard, C. (1938). *The Function of the Executive*. Harvard University Press, Cambridge Mass.

Bass, B. M. (1985). *Leadership and Performance Beyond Expectations*. Free Press, New York.

Bennis, W. G. (1989). *Why Leaders Can't Lead: The Unconscious Conspiracy Continues*. Jossey-Bass, San Francisco.

Bennis, W. G., and Nanus, B. (1992). *Visionary Leadership: Creating a Compelling Sense of Direction for your Organization*. Jossey-Bass, San Francisco.

Berg, P. O. (1986). Symbolic Management of Human Resources. *Human Resource Management*, vol. 25, pp. 557–79.

Berger, P. L., and Luckmann, T. (1966). *The Social Construction of Reality*. Doubleday & Co., New York.

Björkegren, D. (1989). *Hur organisationer lär*. Studentlitteratur, Lund.

Blumer, H. (1969). *Symbolic Interactionism: Perspective and Method*. Prentice Hall, Englewood Cliffs.

Braverman, H. (1977). *Arbete och monopolkapital: Arbetets degradering i det tjugonde århundradet*. Rabén & Sjögren, Stockholm.

Bresnen, M. J. (1995). All Things to All People? Perceptions, Attributions and Constructions of Leadership, *Leadership Quarterly*, vol. 6, pp. 495–513.

Broms, H., and Gahmberg, H. (1983). Communication to Self in Organizations and Cultures, *Administrative Science Quarterly*, vol. 28, pp. 482–85.

Burns, J. (1978). *Leadership*. Harper & Row, New York.

Burns, T. (1957). Management in Action, *Operational Research Quarterly*, vol. 8, no. 2, pp. 45–60.

Calder, B. J. (1977). An Attribution Theory of Leadership, in Staw, B. M., and Salancik, G. R. (eds.), *New Directions in Organizational Behaviour*. St. Clair, Chicago.

Carlson, S. (1951). *Executive Behaviour*. Strömbergs, Stockholm.

Chandler, A. (1962). *Strategy and Structure*. The MIT Press, Cambridge Mass.

Chen, C. C., and Meindl, J. R. (1991). The Construction of Leadership Images in the Popular Press: The Case of Donald Burr and People's Express. *Administrative Science Quarterly*, vol. 36, no. 4, pp. 521–51.

Child, J. (1972). Organizational Structure, Environment and Performance: The Role of Strategic Choice. *Sociology*, vol. 6, pp. 1–22.

Clegg, S., and Dunkerley, D. (1980). *Organization, Class and Control*. Routledge & Kegan Paul, London.

Cohen, M., March J., and Olsen, J. (1972). A Garbage Can Model of Organizational Choice. *Administrative Science Quarterly*, vol. 17, pp. 1–25.

Conger, J. A., and Kanungo, R. (1987). Toward a Behavioural Theory of Charismatic Leadership in Organizational Settings. *Academy of Management Review*, vol. 12, pp. 637–47.

Crozier, M., and Friedberg, E. (1977). *Actors and Systems – the Politics of Collective Action*. University of Chicago Press, Chicago.

Cyert, R., and March, J. G. (1963). *A Behavioural Theory of the Firm*. Prentice Hall, Englewood Cliffs, New Jersey.

Czarniawska-Joerges, B. (1988). *Att handla med ord, – Om organisatoriskt prat, organisk styrning och företagsledningskonsultering*. Carlsons, Stockholm.

Deal, T. E., and Kennedy, A. (1982). *Corporate Cultures*. Addison-Wesley, Reading, Mass.

Durkheim, E. (1933). *The Division of Labour in Society*. Free Press, Glencoe.

Ekman, G. (1999). *Från text till batong*. EFI, Stockholm.

Fayol, H. (1949/1916). *General and Industrial Management*. Pitman Books, London.

Fiedler, F. E. (1967). *A Theory of Leadership Effectiveness*. McGraw-Hill, New York.

Forsblad, P. (1980). *Företagsledares beslutsinflytande. Några försök till identifikation och beskrivning*. EFI, Stockholm.

Frost, P., Moore, L., Louis, M., Lundberg, C., and Martin, J. (eds.). (1985). *Organizational Culture*. Sage, Newbury Park, CA.

Gabarro, J. J. (1987). *The Dynamics of Taking Charge*. Harvard Business School, Boston, Mass.

Gagliardi, P. (1990). *The Symbolic of Corporate Artefacts*. de Gruyter, Berlin.

Galbraith, J. (1973). *Designing Complex Organizations*. Addison-Wesley, Reading, Mass.

Garfinkel, H. (1967). *Studies in Ethnomethodology*. Prentice Hall, Englewood Cliffs, NJ.

Giddens, A. (1981). Agency, Institution and Time-Space Analysis, in Knorr-Cetina, K., and Cicourel, A. V. (eds.), *Advances in Social Theory and Methodology*. Routledge & Kegan Paul, Boston.

Giddens, A. (1984). *New Rules of Sociological Method*. Hutchinson, London.

Gronn, P. C. (1983). Talk as the Work: The Accomplishment of School Administration. *Administrative Science Quarterly*, vol. 28, pp. 1–21.

Gustafsson, C. (1994). *Om Produktion av Allvar*. Nerenius and Santérus, Stockholm.

Hales, C. (1986). What Do Managers Do? A critical review of the evidence, *Journal of Management Studies*, vol. 23, pp. 88–115.

Hales, C. (1994). *Managing Through Organisation: Management Process, Forms of Organization and the Work of Managers*. Routledge, London.

Harré, R. (1982). Theoretical Preliminaries to the Study of Action, in von Cranach, M., and Harré, R. (eds.), *The Analysis of Action*, pp. 5–72, Cambridge University Press, Cambridge.

Harré, R., and Secord, P. F. (1976). *The Explanation of Social Behaviour*. Basil Blackwell, Oxford.

Hemphill, J. K. (1949). Situational Factors in Leadership, Ohio State University Educational Monographs No. 32.

Hemphill, J. K. (1959). Job Descriptions for Executives. *Harvard Business Review*, vol. 37, September–October, pp. 55–67.

Hemphill J. K. (1960). *Dimensions of Executive Positions*. Bureau of Business Research, Ohio State University, Columbus.

Hersey, P., and Blanchard, K. H. (1969). *Management of Organizational Behaviour: Utilising Human Resources*, Prentice Hall, Englewood Cliffs, N.J.

Holmberg, I. (1986). *Företagsledares mandat – ett koncernledningsuppdrag påbörjas*. Studentlitteratur, Lund.

Hosking, D. M. (1988). Organizing, Leadership and Skilful Process. *Journal of Management Studies*, vol. 25, no. 2, pp. 147–66.

House, R. J. (1971). A Path-goal Theory of Leader Effectiveness. *Administrative Science Quarterly*, vol. 16, pp. 321–39.

House, R. J. (1977). A 1976 Theory of Charismatic Leadership, in Hunt, J. G., and Larson, L. L. (eds.), *Leadership: The Cutting Edge*, pp. 189–207. Southern Illinois University Press, Carbondale.

Kanter, R. M. (1982). The Middle Manager as Innovator. *Harvard Business Review*, vol. 60, July–August, pp. 95–105.

Kanter, R. M. (1984). *The Change Masters: Corporate Entrepreneurs at Work*. Allen & Unwin, London.

Kerr, S., and Jermier, J. M. (1978). Substitute for Leadership: Their Meaning and Measurement. *Organizational Behaviour and Human Performance*, vol. 22, pp. 375–403.

Knights, D., and Willmott, H. (1992). *Skill and Consent: Contemporary Studies in the Labour Process*. Routledge, London.

Kotter, J. (1982). *The General Managers*. The Free Press, New York.

Lawrence, P. and Lorsch, J. (1969). *Developing Organizations: Diagnosis and Action*. Addison-Wesley, Reading, Mass.

Lindblom, C. E. (1959). The Science of 'Muddling Through', *Public Administration Review*, vol. 19, pp. 79–88.

Luthans, F., Rosenkrantz, S., and Hennessey, H. (1985). *Organizational Behaviour Modification and Beyond: An Operant and Social Learning Approach*. Scott, Forsman, Blenview.

March, J., and Simon, H. (1958). *Organizations*. Wiley, New York.

McGregor, D. (1960). *The Human Side of Enterprise*. McGraw-Hill, New York.

Mead, G. H. (1934). *Mind, Self and Society: from the Standpoint of a Social Behaviourist*. University of Chicago Press, Chicago.

Meindl, J. R. (1990). On Leadership: An Alternative to the Conventional Wisdom. *Organizational Behaviour*, vol. 12, pp. 159–203.

Meindl, J. R., Ehrlich, S. B., and Dukerich, J. M. (1985). The Romance of Leadership. *Administrative Science Quarterly*, vol. 30, pp. 78–102.

Meyer, J. W., and Rowan, B. (1983). *Organizational Environments: Ritual and Rationality*. Sage, Beverly Hills, California.

Mintzberg, H. (1973). *The Nature of Managerial Work*. Harper and Row, New York.

Mintzberg, H., and Waters, J. (1985). On Strategies, Deliberate and Emergent. *Strategic Management Journal*, vol. 6, pp. 252–72.

Nelson, R., and Winter, S. G. (1982). *An Evolutionary Theory of Economic Change*. Belknap Press, Cambridge.

Norman, R. (1976). *Management and Statesmanship*. SIAR, Stockholm.

Pettigrew, A. (1973). *The Politics of Organizational Decision-Making*. Tavistock, London.

Pettigrew, A. (1985). *The Awakening Giant: Continuity and Change in ICI*. Basil Blackwell, Oxford.

Pfeffer, J. (1977). The Ambiguity of Leadership. *Academy of Management Review*, no. 2, pp. 104–12.

Pfeffer, J. (1992). *Managing with Power: Politics and Influence in Organizations*. Harvard Business School Press, Boston, Mass.

Pfeffer, J., and Salancik, G. (1978). *The External Control of Organizations: A Resource Dependence Perspective*. Harper and Row, New York.

Pondy, L. R., Frost, P., Morgan, Q., and Dandridge, T. (1983). *Organizational Symbolism*. JAI Press, Greenwich Conn.

Powell, W., and DiMaggio, P. (eds.). (1991). *The New Institutionalism in Organizational Analysis*. University of Chicago Press, Chicago.

Quinn, J. B. (1980). *Strategies for Change – Logical Incrementalism*. Irwin, Homewood.

Roethlisberger, F. J., and Dickson, W. J. (1939). *Management and the Worker*. Harvard University Press, Cambridge, Mass.

Rombach, B. (1986). *Rationalisering eller prat: kommuners anpassning till en stagnerande ekonomi*. Doxa, Lund.

Sabini, J., and Silver, M. (1982). *Moralities of Everyday Life*. Oxford University Press, New York.

Sandberg, J., and Targama, A. (1998). *Ledning och förståelse: ett kompetensperspektiv på organisationer*. Studentlitteratur, Lund.

Sathe, V. (1985). *Culture and Related Corporate Realities*. Richard D Irvin Inc., Homewood, Ill.

Schein, E. (1985). *Organizational Culture and Leadership*. Jossey-Bass, San Francisco.

Scott, J. (1995). *Sociological Theory: Contemporary Debates*. Edward Elgar, Aldershot.

Searle, J. R. (1969). *Speech Act*. Cambridge University Press, Cambridge.

Sederberg, P. (1984). *The Politics of Meaning: Power and Explanation in Construction of Social Reality*. University of Arizona Press, Tucson, Arizona.

Senge, P. M. (1990). *The Fifth Discipline: the Art and Practise of the Learning Organization*. Doubleday, New York.

Shotter, J. (1993). *Conversational Realities: Constructing Life Through Language*. Sage, London.

Silverman, P., and Jones, J. (1976). *Organizational Work: The Language of Grading/The Grading of Language*. Macmillan, London.

Simon, H. (1947). *Administrative Behaviour*. Macmillan, New York.

Sjöstrand, S-E. (1973). *Företagsorganisation. En taxonomisk ansats*. EFI, Stockholm.

Sjöstrand, S-E. (1985). *Samhällsorganisation*. Doxa, Lund.

Sjöstrand, S-E. (ed.) (1993a). *On Institutional Change: Theory and Empirical Findings*. M E Sharpe, New York.

Sjöstrand, S-E. (1993b). The Socio-Economic Institutions of Organizing: Origin, Emergence, and Reproduction. *Journal of Socio-Economics*, vol. 22, pp. 323–52.

Sjöstrand, S-E. (1995). Towards a Theory of Institutional Change, in Groenewegen, J., Pitelis, C., and Sjöstrand, S-E. (eds.), *On Economic Institutions – Theory and Applications.* Edward Elgar, London.

Sjöstrand, S-E. (1997). *The Two Faces of Management. The Janus Factor.* Thomson, London.

Smircich, L., and Morgan, G. (1982). Leadership: The Management of Meaning, *Journal of Applied Behavioural Science*, vol. 18, pp. 257–73.

Stein, J. (1993). *Strategy Formation and Managerial Agency: A Socio-cognitive Perspective.* EFI, Stockholm.

Stewart, R. (1967). *Managers and Their Jobs.* Macmillan, London.

Stewart, R. (1976). *Contrasts in Management.* McGraw-Hill, Maidenhead.

Stewart, R. (1982). *Choices for the Manager.* McGraw-Hill, London.

Stogdill, R. M. (1948). Personal Factors Associated with Leadership: A Survey of the Literature. *Journal of Psychology*, vol. 25, pp. 35–71.

Stogdill, R. (1974). *Handbook of Leadership.* The Free Press, New York.

Taylor, F. (1911). *The Principles of Scientific Management*, Harper, New York.

Thompson, J. D. (1967). *Organizations in Action.* McGraw-Hill, New York.

Tyrstrup, M. (1993). *Företagsledares arbete. En longitudinell studie av arbetet i en företagsledning.* EFI, Stockholm.

Watson, T. J. (1994). *In Search of Management, Culture, Chaos and Control in Managerial Work.* Thomson, London.

Weber, M. (1947). *The Theory of Social and Economic Organization.* Oxford University Press, New York.

Weick, K. (1995). *Sensemaking in Organizations.* Sage, London.

Westerlund, G., and Sjöstrand, S-E. (1979/75). *Organizational Myths.* Harper & Row, London.

Wilkins, A. L. (1983). Organizational Stories as Symbols Which Control the Organization, in Pondy, L. R. et al. (eds.), *Organizational Symbolism.* JAI Press, Greenwich.

Williamson, O. E. (1975). *Markets and Hierarchies: Analysis and Antitrust Implications. A Study in the Economics of Internal Organization.* Free Press, New York.

Williamson, O. E. (1985). *The Economic Institutions of Capitalism. Firms, Markets, Relational Contracting.* Free Press, New York.

Wright, P. L. (1996). *Managerial Leadership.* Routledge, London.

Yukl, G. A. (1989). Managerial Leadership: A Review of Theory and Research, *Journal of Management*, vol. 15, pp. 251–89.

Zucker, L. (1988). *Institutional Patterns and Organizations: Culture and Environment.* Ballinger, Cambridge, Mass.

■ CHAPTER TWO ■

The constructions of social constructionism

Jörgen Sandberg

This chapter describes the main features of the social constructionist research approach. A weakness in a wide range of social constructionist studies is the articulation of the assumptions underlying social constructionism. These are often treated superficially, which opens the way for various misunderstandings about constructionism (Hacking, 1999). Therefore, the purpose of this chapter is not only to make explicit the theoretical position adopted in the book as a whole, but also to provide a more extensive elaboration and illumination of the basic assumptions underlying social constructionism in general.

The first part of the chapter considers some common features, as well as the differences and tensions that exist between different research approaches used in social constructionism. The second part elaborates a social phenomenological approach to social constructionism, from which most of the other chapters take their point of departure. In particular, it identifies and describes some of the most basic assumptions underlying a social phenomenological approach, and looks at how social construction is regarded from this standpoint.

What is social constructionism?

For the last two decades, the label 'social construction'[1] has been used more widely in the social sciences. The general tenet within social constructionism is that reality is not objective and given, but is socially constructed. More specifically, it is argued that all aspects of social reality such as male, female, family, identity, sexuality, genius, creativity, management, money, organization and leadership can be seen as socially defined through ongoing actions, negotiations and agreements. However, social constructionism is not a single unified approach but is made up of a large variety of disparate research approaches (Gergen, 1994; Schwandt, 1994; Danzinger, 1997).

As well as the theories explicitly devoted to social construction (Berger and Luckmann, 1966; Farr and Moscovici, 1984; Gergen, 1994; Searle, 1995), the following can also be included under the social constructionist label: certain theories of practice (Giddens, 1984, 1993; Bourdieu, 1990); critical theory (Habermas, 1972); ethnomethodology (Garfinkel, 1967; Heritage, 1984; Atkinson, 1988); symbolic interaction (Mead, 1934); discourse theories (Foucault, 1972; Potter and Wetherell, 1987); post-structuralism (Derrida, 1998); cultural psychology (Bruner, 1996; Cole, 1996; Shore, 1996); theories of culture (Geertz, 1973; Alvesson, 1993); theories of gender (Keller, 1985; Harding, 1986); institutional theories (Meyer and Rowan, 1977; DiMaggio and Powell, 1983; Sjöstrand, 1985, 1993; Scott, 1995); situated cognition (Chaiklin and Lave, 1993; Engeström and Middleton, 1996); theories of sense making (Weick, 1995) and theories of truth (Asteley, 1985; Kvale, 1995).

Common features in social constructionism

Despite the great variety of approaches, there are above all four themes that unify the above research approaches under the label of social constructionism. In particular, what unifies them is a rejection of the assumptions underlying prevalent research approaches in the social sciences: a dualistic ontology, an objectivistic epistemology, the individual as the foundation of knowledge, and language as a mirror of objective reality. This chapter will first describe the general meaning of these assumptions and then discuss why advocates of a social constructionist stance reject them.

Dualistic ontology

Assuming a dualistic ontology means treating subject and object as two separate and independent entities. A dualistic ontology implies a division of research objects into two main separate entities: a subject in itself and an object in itself (cf. Giorgi, 1994). For example, within theories of occupational competence, competence in a particular type of work is identified by looking at the worker and the work as two separate entities. Thereafter, an attempt is made to identify the specific attributes, such as knowledge and skills, that are inherent to the worker and what activities are inherent to the particular work he or she accomplishes (Sandberg, 1994). Similarly, corporate strategy is defined and described by seeing organization and environment as two separate entities. First, the inherent qualities of the organization such as its strengths and weaknesses are described, and then the inherent qualities of the environment such as the threats and opportunities that it offers (Smircich and Stubbart, 1985).

Objectivistic epistemology

The assumption of an objectivistic epistemology stipulates that beyond human consciousness there is an objective reality. Its qualities and the meaning we experience are assumed to be inherent to reality itself. Objective reality is thus seen as given and the ultimate foundation for all our knowledge. Through systematic scientific observations and careful monitoring of the extent to which our theories correspond to the particular aspect of objective reality we are investigating, it is assumed that we will come closer to this true picture of reality.

Individualistic epistemology

Assuming an individualistic epistemology means regarding the individual as the primary creator and possessor of knowledge about reality. The individual is then also regarded as the basic research object. Researchers with an empirical orientation (empiricism) assume that knowledge is produced through the sense experiences of individuals, while researchers with a rationalistic orientation (rationalism) assume that individuals produce knowledge through their inherent reason and their capacity to process and organize incoming sense experiences.

Language as a mirror of objective reality

The core idea of this assumption is that language can represent or, as Rorty (1979) argued, 'mirror' reality in an objective fashion. The relationship between language and reality is thus seen as a relationship of correspondence. As it is assumed that language has the capacity to represent reality, it is treated as a representational system available to the researchers in their endeavour to describe reality objectively.

These assumptions guide advocates of prevalent research approaches in fundamental ways, when it comes to designing and conducting their own research. In particular, research approaches governed by these assumptions focus either on the individual and/or the environment, and treat the individual and the environment as two separate entities, each with their own inherent qualities. For example, the most common approaches in leadership (Yukl, 1994) try either to identify and describe leadership a) by focusing on the specific behaviours of leaders and/or the attributes such as knowledge, skills, attitudes and personal traits that the individual leaders possess, or b) by focusing on situational factors such as the characteristics of the particular leadership task, the staff, the department and the organization in which the leadership is performed. In the former case, leadership is defined in terms of a specific set of attributes inherent to a person; in the latter it is defined by situational factors, that is, a specific set of situational factors requiring a specific type of leadership. Often these two approaches are combined: a specific set of situational factors postulate a specific set of attributes possessed by the leader.

Advocates of social constructionist approaches reject the above assumptions for several reasons. First and most importantly, instead of assuming a dualistic ontology that implies a division of subject and object, advocates of social constructionism regard subject and object as an inseparable relation. As Giorgi (1992) expressed it:

> 'There are not two independent entities, objects and subjects existing in themselves which later get to relate to each other, but the very meaning of subject implies a relationship to an object and to be an object intrinsically implies being related to subjectivity.' (p. 7)

The problem of separating subject and object was originally pointed out by phenomenologists such as Husserl (1970/1900–01) and Heidegger (1981/1927), and later by a series of other researchers such as Schutz (1945, 1953), Berger and Luckmann (1966), Bourdieu (1990), Giddens (1984, 1993) and Searle (1995). Husserl argued that as subjects we are always related to reality through our lived experience of that reality. Heidegger developed Husserl's argument by suggesting that not only is reality mediated through our lived experience, but that it is also mediated through the specific culture, historical time and language in which we are situated.

A number of other researchers in areas such as critical theory, literature theory and social theory have reached similar conclusions to Heidegger. Critical theorists have suggested that our descriptions of reality are often coloured by taken-for-granted ideologies (Alvesson and Willmott, 1996). Advocates of literature theory have argued that such descriptions are furnished by established cultural conventions concerning specific narrative genres and speech codes (Bruner, 1996). Feminist studies have suggested that the dominating theoretical framework for producing knowledge is moulded by and saturated with male imagery (Richardson, 1995). Social scientists have shown that our descriptions of reality are not objective but are socially produced (Danzinger, 1997).

Advocates of these research approaches in social constructionism thus claim that it is not possible to produce objective descriptions of reality. Instead, their basic argument is that our descriptions are always coloured by our specific historical, cultural and linguistic understanding of reality. Thus instead of assuming an objectivistic epistemology in terms of the existence of a given and objective reality, advocates of a social constructionist approach claim that reality is socially constructed by continuous negotiation between people about what their reality is.

The assumption that reality is socially constructed also means a shift from an individualistic to a social epistemology. It is in our relationship to each other that we produce and reproduce reality. More specifically, from the above argument that reality is socially constructed it follows that the social interactions between individuals, rather than the individual mind, is the primary vehicle for developing knowledge. Finally, the assumption that reality is socially constructed means that language is not seen as a representational system that can be used to classify and name objective reality. Instead, language is seen as socially constructed. Thus, language does not achieve its meaning primarily through a correspondence with objective reality, but through the way we socially define and use it in different practices.

Finally, the basic claim of social constructionism, that reality is socially constructed through our activities, does not mean that we continuously produce new realities. Rather, the opposite applies. The fact that our activities are mediated through a specific culture, historical time and language implies that we, to a large extent, reproduce rather than produce reality.

In much the same way that the earlier assumptions guide the advocates of prevalent research approaches, the common assumptions that underlie social constructionist approaches guide its advocates to design and conduct research in specific ways. One of the most fundamental ways in which the assumptions underlying social constructionism govern its specific approaches, is by treating subject and world as an inseparable relation.

For example, within social constructionist approaches, leadership is regarded as a relational or intersubjective phenomenon. First, leadership is seen as intersubjective in terms of an interactive wholeness between the leader and the led (Hosking and Morley, 1991; Hosking, Dachler and

Gergen, 1995; Sandberg and Targama, 1998). More specifically, the leader and the led are seen as part of a social process in which particular forms of leadership are constructed and reproduced over time. Second, leadership is regarded as intersubjective in terms of different forms of conversation or discourse about leadership, such as those that occur within specific organizations, industries, research literature, media and cultures (Calás and Smircich, 1991; Chen and Meindl, 1991; Gemmill and Oakley, 1992; Jönsson, 1995; Alvesson and Willmott, 1996). For instance, Chen and Meindl (1991) explored the construction of leadership over time by investigating how different forms of media produced and reproduced the leadership of Donald Burr and *People Express* between 1981 and 1986.

By regarding leadership as socially constructed, the primary research focus for identifying and describing leadership concerns how certain aspects of leadership are produced and reproduced through the interaction between the leader and the led – that is, both in terms of particular constructions of leadership, and the processes of producing and reproducing these constructions. Moreover, language often becomes a focal point in social constructionist approaches, due to the assumption that we are compelled to report our experiences of reality through a commonly shared language. The way in which we define and use language therefore becomes central to the investigation and understanding of how we construct reality. The focus on language as a central vehicle in constructing leadership is particularly salient in those studies that explore leadership as produced and reproduced through conversation and discourse.

Differences and tensions in social constructionism

Given the great variety of research approaches housed under the roof of social constructionism, there are naturally not only unifying themes but also significant differences and tensions between the different approaches. Three central differences and areas of tension in descriptions of the social construction of reality are micro versus macro levels of social construction; the role of language; and the nature of the relationship between subjectivity and objectivity.

Micro versus macro level of social construction

It is possible to distinguish two major foci within social constructionism (Knorr-Cetina, 1981; Engeström and Middleton, 1996). One set of research approaches, which includes ethnomethodology, symbolic inter-action and cultural psychology, puts its primary focus on the locally constructed reality that is to be found mainly in face-to-face interaction. Another set of approaches, which includes various forms of institutional theory and theories of culture, focuses primarily on a more generally constructed type of reality such as 'the labour market' and 'kinship'. However, a growing number of researchers, such as Knorr-Certina (1981), Callon and Latour (1981), Giddens (1984), Bourdieu (1990), Sjöstrand (1993) and Engeström and Middleton (1996), advocate integrating the micro and macro levels in order to understand how reality is socially constructed.

Approaches that focus on face-to-face interaction only, fail to recognize how that interaction is framed by the larger culture and institutionalized context of which it is a part, while an exclusive focus on the broader social context and culture, fails to recognize how that social context and that culture are produced and maintained in our daily face-to-face interactions.

The role of language in social construction

As was argued before, a general view among social constructionist approaches is that language is not a representational system for classifying and labelling external reality, but that it is instead part of social reality. The debate within social constructionism deals with the extent to which language is part of socially constructed reality, and in what sense it is so. Those who place the strongest emphasis on language are the post-structuralists. Following Derrida (1981/1972, 1998), it is claimed that meaning expressed through language does not refer to an external reality. Derrida (1981/1972) argues further that a specific sign or word within language does not achieve its meaning in relation to an external reality, but only in relation to other words, that is, the meaning of a word is constructed through the play of differences between words. And since meaning is constructed within language, reality appears as language.

A somewhat weaker, albeit still strong emphasis on language is proposed by advocates of discursive approaches. For example, Gergen (1994) argued that social constructionism does not deny:

'... the world out there more generally [...]. Once we attempt to articulate "what there is", however, we enter the world of discourse. At that moment the process of construction commences, and this effort is inextricably woven into processes of social interchange and into history and culture.' (p. 72)

The argument that we construct reality through language and discursive practices implies that they are in focus when exploring the social construction of reality.

Although a number of researchers regard language and discursive practices as the primary vehicle in the social construction of reality, there are also many others such as Wittgenstein (1953), Berger and Luckmann (1966), Habermas (1972), Giddens (1984), Bourdieu (1990), Chaiklin and Lave (1993) and Searle (1995) who place less emphasis on language. Giddens (1984), for example, claimed that reality is only partly constructed through discursive practices, or what he called 'discursive consciousness'. He claims instead that the greater part of the social construction of reality takes place in 'practical consciousness'.

'Practical consciousness consists of all the things which actors know tacitly about how to "go on" in the context of social life without being able to give them direct discursive expression.'

In his theory of practice Bourdieu (1990) argued along lines similar to Giddens. More specifically, in elaborating the concept of habitus as a theory for bridging the distinction between individual and social, Bourdieu argued that habitus is primarily bodily rather than discursive. Moreover, as Bourdieu (1990), Engeström (1993) and even Derrida in his later writings (see Debrix, 1999) have pointed out, various forms of material conditions, such as economic capital and material tools, are also central components in social construction, since they constrain and enable the social construction of reality in specific ways.

The nature of the relationship between subject and object

As was described earlier, most social constructionists embrace a relational ontology, in the sense that subject and object are regarded as inextricably related. However, there is tension between those researchers who put the focus on the subject pole and those who focus on the object pole of the relation, and there is an ongoing debate between the two sides. The theoretical path within constructionism originating from Piaget (1954) and Kelly (1955) in cognitive psychology (Schwandt, 1994; Gergen, 1995) falls close to the subjective pole. Post-structuralists who tend to equate reality with language, as well as researchers who mainly adopt a discursive approach, also come close to the subjective side. A number of institutional theorists, on the other hand, are closely related to the objective pole.

Researchers such as Berger and Luckmann (1966), Bourdieu (1990) and Giddens (1984) are critical of these approaches, whose primary focus falls on either the subject or the object pole of the relation. The greatest risk in taking a strong subjectivistic or objectivistic stance here is that the indissoluble relation between subject and object may be neglected. For example, a strong focus on individuals may fail to take into account the way in which institutions such as money, property, marriage and leadership influence the subjective construction of reality. Taking a strong subjective stance also implies the risk of falling into idealism. On the other hand, a strong objective focus may fail to take into account how these institutions are subjectively produced and reproduced, and thus lead to realism.

A social phenomenological approach to social constructionism

The social constructionist approaches adopted in this book are primarily rooted in a social phenomenological framework as proposed and developed by scholars such as Berger and Luckmann (1966), Giddens (1984) and Bourdieu (1990). As has been indicated, the approach proposed by these researchers and others falls somewhere midway between the above mentioned controversies within social constructionism. First, advocates of a social phenomenological approach emphasize the importance of treating the micro and macro level of the social construction of reality as integrated. Second, they emphasize the importance of taking into account both the symbolic and the material dimension in describing the social construction of reality. Third, they emphasize the need to treat the relation between subject and object as a dialectic wholeness.

The aim of the rest of this chapter is to further elaborate and describe the most central features of a social phenomenological approach to social constructionism. This elaboration will be based primarily on Berger and Luckmann's (1966) theory of social construction. There are two reasons for this choice. The most important is that most of the other chapters in this book explicitly or implicitly utilize Berger and Luckmann's theory of social construction in their analyses. The second reason is that Berger and Luckmann's theory is still one of the most comprehensive theories of social construction.

Life-world as the basis for the social phenomenological approach to social constructionism

The basis for a social phenomenological approach to social construction-ism is the notion of life-world, stipulating that subject and world are inextricably related through the subject's lived experience of the world. The concept of life-world was first proposed by Husserl (1970/1936) but has been further developed by other phenomenologists such as Heidegger (1981/1927), Merleau-Ponty (1962/1945) and Gadamer (1994/1960). However, it is primarily Schutz's work (1945, 1953, 1967) and Schutz and Luckmann (1973) that has laid the groundwork for the social phenomenological approach to social constructionism.

Bengtsson (1989, p. 72) captured the basic idea of life-world, that subject and world are inseparable through the subjects' experience of the world as follows:

'[...] even if life-world is objective both in the sense that it is a shared world and in the sense that it transcends (exceeds) the subject, that is, its qualities are not qualities within the subject, it is likewise inseparable from a subject, namely, the subject who experiences it, lives and acts in it. The world is always there in the first person from the perspective of my space and time here and now.'

As Bengtsson (ibid.) points out, life-world is the subject's experience of reality, at the same time that it is objective. It is not objective, however, in the sense of being an objective reality independent of the subject. Instead, it is objective in the sense that it is an intersubjective world. We share it with other subjects through our experience of it, and we are constantly involved in negotiation with other subjects about reality in terms of our intersubjective sense-making of it. The agreed meaning constitutes the objective reality. Furthermore, life-world is objective in the sense that it transcends its subjects. This is because its qualities are not solely tied to the subjects' lived experience of it. At the same time, however, it is inseparable from the subjects through their experience of it. For example, most European countries have agreed to have daylight saving and move the clock one hour ahead for the period of March to October. Daylight saving thus becomes an objective fact through this agreement. Even if some of us try to ignore the agreed daylight saving time, we encounter difficulty in doing so because its qualities extend beyond our experience of clock time.

As became apparent in the above example, subjective and objective realities reflect each other. On the one hand, a basic condition for individuals to survive in society is that their subjective reality corresponds with objective reality. If my subjective construction of clock time deviates considerably from the general construction of clock time, I encounter difficulties in getting by. On the other hand, the construction of objective reality must correspond to the subjectively constructed reality. If not, a particular constructed reality will not achieve the status of objective reality. It is first when there is a correspondence between a number of subjectively constructed realities, such as agreement among most countries in Europe concerning the introduction of daylight saving, that an objective reality can appear.

However, subjective and objective reality can never correspond completely, because objective reality always exceeds subjective reality in a number of ways. One reason for this is the division of labour, which gives rise to a particular distribution of knowledge of reality among members of a society. For instance, even if a trade unionist and a board member of a company are in agreement that the failure of their company to produce a desirable profit stems from a leadership problem, their construction of leadership and the solution to that problem may differ. Another central factor is our social position, such as class and gender in the social structure in which we live and act. If the trade unionist is a woman and comes from the working class, and the board member is a man who comes from the upper class, this may mean an even larger difference in their construction of the problem of leadership. Moreover, other factors such as differences in culture and the geographical area (urban or rural) in which a person has grown up and lives, or differences in age, may also lead to a lower level of correspondence between the subjective and objective construction of reality. For example, Hofstede's (1980) study of cultural differences in 40 countries illustrates that the construction of leadership varies from culture to culture.

Subjective and objective reality as a dialectic wholeness

But how can reality exist as subjective and objective at the same time? As well as Berger and Luckmann, both Bourdieu and Giddens have each offered a comprehensive account of the problem of the simultaneity of subjective and objective experience. Through his concept of *habitus*, Bourdieu (1981, 1990) tried to describe the inextricable relation between subject and object. According to his view, every action brings together two states of history: objectified history and embodied history in the form of habitus. Objective reality exists in terms of an objectified history accumulated in material objects such as machines and buildings, and in immaterial objects such as theories and customs. Subjective reality exists as embodied history, which consists of an internalized objectified history or objective reality. In our activities and actions, objectified and embodied history appears simultaneously in habitus. As Bourdieu (1981) exemplified it:

> 'A man who raises his hat in greeting is unwittingly reactivating a conventional sign inherited from the Middle Ages, when as Panoflosky reminds us, armed men used to take off their helmets to make clear their peaceful intentions.' (p. 305)

What Bourdieu's example shows is that the habitus of 'greeting' is part of objectified history or objective reality, while at the same time it is part of embodied history or subjective reality, in the sense that 'greeting' carries the agent's action and is carried by the agent simultaneously.

In his theory of structuration, Giddens (1984, 1993) gives a similar account of how subjective and objective reality can exist simultaneously. In his view, the dialectic relation between subjective and objective reality can be described as a duality of structure. By duality of structure he means 'that social structure is both constituted by human agency and yet is at the same time the very *medium* of this constitution' (Giddens, 1993, p. 128). The theory of duality of structures can also be illustrated by Bourdieu's example of greeting, where we see how the social structure of greeting is produced by the man who raises his hat to the person he meets, while at the same time the social structure of greeting produces the way in which the two people interact when they meet each other.

The simultaneous dialectic between subjective and objective reality is also the most central feature of Berger and Luckmann's (1966) theory of social construction. In the social construction of reality, they see an ongoing dialectical process between subjective and objective reality, which can be described in terms of externalization, objectivation and internalization.

Externalization means that we produce our reality through activities such as talking, thinking, building, managing, curing, eating, writing and driving. The agreement on daylight saving time is an externalization of human activities. Objectivation means that we experience our activities as having an objective existence independent of ourselves as individual subjects. For instance, the agreed change in time is experienced as objective because it influences our daily life in various ways. Internalization refers to the socialization process whereby we become part of the reality we have produced. For example, we internalize daylight saving time by living and acting according to that time. These three dialectical elements appear not sequentially, but simultaneously. At the same time that we act in accordance with the stipulated daylight saving time, we externalize, objectify and internalize it. More precisely, by following this time, we reproduce it; and because of our doing so, daylight saving time achieves the status of objective reality, which we internalize by being socialized into daylight saving time.

Socialization: from subjective to objective construction of reality

Although we participate simultaneously in the societal dialectics between subjective and objective reality, there is a sequential time span in which each one of us becomes part of these societal dialectics. The starting-point for this is the internalization process, the immediate experience of an activity that expresses meaning, that is, as a manifestation of someone else's subjective processes that become subjectively meaningful to me. Through the externalization, this person's subjectivity becomes objectively available to me, and thus also meaningful to me irrespective of whether my interpretation is in line with the other's intention.

There are two central processes by which an individual internalizes society: primary and secondary socialization. Primary socialization is the first and most fundamental step in the internalization of the construction of objective reality. In primary socialization we internalize the most basic constructions of reality such as language, greetings, mother, father and gender that regulate the most common activities and interactions among people. Secondary socialization includes any of the subsequent socialization processes by which individuals internalize central aspects of reality, such as professions, and institutions such as money, banks and tax authorities.

A central feature in both primary and secondary socialization is that the internalization of roles and attitudes from significant others such as parents, relatives, friends and teachers becomes progressively abstracted to roles and attitudes in general. When the generalized other has been incorporated into consciousness, a symmetrical relation between objective and subjective reality is established. As Berger and Luckmann (1966) expressed it: 'What is real "outside" corresponds with what is real "within"' (p. 153).

An important conclusion to be drawn from the above discussion is that our experience of reality as meaningful is not primarily a result of our own sense-making of it. Rather, meaningfulness originates in the process by which we as individuals internalize the reality in which others already act and live. In other words, the socially constructed reality that we internalize becomes our framework for making sense of reality. This means that those activities and actions in which individuals are involved, achieve their meaning through the specific social constructions of reality that they have internalized via primary and secondary socialization.

From the above description, it may appear as though the interaction between subjects in the process of constructing reality is primarily harmonious and symmetrical. This, however, is not always the case. As was pointed out earlier, the symmetry between subjective and objective reality can never be complete, because there is always more objective than subjective reality available. In addition, the interaction is largely asymmetrical, in terms of both knowledge and power (Foucault, 1972). This asymmetry is obvious between parents–children and teacher–pupil, but is also particular salient in leadership. In Berger and Luckmann's words (1966):

> 'He (sic) who has the largest stick has the better chance of imposing his definitions of reality. This is a rather safe assumption to make with regard to any larger collectivity, although there is always the possibility of politically disinterested theoreticians convincing each other without recourse to the cruder means of persuasion.' (p. 127)

The role of language in the social construction of reality

In the social phenomenological approach, language plays a crucial role in the social construction of reality. However, while language is funda-mental to the social construction of reality, it is at the same time socially constructed itself. As Searle (1995) argued, language can be seen as the most basic socially constructed institution, since all other socially constructed institutions presuppose language. Therefore, before the role of language in the social construction of reality is discussed in more detail, there follows a brief description of how language is socially constructed.

Language can be characterized as a system of vocal signs. It is produced when we externalize ourselves through specific forms of vocal expression. Through vocal expressions, language becomes objectively available to others, and objectified as having an objective and indepen-dent existence. We are also concerned about constructing the same language. For example, we often correct each other when we deviate from objective language. Some countries have also gone so far as to establish language authorities whose aim it is to monitor, and in some cases even dictate, how a particular language develops. This concern for constructing a single language is based on the idea that the social construction of reality presupposes an objective language. A high correspondence between subjective and objective language construction is a prerequisite for achieving a high correspondence between subjective and objective constructions of other aspects of reality.

The need to have a strong correspondence between the subjective and objective construction of reality becomes particularly obvious when we learn an additional language in order to communicate adequately. To achieve a high level of correspondence, a successful internalization of language is fundamental in both primary and secondary socialization. In the first phases of primary socialization, there is a big distance between subjective and objective language. Gradually, subjective and objective languages begin to come closer and closer together. The same applies to secondary socialization. For example, to become a corporate leader in a Swedish company the person concerned has to internalize the specific language and vocabulary developed and used by Swedish leaders when exercising leadership.

If language, then, is socially constructed, what role does it play in the social construction of other aspects of reality? From a social phenomenological perspective (e.g. Berger and Luckmann, 1966; Giddens, 1984; Bourdieu, 1990; Searle, 1995), language plays the following roles in the social construction of reality:

- it objectifies our experiences by categorizing and organizing them into meaningful wholes;

- it functions to a large extent as interpretative schemes of reality in the sense that our experiences of reality are objectified through language;

- through the objectivation of our experiences, it functions as a storage room for our accumulated experiences; and

- it works as the primary medium through which our accumulated experiences are transmitted between people and between generations, that is, between subjective and objective reality.

It is primarily in conversations between people that language plays an important role in the social construction of reality. The construction of reality through conversation is often described as discourses (Potter and Whetherell, 1987). However, the term 'discourse' does not have one single meaning, but is defined and used in a whole range of ways (Mills, 1997). In its most general sense, discourse can be described as a particular set of linguistic expressions, statements and concepts that form a kind of wholeness of particular topics.

In an overview of discourse studies in organization and management, Alvesson and Kärreman (1998) identified two key dimensions. One dimension refers to the extent to which discourse determines the construction of reality and enjoys a wide range of advocates, from those who assume that discourse determines the construction of reality completely to those who regard discourse as relatively independent of the construction of social reality. As was argued in the first part of the chapter, social phenomenology falls between the end positions on this dimension. The second key dimension refers to the level of discourse, from local discourse in which most face-to-face conversations take place, to mega discourse such as general conversation about medicine or leadership in the Western world. The second dimension corresponds to a large degree with Berger and Luckmann's (1966) description of the legitimation of socially constructed reality as being objective. This correspondence can be used as a further exemplification of the role of language and discourse in the social construction of reality.

Following Berger and Luckmann (ibid.), legitimation can be seen as a second-order objectivation of our construction of reality. These authors distinguish four levels of legitimation. The first is described as a pre-theoretical and taken-for-granted stipulating that 'this is the way we do things here'. This level in particular provides a basic vocabulary which legitimates the social construction in question, and parallels a range of discourse studies in Alvesson and Kärreman's (1998) overview that emphasise the importance of detailed studies of local discourse in the understanding of particular social constructions of reality, such as leadership.

At the second level of legitimation, rudimentary theoretical statements are introduced. Proverbs and different forms of words of wisdom are commonly used. This second level of legitimation parallels the studies cited by Alvesson and Kärreman (ibid.), in which researchers acknowledge not only the need to be sensitive to specific expressions and statements used in local discourse, but also the need to go beyond local discourse and to make comparisons with other similar discourses in order to find broader discourse patterns. For example, instead of focusing only on the leadership discourse of a specific company, we could also investigate discourses of recruitment, incentives, training and career planning in an effort to explore in greater depth how leadership is socially constructed in that company.

The third level of legitimation provides more explicit theories on a range of institutions, which in turn often provide a more comprehensive framework to legitimate a specific social construction of reality. This level corresponds with the discourse researchers in Alvesson and Kärreman's (ibid.) overview present, which focuses on the higher-level discourses that order more local discourses into an integrated frame constituting a particular institution. For example, a higher level discourse of leadership is often provided by business schools, leadership institutes and research literature.

Finally, a particular construction of reality is legitimated at a fourth level, comprised of overarching theories. These theories integrate a range of related activities into a meaningful whole, or what Berger and Luckmann (1966) labelled a 'symbolic universe'. The aim of this symbolic universe is to produce an exhaustive framework that gives meaning to, and justifies the existence of a range of related institutionalized activities. The symbolic universe corresponds to what Alvesson and Kärreman (1998) called 'mega discourse'. Mega discourse refers to the most general and standardized ways of conversing about certain practices, such as leadership. The market economy can be regarded as one mega discourse in which different forms of leadership discourse take place.

Concluding remarks

The aim of this chapter has been to describe the main features of social constructionism and to provide some background for the analysis in subsequent chapters of how leadership is socially constructed in different arenas. I first looked at the different research approaches covered by the label of social constructionism, to explore what they have in common and what differences and tensions exist among them. I then examined the basic features of a social phenomenological approach in greater detail, with a view to highlighting the theoretical framework behind the analysis of leadership in the chapters that follow.

A central claim arising from this more detailed examination of the social phenomenological approach is that the social construction of reality consists first and foremost of an ongoing reproduction, rather than an ongoing production, of reality. Using Bourdieu's (1981, 1990) terminology, the social construction of reality is largely a reproduction of objectified history embodied in our subjective activities in the form of habitus. No sooner are we born than we begin to internalize and embody reality as an objectified history. The more we become part of reality, through primary and secondary socialization, the more we begin to reproduce it ourselves. It is when we as subjects are first able to reproduce objective reality through our activities that we are regarded as fully fledged members of socially constructed reality.

That individuals to a large extent reproduce reality does not mean that they are some kind of mechanical robots that have been programmed in a certain way through socialization into society. We also have an ability to stand back and reflect on our performance, and to become aware of the ways in which our activities and actions are a result of what we have internalized through our participation in society. In other words, through reflection we are able to discover that society is a social construction rather than something given by nature. If we have created society, it also means that we can change it. However, changing requires an awareness and knowledge about how we socially construct reality, and its specific aspects such as leadership. Without such knowledge, we are more or less doomed to reproduce society in its present form.

A central aim in the chapters that follow is to identify and describe what constructions of leadership exist within organizations and how they are (re)produced in the interaction between people. In particular, the ongoing (re)production in terms of the dialectical wholeness between the subjective and objective construction of reality is the main focus in our attempts to identify and describe how managerial leadership is socially constructed in different arenas.

Note

1 In social science, the terms 'constructivism' and 'constructionism' are sometimes used interchangeably. But as Gergen (1985) and others have pointed out, these terms have quite different origins. The term 'constructivism' is used primarily with reference to the Piagetian theory of perception, while 'constructionism' refers mainly to Berger and Luckmann's (1966) work on how reality is socially constructed. As the main focus in this book is on theories more closely linked to Berger and Luckmann than to Piaget, the term 'constructionism' is used.

References

Alvesson, M. (1993). *Cultural perspectives on organizations*. Cambridge University Press, Cambridge.

Alvesson, M., and Kärreman, D. (1998). *Discourses and grand discourse. Discourse and the study of organizations*. Paper presented at the conference Organizational Discourse: Pretext, Subtext and Context, London, UK.

Alvesson, M., and Sköldberg, K. (1999). *Toward reflexive methodology*. Sage, London.

Alvesson, M., and Willmott, H. (1996). *Making sense of management. A critical introduction*. Sage, London.

Asteley, W. G. (1985). Administrative science as socially constructed truth. *Administrative Science Quarterly*, vol. 30, pp. 497–513.

Atkinson, P. (1988). Ethnomethodology. A critical review. *Annual Review of Sociology*, vol. 14, pp. 441–65.

Bengtsson, J. (1989). Fenomenologi: Vardagsforskning, existensfilosofi, hermeneutik. In P. Månson (Ed.), *Moderna samhällsteorier: Traditioner riktningar teoretiker*, pp. 67–108, Prisma, Stockholm.

Bengtsson, J. (ed.). (1999). *Med livsvärlden som grund*. Studentlitteratur, Lund.

Berger, P. L., and Luckmann, T. (1966/1981). *The social construction of reality*. Penguin, Harmondsworth.

Bourdieu, P. (1981). Men and machines, in Knorr-Certina, K., and Cicourel, A. V. (Eds.), *Advances in social theory and methodology. Toward an integration of micro- and macro-sociologies*. Routledge, Boston.

Bourdieu, P. (1990). *The logic of practice*. Polity Press, Cambridge.

Bruner, J. (1996). *The culture of education*. Harvard University Press, Cambridge.

Calás, M. B., and Smircich, L. (1991). Voicing seduction to silence leadership. *Organization Studies*, vol. 4, pp. 567–602.

Callon, M., and Latour, B. (1981). Unscrewing the big Leviathan: how actors macro-structure reality and how sociologists help them to do so, in Knorr-Certina, K., and Cicourel, A. V. (eds.), *Advances in social theory and methodology. Toward an integration of micro- and macro-sociologies*. Routledge, Boston.

Chaiklin, S., and Lave, J. (1993). *Understanding practice. Perspectives on activity and context*. Cambridge University Press, Cambridge.

Chen, C. C., and Meindl, J. R. (1991). The construction of leadership images in the popular press: The case of Donald Burr and People Express. *Administrative Science Quarterly*, vol. 36, pp. 521–51.

Cole, M., (1996). *Cultural Psychology. A once and future discipline*. Harvard University Press, Cambridge.

Danzinger, K. (1997). The varieties of social construction. *Theory & Psychology*, vol. 3, pp. 399–416.

Debrix, F. (1999). Specters of postmodernism: Derrida's Marx, the new International and the return of situationism. *Philosophy & Social Criticism*, vol. 1, pp. 1–21.

Derrida, J. (1981/1972). *Positions* (translated by Alan Bass). The Athlone Press, London.

Derrida, J. (1998). *Rösten och fenomenet*. Thales, Stockholm.

DiMaggio, P. J., and Powell, W. W. (1983). The iron cage revisited. Institutional isomorphism and collective rationality in organizational fields. *American Sociological Review*, vol. 148, pp. 147–60.

Engeström, Y. (1993). Developmental studies of work as a testbench of activity theory: The case of primary care medical practice. In Chaiklin, S., and Lave, J. (eds.) *Understanding practice. Perspectives on activity and context*. Cambridge University Press, Cambridge.

Engeström, Y., and Middleton, D. (1996). *Cognition and communication at work*. Cambridge University Press, Cambridge.

Farr, R. M., and Moscovici, S. (eds.). (1984). *Social representations*. Cambridge University Press, Cambridge.

Foucault, M. (1972). *The archeology of knowledge*. Routledge, London.

Gadamer, H-G. 1994/1960. *Truth and method* (translated by Sheed and Ward Ltd). Continuum, New York.

Garfinkel, H. (1967). *Studies in ethnomethodology.* Prentice Hall, Englewood Cliffs, NJ.

Geertz, C. (1973). *The interpretation of cultures.* Fontana Press, London.

Gemmill, G. and Oakley, J. (1992). Leadership: An alienating social myth? *Human Relations,* vol. 2, pp. 113–29.

Gergen, K. (1985). The social constructionist movement in modern psychology. *American Psychologist,* vol. 3, pp. 266–75.

Gergen, K. (1994). *Realities and relationships. Soundings in social construction.* Harvard University Press, Cambridge.

Giddens, A. (1984). *The constitution of society. Outline of the theory of structuration.* Polity Press, Cambridge.

Giddens, A. (1993). *New rules of sociological methods. A positive critique of interpretative sociologies.* Polity Press, Cambridge.

Giorgi, A. (1992). *The theory, practice and evaluation of the phenomenological method as a qualitative research procedure for the human sciences.* Université du Québec à Montréal, Quebec.

Giorgi, A. (1994). A phenomenological perspective on certain qualitative research methods. *Journal of Phenomenological Psychology,* vol. 25, pp. 191–220.

Habermas, J. (1972). *Knowledge and human interest.* Heinemann, London.

Hacking, I. (1999). *The social construction of what?* Harvard University Press, Harvard.

Harding, S. (1986). *The science question in feminism.* Cornell University Press, London.

Heidegger, M. (1981/1927). *Varat och tiden,* vols. 1–2 (translated by Richard Matz). Doxa, Lund.

Heritage, J. (1984). *Garfinkel and ethnomethodology.* Polity Press, Cambridge.

Hofstede, G. (1980). *Culture's consequences: International differences in work-related values.* Sage, Beverly Hills.

Hosking, D-M., and Morley, I. E. (1991). *A social psychology of organizing.* Harvester Wheatsheaf, New York.

Hosking, D-M., Dachler, P. H., and Gergen, K. J. (1995). *Management and organization: Relational alternatives to individualism.* Avebury, Aldershot.

Husserl, E. (1970/1900–01). *Logical investigations,* vol. 2 (translated by J. N. Findlay). Routledge & Kegan Paul, London.

Husserl, E. (1970/1936). *The crisis of European sciences and transcendental phenomenology* (translated by D. Carr). Northwestern University Press, Evanston.

Jönsson, S. (1995). *Goda utsikter. Svenskt management i perspektiv.* Nerenius & Santérus, Stockholm.

Keller, E. F. (1985). *Reflections on gender and science.* Yale University Press, New Haven.

Kelly, G. A. (1955). *The psychology of personal construct.* Norton, New York.

Knorr-Certina, K. (1981). The micro-sociological challenge of macro-sociology: toward a reconstruction of social theory and methodology. In Knorr-Certina, K., and Cicourel, A. V. (eds.), *Advances in social theory and methodology. Toward an integration of micro- and macro-sociologies.* Routledge, Boston.

Kvale, S. (1995). The social construction of validity. *Qualitative Inquiry,* vol. 1, pp. 19–40.

Mead, G. H. (1934). *Mind, self and society from the standpoint of a social behaviorist.* Chicago University Press, Chicago.

Merleau-Ponty, M. (1962/1945). *Phenomenology of perception* (translated by C. Smith.). Routledge & Kegan Paul, London.

Meyer, J., and Rowan, B. (1977). Institutional organizations: Formal structure as myth and ceremony. *American Journal of Sociology,* vol. 83, pp. 340–63.

Mills, S. (1997). *Discourse.* Routledge, London.

Piaget, J. (1954). *The construction of the reality in the child.* Basic Books, New York.

Potter, J., and Wetherell, M. (1987). *Discourse and social psychology: Beyond attitudes and behaviour.* Sage, London.

Richardson, L. (1995). Poetics, dramatics, and transgressive validity: The case of the skipped line. *The Sociological Quarterly,* vol. 4, pp. 695–710.

Rorty, R. (1979). *Philosophy and the mirror of nature.* Princeton University Press, Princeton, NJ.

Sandberg, J. (1994). *Human competence at work: An interpretative approach.* BAS, Göteborg.

Sandberg, J., and Targama, A. (1998). *Ledning och förståelse. Ett kompetensperspektiv på organisationer.* Studentlitteratur, Lund.

Schutz, A. (1945). On multiple realities. *Philosophy and Phenomenological Research, A Quarterly Journal,* vol. 5, pp. 533–75.

Schutz, A. (1953). Common-sense and scientific interpretation of human action. *Philosophy and Phenomenological Research,* vol. 14, pp. 1–37.

Schutz, A. (1967). *The phenomenology of the social world.* North Western University Press, Vienna.

Schutz, A. and Luckmann, T. (1973). *The structures of the life-world,* vols. I and II. Northwestern University Press, Evanston.

Schwandt, T. A. (1994). Constructivist, interpretivist approaches to human inquiry, in Denzin, N. K., and Lincoln, Y. S. (eds.), *Handbook of qualitative research,* pp. 118–137, Sage, Thousand Oaks, CA.

Scott, R. W. (1995). *Institutions and organizations.* Sage, Thousand Oaks.

Searle, J. R. (1995). *The construction of social reality.* Free Press, New York.

Shore, B. (1996). *Culture in mind. Cognition, culture, and the problem of meaning.* Oxford University Press, New York.

Sjöstrand, S-E. (1985). *Samhällsorganisation.* Doxa, Lund.

Sjöstrand, S-E. (1993). The socioeconomic institutions of organizing: Origin, emergence, and reproduction. *The Journal of Socio-Economics,* vol. 4, pp. 323–52.

Sjöstrand, S-E. (1997). *The Two Faces of Management. The Janus Factor.* Thomson, London.

Smircich, L. and Stubbart, C. (1985). Strategic management in an enacted world. *Academy of Management Review,* vol. 4, pp. 724–36.

Townely, B. (1993). Foucalt, power/knowledge, and its relevance for human resource management. *Academy of Management Review,* vol. 3, pp. 518–45.

Weick, K. E. (1995). *Sensemaking in organizations.* Sage, Thousand Oaks.

Wittgenstein, L. (1953). *Philosophical investigations.* Blackwell, Oxford.

Yukl, G. (1994). *Leadership in organizations.* Prentice Hall, Englewood Cliffs, NJ.

CHAPTER THREE

The tough ones

Markus Kallifatides

An internal programme of interaction between top management and selected young managers, known as *Top Selection,* is interpreted as a process of the managerial constructing of managerial leadership/leaders. A one-day meeting is described in some detail, and its proceedings are interpreted in terms of well-established legitimating conceptual machinery of the manager as a social institution. It is shown that the process of constructing managerial leadership is not neutral relative to its constructions. On the contrary, the process of constructing is fuelled by the constructions, and vice versa. In this case, both the constructing and the construction are permeated by what could be called the virtue of toughness.

Introduction

In this chapter social constructions are seen as comprising a cultural base, unequally accessible to different individuals, and unequally appropriated by them. This cultural base can be, and is, drawn upon so that people can act in their daily lives. It is my firm assumption that drawing upon a cultural base is generally a subconscious or preconscious process, rather than a conscious one. In retrospect, however, much can be made conscious. This chapter is an attempt to bring one such significant construction into the realm of consciousness.

The relation between constructions and constructing processes is an intricate one. A construction may or may not include ideas about how the construction itself is to be constructed. Constructions of leadership, for example, may include ideas about how leadership is to be constructed, i.e. both processes and outcome are included in the construction. To indicate where such constructions are infused with normative value ('this is the way it should be'), the concept of virtue is introduced.

The following pages will consider the creation of managerial leadership constructions in the western world. I suggest that this process has created images of managerial leadership which are infused with normative value (after much ideological work had been done), and which have thus been transformed into virtues. These virtues will be considered as they are enacted in the contemporary setting of ordinary managerial activity, namely in the socialization of new managers, or in other words the managerial constructing of managerial leadership.

The constructing of managerial leadership constructions

Management as a social institution has many roots. When it comes to the formation of this particular institution, it is always possible for instance to invoke the idiosyncrasies of particular cultures, national or otherwise. Here, it is proposed instead that there is a fairly general and widely held idea of management's, or the manager's, status as an institution in the western world.

The complexity of managerial life has had its counterpart in the cultural and/or social construction of managerial leadership. There is simply no single set of beliefs about what makes for a good manager out there in the human world. I am prepared to argue, however, for the existence of a set of beliefs that do seem to be prevalent. In doing so I will follow Bendix (1956) in offering a description of the constructing of managerial leadership constructions that today are part of the cultural base in much of the western world.

Managerial ideologies

In Great Britain, capitalism arose as a subversive social movement, its advocates consciously aspiring to break down established social structures (both physical and mental). This was indeed a hard battle, and at the beginning the capitalist was often the underdog. Over the decades, however, all this naturally changed. In the United States the Protestant ethic, which embraced and fuelled the capitalist spirit, was the dominant social ideology from the very beginning (as eloquently described by Weber, 1905). Bendix (1956, pp. 254–67) highlights the importance of Social Darwinism in the formation of managerial ideology at the beginning of the twentieth century. A veritable gospel was created, whereby success in industrial activities was seen as the fruit of possessing the right attitude, of being 'made of the right stuff' (which parallels the doctrine of predestination in Reformist Protestant theology).

With Taylor (1911) and the scientific management movement, a second image of the manager was born, that of the manager as scientist or, if you will, as expert. The manager *qua* expert studies and documents, measures and calculates; his[1] task is to optimize activities.

The human relations movement – the birth of which is often said to have occurred with the Hawthorne studies (Roetlisberger and Dickson, 1947), but is sometimes also traced back to the work of Barnard (see Perrow, 1986, Ch. 2) – adds a third image to the modern arsenal of managerial ideology, namely that of the manager as a father figure, who with his patriarchal hand helps his subordinates to develop, guided by his knowledge of their emotional status, in particular their desire 'to stand well with [their] fellows' (Mayo, cited in Bendix 1956, p. 313). What natural science is to scientific management, social science is to human relations.

This depiction of the cultural base needs extending somewhat for our present purposes. Alongside the development of the ideology of free enterprise, the ideal of bureaucracy, most clearly investigated by Weber, has also emerged. This emanated in part outside the realm of free enterprise. Holding office in a bureaucracy means, more than anything else, that you have been selected for that office by someone possessing the authority to choose you and that you have been chosen on grounds of formal criteria of merit. I argue that this ideal has been resolutely appropriated by private enterprise, and 'being chosen by someone' is now a fundamental legitimating mechanism (possibly even *the* such mechanism), not only for individuals holding public office but also for managers in the world of private enterprise.

Managers today thus have access to four images of management that are well established in the cultural base (transmitted in public debate and the media, as well as in academia). These are: being made of the right stuff, the calculating expert, the father, and being chosen by someone. Images are quickly transformed into virtues, and virtues are enacted. This will be illustrated below.

Methodology and empirical base

In order to trace these four cited virtues in the contemporary world, I use observations from a one-day meeting in an industrial sales company. Although the meeting constitutes only a fraction of a much larger and somewhat differently oriented case study of the company in question,[2] the observations described below were made with the specific purpose of providing a basis for this chapter.

The top selection programme

Top management (CEO, Financial Director and Personnel Director) has put together, largely according to group standards, a set of programmes to help secure for the company a steady internal supply of qualified candidates for manageriai positions. A trainee programme has been initiated, as well as a multi-level training programme for managers (with internal and external educational activities), and a job rotation programme. It has not been uncommon for trainees to be looked upon with some degree of suspicion and envy, partly because of all the attention they receive within the organization, and particularly because they are permitted to 'float' between various departments over fairly short periods of time. To balance this relatively high profile of newly recruited trainees, top management instigated a programme that we can call Top Selection (TS).

Top Selection assembles employees possessing a certain amount of experience of operative work within the organization for one-day meetings with top management. The meetings are not planned as classroom lessons. The explicit intention on the part of top management is to set up activities conducive to developing and stimulating these individuals in their careers, as well as 'enhancing their identification with, or loyalty to, the company'. Straightforward information, internal and external lectures, discussions, presentations, workshops, problem solving, and visits to other companies are examples of such activities. 'Open and straightforward dialogue' is said to be sought after, and this is also stated in documents pertaining to the programme.

What follows is a fairly detailed description of one of these one-day sessions.

A day in the sun

The CEO placed himself in the centre of the conference room – something he almost always does when it is his turn to speak. He began with a review of Group activities over the last six months, glancing at a document in his hand to recall important figures from the latest accounts, all in his usual calm and rather grave manner.

'Orders are up, as is turnover. Profits, however, lag behind, and the company's shares are falling on the market. This is a problem, and it explains the recent initiatives from headquarters. There is reorganization in the pipeline. Three central product divisions, one of which has had serious problems achieving profitability, are to be reorganized into three new ones, moving bits and pieces to and from other divisions as well. Now, how are we to handle all this locally? How are we to integrate subsidiary X into our own organization? Is division X going to be a legal entity of its own? These are the things we'll be forced to discuss in the near future.'

Only one young manager, Ivan, interrupts with a few questions. The CEO moves on to the local company activities and figures.

Then he lays aside his papers: 'I thought we might begin today by asking ourselves a philosophical question. Why are we here?' (At the same time, he turns on the overhead projector and the first point on the slide is shown.)

'This is not a sports club or anything like that. It's not a voluntary organization, we have an assignment, and we are not here just to have fun. This is serious. Top management, product division managers, lower unit managers, indeed everyone – there is an assignment behind it all. We are here to create terminology, goals and strategies. Then there are of course conflicting interests in such a large Group. Headquarters, product divisions, geographically organized units.'

There's a lot of bad mouthing going on. I guess that's part of the game in a large group. There are a lot of people, and there are many ways of swerving away from what has been said. Still, we, [the Financial Director and I], we have an assignment. Most importantly, we are here to protect the interests of the group's total mass of activities here in Sweden. Now, what does that mean?

Ivan tries to explain what the assignment implies. The CEO nods affirmatively and continues: 'That is, it's about balancing the interests of various product divisions. Now, you can see the problem we have when we appoint a product division manager.' He goes on to explain that tension exists between different dimensions in the global matrix at every level down the corporate ladder. 'You are all first and foremost responsible for the whole, you are employed by the [Swedish company]. Of course there are tensions, the Group is set up that way, but the whole is what counts.'

Here, Ivan adds: 'It mustn't cost too much energy, these internal matters.' The CEO voices his agreement. Another young TS, Ethan, makes his second comment: 'It's also a question of the management systems one builds up at every level in the organization ... all these figures at all levels.' The Financial Director jumps in: 'Yes, but we need the figures to be able to govern activities. It's a kind of trade-off between governability, incentive systems and the whole. Sure. But you have to live with that.'

The CEO takes charge: 'All this works when you have a very powerful central leadership, like [major competitor X] has had for example. We have another kind of culture. I mean, we have to agree on things somehow, a whole lot of people. But we're getting somewhere anyway. And we may have another kind of discussion than [competitor X] during the reign of [President P]. Maybe they've had clearer briefings than we have.'

A few more points are briefly discussed, and the supposed prevalence of the totality is underlined again when Ethan asks: 'But the whole is supposed to take over [...]?' To which the CEO replies: 'Sure.' He goes on to tell a story about the management of one product division that wanted to move to offices outside the present headquarters. 'They said it was too expensive for them to stay here. I just sent him a letter explaining that we're both obliged to see to everything here. Every square inch of office space outside this building is an extra cost for the Group as a whole.' The Financial Director adds: 'And that's apart from the fact that it isn't too expensive here. But that's another issue.'

The CEO moves on to the fifth point on his overhead. 'We are obliged to safeguard the interests of all other companies belonging to the Group. It's always possible to question whether we've met that demand. I mean, it all depends on having the right kind of mentality from the beginning. Always to try to have the energy to have the whole in mind. I guess we have work to do here.' Nobody protests.

The final point on the list of top management responsibilities is 'to do everything possible to create a positive reputation for the Group.' 'How do we do that?' the CEO asks. To which the Financial Director replies, glancing across the room: 'Don't criticize the company as rubbish outside this building.' The CEO continues: 'For example, when we send out a service engineer, and he's muttering out there that everything's a mess and that this and that is missing or badly installed; I mean, that's bad for us. We've got to handle things like that.'

Ethan jumps in, trying to qualify the issue in terms of image. The CEO picks up on this and goes on: 'It's about internal and external communication. And we've said that we have to begin here [i.e. internally].' Ivan takes over: 'It's important to make our business mission concrete for everybody around here.' The CEO nods affirmatively.

The Financial Director shifts focus, beginning to frame the issue in terms of a balancing of crisis awareness and not bad-mouthing the company. 'Would it all be easier with another structure?' Steve asks. The CEO and the Financial Director pool their efforts: 'Sometimes one would wish ... I mean x thousand people worldwide aren't too easy to turn around. But it seems that the new President of Finance [at headquarters] stands for something new. He keeps pushing out new things and everybody's screaming, but he keeps on anyway.' Ivan breaks in again: 'We keep treating symptoms in this Group. When are we going to get to the cause of everything?' The Financial Director latches on: 'Everybody's got to think that way.'

A lot of small talk breaks out, leading to the CEO summing it all up: 'We are a corporation, not a family foundation. All the money is at the centre. And there's a shortage of money.' This last statement sets the stage for the next point on the agenda for the day, the new financial management programme for the Group.

The Financial Director takes the floor. He too, like the CEO, commands the room by moving into the middle in front of the desk and picking up a pointer. His style is also relaxed, but somewhat sharper than that of the CEO. He addresses questions to the TSs and makes ironic remarks when they respond with silence. After making it clear that he is not happy about people not really taking information on board, the Financial Director goes on to give the background to the Group's financial situation and the development of the Group's stock on the market. Things aren't looking so good and '... we have to turn this trend around'. He goes on to explain that the problems are primarily due not to activities in Sweden or Scandinavia, but to those in other parts of the world. Referring to the aforementioned principles of ethics and morals, he exhorts his audience to '... keep this in the building'.

Put on the spot

Four TSs have had a home assignment to do since the last meeting. The assignment was to present a number of financial ratios and to explain their significance. The four position themselves at the front of the room, staying close to the walls, standing stiffly, hands clasped in front of them.

The first up, Robert, stands next to the overhead projector. He puts in a slide showing a couple of ratio definitions. He reads what it says on the picture. Another TS makes a comment, pointing out that the ratio in question includes a measure of operating profit after taxes. Everybody 'hums' approvingly. The presenter moves on to his next definition, again simply reading what is on the overhead. He turns to the Financial Director asking: 'Do you have anything there, [Financial Director]'? And the Director replies in a low voice: 'Well, yes, I'm wondering if you've really understood all that.' He then goes on with rather an elaborate monologue on various methods used in financial analysis. Robert indicates silently that he has finished.

Steve, his face crimson, takes the floor. His assignment is to illustrate how to explain the Group's financial situation to company employees, and what is to be done about it. He too puts in an overhead and starts to go through the points. After only a few minutes, the CEO interrupts with a joke, and asks if Steve thinks he has now explained to employees what all this is about. The Financial Director also mutters something. Ivan, to the Financial Director, laughing: 'You can't just jump in and say things like that.'

Steve continues his presentation, as he had prepared it, with the top management duo continually interrupting with similar questions. After a while Steve is asked to 'speed things up a bit', and he tries to work his way up to his final slide which is a list of implications, concluding that: 'So all this means that we must work with decentralized responsibility ... everybody is responsible for their own profitability. It's about initiatives and creativity. We must have the resources to make quick and correct decisions.'

The CEO takes over again, asking: 'Me, as an ordinary employee, what am I supposed to do?' He goes on for a while about this being a question of culture. 'Everyone must think.' Ethan counters, referring to Steve's presentation: 'Sure, it's about responsibility, but you must also have the authority to make decisions and take action.' His comment is left unanswered.

The Financial Director reverts to the question of why this initiative has been taken at this particular point in time. He gives his own view of things, which is different and much shorter than the one presented by the group of TSs. Ethan tries to say something about this particular approach being in fashion, but is interrupted by the Financial Director who claims that there is a real need for the programme.

Luke makes the sudden announcement that '... with x per cent return on capital, something is sick.' The CEO objects to this description. 'You must look at the history. We've been around for y years and we've always had [this or that] direction of activities.' He continues on this theme, and the Financial Director soon takes over and develops the argument further. The CEO sums up by saying that 'We must get rid of the rubbish, and take in good stuff'. Luke asks if there are any guidelines for these new directions, and the CEO is forced to admit that there has not really been anything specific on that subject. Luke and Ethan together try to bring up the question of incentives, but the CEO brushes their attempt aside, closing the subject with '... incentives are damn difficult'.

The Financial Director zooms in on a new issue. 'We've got to break this down into concrete examples [referring to the implications of the new programme for individual employees].' Several TSs point out the importance of this and the importance of the programme as such. 'We have to be profitable, we have to make people understand'. The Financial Director then asks: 'How are we to communicate this?' There is a lengthy debate about the concept of culture and how long it takes to change it. The young TS, Ivan, who has spoken on several occasions and at some length, tries to refer back to Ethan's remarks on the importance of the authority to make decisions. This time his theme is not taken up. It's time to break for lunch.

A new way of working

After lunch and a guest lecture, it is time to discuss the new key account programme, which is presented by Robert. The Financial Director asks why this is being done now, and Ivan explains that because it's part of ordinary sales work, it is actually something that should always have been done. The CEO takes over to explain that both new and tenured sales people can gain from these activities. After Ivan, the Financial Director takes the initiative, and asks if this means that '... we are more focused on the whole now?' to which he does not get an answer.

Luke then poses the question: 'Do all product groups work with this?' The CEO responds 'Yes, the plan comes from headquarters.' Luke again: 'Are there any concrete results yet in terms of sales?' The CEO answers that there are no definite results yet and that it will take some time, but the signals are clear about the importance of this program. Ivan steps in, emphasizing the importance of formulating concrete goals for the programme. Luke says that the die is cast and that they can't give up on this now. The CEO calms him: 'No, no, no-one would dream of doing that.' The Financial Director goes on: 'We are investing about x million a year in this programme.'

Calm is restored and Robert is allowed to continue, explaining that the purpose of the programme is to present a unified front vis-à-vis the customers. He goes on to describe the internal organization of the programme.

The CEO leaves the room for a moment to greet yet another guest who is coming to the meeting. The Financial Director opens up a new line of reasoning: Has the process permeated the organization in a satisfactory manner? Robert believes that there are some difficulties. The process seems to be blocked at the level of product division management. This opens up a veritable flow of comments from several other TSs.

'There is a conflict here between the long term and the short term, between product division priorities and company-wide priorities. Not all product divisions see their business opportunities as clearly with these key accounts.'

Luke sums up by claiming that it is all due to a basic lack of resources. The number of salespeople and the present organization just do not match the sales volumes in question. Ivan tries to convince the others that one must also be able to demand something of the customers.

'We can't always come up with an offer right away. Sometimes it's all right to say that we can produce an offer by this or that date.'

Robert interrupts, stating that many seem to see the programme as something of a burden. The CEO has returned in the middle of this heated discussion, and puts a stop to it: 'We could go on all night but now we have a guest.'

The final round

Several hours later, after presentations by two guests and yet another TS, the central topic is brought back on stage again by the CEO. 'We were discussing the key account managers and resources [...] that subject hasn't perhaps been fully dealt with?' Luke immediately expands on the topic, stating: '[...] we all have a lot of stuff going on and we're all forced to set priorities'. The CEO counters: 'We have set the priorities together, across the product divisions. I mean, these key accounts have not been picked out at random. There has been a lot of thinking, you know. We've selected these particular customers because we have judged that that's where the potential for us lies. In fact, those that scream the loudest about this are the ones who already have big volumes with these customers.' He goes on, giving more details about volumes and screaming, and then concludes: 'We're supposed to act, not react. We end up feeling stressed because we're reacting to every call from the customers.' The Financial Director steps in: 'Ivan, what do you have to say?'

Ivan is glad to elaborate on how the system is supposed to work, for the most part repeating what he had said several hours ago. This time, however, he finishes by identifying the need for an analysis of communications needs. Robert agrees with Ivan. The Financial Director tones this down: 'We mustn't take on more than we can handle.'

Luke: 'They [the key accounts] ask a lot of us. It swallows a lot of resources. Nobody wants to drop things.' The CEO interrupts: 'And nobody wants to say no to a customer [. . .]. Not everything can be prioritized. Damn, we can't go on taking care of everybody.' Ivan and the CEO have another exchange and the CEO concludes: 'This is a long-term effort. It costs a lot of money and it's important that product division management is a driving-force in the process.' He goes on to claim that between 25 per cent and 50 per cent of those appointed to key account teams display some kind of resistance, for various reasons. The priority of key accounts does not seem to have 'reached out' in the organization.

One TS who has been silent practically all day begins to speak about measurements and incentive systems. 'I mean, when you stand there with a deviation from budget, the claim that you've been working with the key account team just doesn't cut any ice, does it?' The CEO replies, rather softly: 'But you know we have a system of paying bonuses even to people who have not exceeded budgeted sales. I don't think that people have understood that when you're selected for a key account team, you have eyes on you. Maybe not everybody is aware of that?'

Ethan: 'This is also a matter of communication. Maybe it has to be pointed out in some way that you have this system of bonuses?' Someone says: 'Maybe one should tell people that it's not such a disaster if you miss out on your sales budget, so long as . . .'. Everybody laughs, and the Financial Director adds: 'I'm not sure that we'd want to send out that message.'

After this, there is a switch in the discussion, away from the question of incentives, resources and resistance, and towards the question of the merits of the key account programme, how it can be conducive to learning in the organization, and how it helps to reveal a lack of knowledge about even the most established customers.

Mario, however, goes back to the former topic: 'At product division [x], there sure isn't any acceptance of the fact that salespeople have a new boss in the key account manager.' The CEO is surprised to hear this, since the division in question has actually been very good at showing up in key account teams, although it is said to have the lowest current sales potential with the key accounts.

Luke repeats his argument about the lack of resources. The CEO counters: 'Sure, we need more salespeople, we're good at hiring technicians, we're worse at hiring salespeople.' 'Are we?' someone mutters.

Luke again: 'It hurts to teach new people.' Ivan jumps in with: 'Yeah, sure it hurts, but it has to be done. If you're sloppy in that department you can throw the whole damn package away.' He then goes on to say something to the effect that the present organization must be accepted as the starting point. 'There are simply no alternatives to trying to use present resources, set priorities, and then develop activities.'

The CEO adopts a line of reasoning about the merits of the new system and gives a practical example. 'Look at Mr X. He didn't know a thing. I mean he didn't know anybody at key account Y, but it works fine. Sure, he knew the business, and he knows our products, so we didn't have to put in a lot of product training, but it seems that relationships can be built up rather quickly.'

The Financial Director breaks in: 'So what's the bottom line here?' Luke: 'We'll hire people.' CEO: 'We need more salespeople. We all have to communicate the importance of the key accounts. I mean, if it's wrong, if it goes to hell, top management will have to accept responsibility.'

Ivan breaks in, urging the CEO to take strong action against anyone who doesn't fall into line, for example, those who aren't sending people to the key account teams. The CEO remarks: 'It's this discussion climate that we have in the Group ...'. Ethan tries to get a word in: 'But if you don't know, how are you supposed to communicate?' The Financial Director responds, rather angrily: 'But why don't they know?' The CEO continues: 'Yeah, what the hell, these are decisions that we've made in the top management team, a lot of managers together.'

It's getting late and the Financial Director breaks off the discussion.

Analysis

The various managerial virtues are reflected in different aspects of the programme. The Manager *qua* Expert image is reproduced in the formal programme requirements, as well as in the one-day seminar itself. The Financial Director is clearly the most formidable bearer of this virtue, assuming the role of teacher and examiner.

The Father image of managerial leadership, however, is not particularly strong here. This is not too surprising, since that particular role is thought to be fulfilled in relation to the lower 'classes' (who mainly want to stand well with their fellows), and not perhaps so much among the managers themselves.

The 'chosen-ness' of those attending the seminar is mentioned a couple of times, but formal criteria of merit are not in focus here. Rather, this is the time for the real stuff, the time for reinforcing what seems to be the most fundamental of managerial virtues in this context. It is about showing what it means to have the right attitude – showing what it takes to get somewhere. Not just saying it, but showing it by saying and by other means of action, at times quite aggressively.

The two top managers are the ones who set the rules of interaction, and they are the ones who take many lengthy conversational turns. This, I would imagine, is the most basic mechanism in the externalization of these managers' own subjective reality, whereby they expect to set the rules themselves and to do most of the talking. The power of the mechanism lies in the fact that this is probably also part of the objective reality, already internalized by most of the other participants; they too expect top management to do most of the talking. No matter what has been said in written documents or verbally, the meeting does not transcend, but rather reinforces the social construction of managerial leadership that was there from the start. But what is that construction all about?

The virtue of toughness: the subject

Young Ivan has a vital role to play in this drama. He is socially positioned as a spokesperson for the manager as being made of the right stuff; he gets to formulate the possibilities, the openings, the optimism and drive, which I would claim to be an important aspect of the virtue of toughness. He also flaunts this toughness, by being the only one to make meta-statements about the rules of interaction in the situation, which are otherwise completely determined by the two top managers, including the overall organization of the meeting and the programme of which it is a part. Ivan's entire participation is marked by toughness, simply by the number and length of his discursive turns. This toughness is further reinforced by the fact that he is the only one besides top management to make lengthy interruptions of other people's presentations. All this is in turn vigorously reinforced by the two top managers who directly and indirectly provide him with discursive opportunities: directly, by soliciting his comments on certain matters, and indirectly by praising what he has said.

Being made of the right stuff is perhaps the most persistent aspect of the 'accumulated' construction of managerial leadership. If we are to believe Bendix (1956), it is also the oldest, the remains of the construction of the capitalist entrepreneur transmitted into the age of managerialism. By what mechanism did this occur, one might then ask.

The handling of political vagaries is believed by both managers and non-managers to be an important everyday activity of managers in complex organizations, indispensable to self-defined managerial success

(Dalton, 1959; Pfeffer, 1981; Kotter, 1982; Jackall, 1988). (Not to mention the struggle in the market-place.) This is also what I believe is hinted at in the CEO's opening statements. There are at least two important aspects to this problem. First, you must be tough enough to stand your ground against others. You must be prepared to negotiate, or else you will be brushed aside by others, often to the detriment of the organization as a whole. Second, it is very useful to be good at picturing ways out of what appears to be a deadlock. The persistent dream of the managerial class is the win-win situation, which constitutes the overall legitimization of the capitalist mode of production, and is intrinsic to managerial life.

Cunning or cleverness, the predominant attributes of epic heroes, maintain their position in the cultural ambience of the manager's world (Gustafsson, 1992). There is a constant element of admiration for the political skill of others, even if you lose something yourself because of it. From above, senior management comes across much more strongly, if its subordinates are not excessively compliant, but instead are themselves quite strong people with at least some Machiavellian skill of their own. This probably explains why breaches of social rules that are standard in many other settings are often left unpunished in the managerial setting. Construction flows through into construction processes. At the particular meeting described here the construction engineers (top management) appear to exhibit this toughness directly and indirectly via the others present by interrupting with what are sometimes quite sharp comments or by not responding to questions at all, and by constantly laying down their rules for interaction.

The Financial Director is the embodiment, in this meeting, of this kind of toughness. He makes sharp remarks and puts people on the spot by asking questions they cannot or dare not answer. Can anyone really be surprised to learn that these sessions do not lead to the open dialogue that according to management talk and documents is so eagerly sought?

Another aspect of having the right attitude is the ability to keep people's spirits up. Analysis and critical reflection are certainly valued activities, but management – as managers claim – is ultimately the sphere of action, optimism and drive; management is the art of practical action, and managers are people of practical action (Berglund, 1999). Having the right attitude is about expressing optimism, possibilities, opportunities, and 'ways out'.

There is of course another side to this coin: there cannot be too much whining about deadlocks and difficulties. While it's necessary to be able to see such things, doubts should not be expressed too often or too publicly. Criticism must have its limits. The comment that an organization reporting a certain level of profitability is somehow 'sick', has crossed that line. The CEO in our example was very quick indeed to defend his company against such an accusation.

A plea for trust in the value of virtue

In rather a fleeting fashion the CEO hints that managers should show themselves willing to work for the best of the company as a whole and not only for their own department. Selecting someone to join a cross-departmental work group should mean something, though the CEO is not altogether clear exactly what. It is likely that he means it as a signal to the chosen one that he has promise, and may well get financial remuneration if the job is well done. And what is more, participation in work of this kind has important implications for possible future promotion ('. . . you have eyes on you').

One participant immediately tried to suggest that this ought perhaps to be made clearer. Unfortunately, I failed to pick up any reaction to his remark from top management, as the discussion turned to an even more heated topic (see next section). It is likely that the spontaneous reaction of the CEO would have been that further clarity was not necessary, since such things should not need pointing out at all: it should be obvious that hard work and loyalty will be rewarded. The virtuous will ultimately prevail, and pointing out something so obvious might lessen its impact.

A crescendo of socialization: the subjected

The meeting moved towards something of a crescendo, at least in the eyes of this observer. It was a crescendo of socialization into the managerial attitude. When someone drew a very logical conclusion from the discussion of the key account programme, incentives and matrix relations, he was met by laughter all round. The particular logic that says that you can't have your cake and eat it is not accepted in such a context. Whatever the reason, you cannot simply tell people that it's all right to miss their budget, although this may well be tacitly accepted. One smart thing to do is to adjust the figures downward a bit. In fact, of course, managers should always strive to meet budgets and participate in the key account programme (i.e. eating their cake yet making it grow).

This is the route to the kind of universe-maintenance that Berger and Luckmann described as therapy. As they pointed out (1966, pp. 130–31) therapy targets individual cases. Here, the case presents itself neatly in conversation, and was instantly homed in on by the group as a whole. By observing the way the group reacted to the aberrant view, we can get an idea of the kind of explanatory therapeutic conceptual machinery used to account for the aberration in the first place: youthful naiveté, best dealt with by way of condescending, and perhaps forgiving, laughter.

Conclusion: constructing and construction linked by virtue

This chapter has tried to show how the process of constructing managerial leadership and managerial leaders is in itself one of the cornerstones of the dominant constructions of managerial leadership. One way of linking constructing and construction is to introduce the concept of virtue.

Constructions of managerial leadership are not neutral relative to the constructing processes. This could be said to mean that managerial leadership is a non-rationalistic, anti-enlightenment, or perhaps a pre-enlightenment construction. As far as the virtue of toughness is concerned, this is fairly evident, since this particular virtue has already been traced back to Reformist Protestant theology (with its doctrine of predestination).

One might be tempted to ask whether all constructions are like this. To which the answer is an emphatic no! Rationalism separates the ends from the means. To a rationalist, war can be a good means for achieving peace. To a non-rationalist, only peace can engender peace. A rationalist conception of leadership would entail one view of the best way of exercising leadership, and another and perhaps radically different view about how to become a leader. In a rationalist approach there is plenty of room for the idea that leaders, for example tough leaders, could be created by way of warm, caring, dialogic-cum-pedagogic processes, whereby the individual is carefully taught how to be tough when necessary.

Rationalism has no room for the concept of *éducation sentimentale* (MacIntyre, 1981), i.e. the idea that individuals orientate themselves to the world in one way or another, as a result of the way socialization is effected. Rationalism offers even less room for the idea that the outcome of *éducation sentimentale* can explain much of what goes on in society or in organizations.

The concept of virtue takes us to the particular level of consciousness that is called practical consciousness (Giddens, 1984). Virtue is then defined as the patterns of acts (including speech) exhibited by an individual over time, as judged by someone else. It is my belief, moreover, that such judgements are located primarily in practical rather than discursive consciousness. And while the virtue possessed by one individual, A, may at times be reflected upon consciously and formulated in discursive consciousness by another one, B, the important thing is the particular feeling that B has about A.

Virtues are supposed to be displayed by individuals in a non-calculating fashion, through ongoing activities. Managerial virtues are no exception. There is no spoken discourse in this empirical context about managerial virtues or the like. The spoken word is concerned with market shares, organizational structures, customer relations, financial management and so on. But possession of virtues is thought, or rather felt, to be displayed. People are being judged. People are being selected. People are being chosen to be chosen even more and all this is accomplished around spoken discourse. The consequences of this 'chosen-ness' are of course announced discursively: Mr Y is the new head of department X; Mr Z gets a layoff notice.

Naturally, most people understand that selection is taking place. It is not certain, however, that everybody understands how the process of selection works. For instance, in the larger study that I am undertaking in the same company, several of the TSs interviewed have explicitly asked about the criteria for being accepted for the TS-programme, and how inclusion in or exclusion from the programme would be conducted in the future.

One important consequence of the importance attached to an admired virtue in a particular context is that it stabilizes the social setting in question, since people already possessing the virtue acquire the chance to develop it further, while others who do not possess it are gradually edged out. Another consequence could be that possession of the particular virtue reinforces certain conditions in the organization, like those that the CEO in our example referred to in his opening address as being problematic. A further result could be that the predominance of a virtue determines who talks and when, which in turn tends to reinforce the image of any existing self-identified managerial leaders as being made of the right stuff.

The virtue of toughness and its implications

In the empirical material, the virtue of toughness forms a solid background for the social situation described. It is both that which is sought after (in a teleological sense) and that which is enacted. It is both the means and the end. This hardly comes as a surprise since the virtue of toughness is an integral part of the oldest of legitimating conceptual machineries of the managerial class inherited from the entrepreneurs of early industrialism. At the same time, a plea for faith in the justice of the system informed by toughness is registered.

The virtue of toughness is legitimized in a universe of symbols that is transmitted in a wide variety of ways (for instance in the biographies of managerial leaders and in the business press). I would suggest, however, that this particular virtue has its anchorage in the social organization of managers themselves, in the daily small talk and other interaction between managers. This implies that the construction of the managerial leader as someone who exhibits the virtue of toughness is most accessible to managers themselves and to those who 'happen' to be their conversation partners. It also means that there will be many individuals within organizations who are not equally familiar with this construction, and who are more likely to be surprised or even frightened when they are exposed to its externalization.

Were we to seek an understanding of the underpinnings of the preconscious conceptions of the managerial virtue of toughness, we might find it in the lay-psychology characterization of individuals as a collection of stable – or perhaps potential – traits that are not situational and that do not stem from patterns of life. People either have this virtue – or they don't. The managerial task of finding new managers is essentially one of finding out who is made of the right stuff – a task that is being constantly performed 'around' other work, including our one-day meeting. The point is that it is something that is not discussed openly, since – as lay psychology might have it – people would then begin pretending to be what they are not.

Berger and Luckmann (1966, p. 192) see the fact that we all have access to multiple worlds as a dominating feature of the modern condition. And by access to multiple worlds, they mean that we know of more than one institution and more than one set of role definitions that could be applied to every phenomenon. This opens up the possibility for us to pretend we are something we are not. But more importantly, Berger and Luckmann claim, with the aid of Schelsky and Gehlen, this enables us to play at what we are, reducing or sharpening man to a stereotype, a character (MacIntyre, 1981). It is worth noting here, however, that MacIntyre was concerned primarily about the reduction of man to a character in connection with another of the images of management, namely that of the Calculating Expert. My concern here is for the Tough One, were he to become dominant in most areas of life, in and around organizations.

The importance of the virtue of toughness as depicted here is, of course, in sharp contrast to much of the public and even the semi-private discourse in which leadership is discussed in terms of humanism, participation, empowerment and so on. The dissonance between espoused theories and theories in use, or between saying and doing (including saying something else), has been observed before (Kaplan, 1964) One interpretation of this condition of de-coupling is that it is a case of blatant hypocrisy. Another interpretation is that participation etc. pertain to the relation between managers and for-ever-to-be-subordinates, not to relations within the managerial class (which includes managers-to-be).

Notes

1 Masculine pronouns are used throughout this chapter. There are several reasons for this. Firstly, it serves to anonymize the empirical material. Secondly, the majority of the people in the empirical material, as well as in the organisation in question as a whole, are men. Thirdly, the history of management is to a large extent a history of men. And finally, the interpretations offered here are largely in line with interpretations of managerial leadership as a construction with a strong masculine flavour.
2 The larger project is being conducted in the ethnographic spirit of, for example, Geertz (1973), enriched by a phenomengraphic approach to interviewing (see Sandberg, 1994).

References

Barnard, C. (1938). *The Functions of the Executive.* Harvard University Press, Cambridge, Mass.

Bendix, R. (1956). *Work and Authority in Industry.* UC Press, Los Angeles.

Berger, P., and Luckmann, T. (1991/1966). *The Social Construction of Reality. A Treatise in the Sociology of Knowledge.* Penguin Books, London.

Berglund, J. (1999). The Practical Men of Action. The Construction of Masculinity and Model Leaders in Business Magazine. *Center for Advanced Studies in Leadership School of Economics,* Stockholm, no. 4.

Dalton, M. (1959). *Men Who Manage.* John Wiley & Sons, New York.

Geertz, L. (1973/1993). *The Interpretation of Cultures.* Fontana Press, London.

Giddens, A. (1984). *The Constitution of Socity.* Policy Press, Cambridge.

Gustafsson, C. (1992). Den dygdige företagsledaren, in Sjöstrand, S-E., and Holmberg, I. (eds.), *Företagsledning bortom etablerad teori,* pp. 31–45, EFI, Stockholm.

Jackall, R. (1988). *Moral Mazes. The World of Corporate Managers.* Oxford University Press, New York.

Kaplan, A. (1964). *The Conduct of Inquiry.* Chandler, Scranton, Penn.

Kotter, J. P. (1982). *The General Managers.* The Free Press, New York.

MacIntyre, A. (1985/1981). *After Virtue.* Duckworth, London.

Perrow, C. (1986/1972). *Complex Organizations – A Critical Essay.* McGraw-Hill, New York.

Pfeffer, J. (1981). *Power in Organizations.* Pitman, Marshfield, Mass.

Roethlisberger, F. J., and Dickson, W. J. (1947). *Management and the Worker.* Harvard University Press, Cambridge, Mass.

Sandberg, J. (1994). *Human Competence at Work: An Interpretative Approach.* BAS, Gothenburg.

Taylor, F. W. (1913/1911). *The Principles of Scientific Management.* Harper and Brothers, New York, NY.

Weber, M. (1997/1905). *Den protestantiska etiken och kapitalismens anda (The Protestant Ethic and the Spirit of Capitalism).* Argos, Lund.

CHAPTER FOUR

The rhetorical dimension

Johan Stein and Lena Andersson

This chapter considers the role of rhetoric in management communication, and in particular the way three facets of rhetoric – ethos, pathos
and logos – influence the construction of leadership. Rhetoric is broadly
defined here as the art of persuasion. In line with the overall theme of this
book, the present chapter examines leadership rhetoric in a social
context. Ethos, pathos and logos can appear in various guises in the
service of persuasion, depending on the situation. Hence, the construction of successful leadership – i.e. leadership that works – is also
contingent on context. By focusing on rhetoric, our aim here is to throw
some light on the interactive nature of leadership.

The top management rhetoric demonstrated in a set of videotapes
from a meeting in a large firm has provided the empirical base. Attention
will be given specifically to the qualities of ethos, pathos and logos and
the relationship between them as it is expressed in the tapes. By
addressing the question of leadership rhetoric, this chapter will contribute
to our understanding of leadership in a social constructionist perspective.

Rhetoric as the art of persuasion

The word rhetoric has been used in a variety of ways. Nowadays it is
frequently misused. In the media, for instance, it often seems to mean
empty phrases, pretty words without content, or even nonsense. From a
theoretical point of view, however, rhetoric is supposed to be neutral.
More than 2000 years ago Aristotle was the first to suggest this aspect of
its nature (Aristotle, 1991, p. 35). His, too, was the classical definition of
rhetoric as the art of persuasion (Aristotle, 1991, pp. 36–7). This broad
definition is the one that has been adopted in this chapter.

Our understanding is that rhetoric is both theory and craftsmanship. The systems of rhetoric can be used for building persuasive messages as well as for analysing the communication of messages. The messages themselves may be anything from pictures, music, acting or silence, to written or spoken language. As noted in Chapter 2 above, the importance of language systems has often been observed in the literature of social constructionism. However, rhetorical schools of thought add to this literature by addressing the often asymmetrical conditions in the interrelationship between the leader and the led (cf. Burke, 1969; Perelman, 1990). A person with the legitimacy and ability to lead is likely to be more influential in such relationships. Hence, according to several scholars of rhetoric, the intersubjective construction of reality is not a symmetrical process among individuals.

Aristotle (1991) identified three modes of persuasion based on the devices of ethos, pathos or logos. Combining these three elements in a communication offers a powerful means of persuasion (Johannesson, 1990).

Ethos is bound up with the character of the individual, as expressed in the values and beliefs that they uphold. Hence, speakers who are trying to project a particular image of themselves are exploiting the rhetorical tools of ethos for the purpose (cf. Corbett, 1990; Aristotle, 1991). Ethos can thus be used to generate in an audience the perception of a speaker as competent, trustworthy, friendly, etc.

Successful persuaders seem to be very good at signalling their possession of attributes that are valued among those who are to be persuaded (Willner, 1984). It has been observed, for example, that advertising workers portray themselves as aesthetic, creative and emotional, among other things (Alvesson, 1993).

Pathos is about the arousal of feelings. Hence, if a message makes people feel happy, sad, hopeful, fearful, confident, etc., this has to do with its pathos. Finally, logos concerns persuasion by invoking hard facts like figures, diagrams or proofs. Messages that are regarded as logical can be persuasive. The notion of logic can be linked to rationality. What is interpreted as logical and rational, however, can vary with context (Weber, 1947; Sjöstrand, 1985).

The classical literature on rhetoric is normative, providing the reader with guidelines for becoming a successful persuader. More recent contributions are much more descriptive and explorative. The reader is not given any recipes for being persuasive.

One example of the 'new' rhetorical tradition is provided by Corbett (1990, p. 3) who redefines the notion of rhetoric in order to emphasize its contextual embeddedness:

'Rhetoric is the art or the discipline that deals with the use of discourse, either spoken or written, to inform or persuade or motivate an audience, whether that audience is made up of one person or a group of persons.'

Here, Corbett stresses that rhetoric is discursive. He adds that rhetors can be more or less conscious of the discourse they are reproducing. Further, a person can be part of several discourses.

Management of pathos and logos

Individuals are active constructors of meaning (Weick, 1979). Information is decoded with the help of cognition and emotions into something that makes sense for the individual (Bourne et al., 1986; Weick, 1995). Hence, in order to be persuasive, managers need to be able arouse feelings (pathos) and to be understood (logos). Emotional arousals are most often automatic and subconscious rather than intentional and planned (Locke and Henne, 1986). Hardly surprisingly, the literature on rhetoric places much emphasis on how to get people interested in a message. People are less likely to use their cognitive capabilities in order to interpret, question, understand and otherwise attend to messages, if they are not interested.

The specific meaning that a receiver attaches to a message may be different from the original meaning intended by the sender. There are several reasons why receivers do not interpret information in the way intended by the senders. These reasons may depend on the senders, the receivers or the social context. From a cognitive perspective, such divergence is primarily caused by the variety of individual experiences – i.e. different frames of reference within which the information is interpreted. Among other explanations we find that knowledge can be tacit (Polanyi, 1966). People are sometimes unable to find a written or oral representation of the things they want to express. Further, individuals may have different skills in creating symbols which enable others to decode what they are trying to communicate (Goldhaber, 1993). The nature of needs, values, and interests also comes into play. The emotional dimension is obviously important – individuals tend to see and hear things that have triggered their emotions (Ortony et al., 1988).

Notably, in writings on the management of meaning authors seldom address the issue of feelings or pathos in depth (cf. Starbuck, 1976; Weick, 1979; Sims and Gioia, 1986; Smircich and Stubbart, 1985;

Spender, 1989). Thus, in considering the rhetorical dimension in the construction of leadership, current writings on the management of meaning can be fruitfully complemented by also observing the element of pathos or feeling.

Ethos, trust and charisma

In a social constructionist perspective, a leader's ethos can be described as the beliefs held by other people about the leader's character. Hence, there is no objective definition of ethos, and the ethos of a person can differ depending on the context (Willner, 1984). Within these contexts, a successful persuader is often regarded as trustworthy. Personal traits like gender, ethnical background, education, looks and so on are ingredients in the social categorization of a person.

The notion of charisma derives from a Greek word meaning, 'divinely inspired gift' (Yukl, 1994). Many attempts have been made by scholars in the field of sociology, political science and business administration to conceptualize this 'gift'. According to Yukl (1994), there has been a converging tendency to think in terms of an interactive capability. Pettigrew (1973, p. 25) appears to be thinking along similar lines when he observed:

'A position may give a leader authority, but the exercise of authority requires interaction. It is at this point that the leader's problems begin.'

This means that a person's 'charisma' is highly dependent upon context. For instance, Weber (1947) argues that in times of uncertainty, perhaps during a crisis, someone who can take charge of the situation and reduce people's uncertainty is likely to be perceived as charismatic. The behaviour of charismatic leaders is thus also important. Charismatic leaders often appear confident, express strong convictions, make self-sacrifices, set visions that are radical but realistic, communicate high expectations and create the impression of being competent (cf. House, 1977; Conger and Kanungo, 1987; Yukl, 1994). According to Perelman (1990, p. 1081), a persuasive orator has the ability to bring to the surface the wishes of the listeners.

'The orator's aim in the epidictic genre is not just to gain a passive adherence from his audience but to provoke the action wished for or, at least, to awaken a disposition so to act.'

Ethos can also be linked to trust, which can be seen as the credibility of a person in the minds of others. This credibility is dependent upon a number of attributes, such as whether a person is perceived to be knowledgeable, honest and sincerely concerned about the well-being of others (Yukl, 1994). It should be noted that trust is not the same as charisma, although some of their attributes coincide. The primary difference seems to be that trust doesn't require the same amount of emotional attractiveness as charisma does. It is our conclusion that trust is a necessary requirement for ethos, whereas charisma is more of a reinforcer of ethos.

A manager's legitimacy to lead is linked to his or her ethos, including the elements of trust and charisma. Rothschild (1977) among others observes the importance of leaders being aware of their legitimacy to lead. He describes how risky it is (at least in the long run) to misjudge one's own legitimacy in this respect. Likewise, Scott emphasizes the contextual influence on legitimacy.

'Legitimacy refers to a set of social norms that define situations or behaviours as correct or appropriate. Thus to speak of legitimate power is to indicate: 1) a set of persons or positions linked by power relations; 2) a set of norms or rules governing the distribution and exercise of power and the response to it.'

(Scott, 1981, p. 280)

Managers can also be seen as legitimizers (Müllern and Stein, 1999). That is, by communicating priorities they signal to the organization that it is legitimate to act in a certain direction. The mission, vision, strategies and values of a firm are examples of tools that top management uses in order to communicate such priorities (ibid.). However, these and other tools don't seem to be enough, since it can be difficult for the organizational members to understand the various expressions of top management. Müllern and Stein (1999) observe that this lack of understanding is caused by several factors. For instance, words that are abstract and uncommon (like some fashionable management words) can confuse the meaning of what is being communicated.

Berger and Luckmann (1966, p. 37) underline the importance of continuous interaction in order to bridge gaps in understanding:

'Indeed, I cannot exist in everyday life without continually interacting and communicating with others.'

In sum, the construction of leadership is dependent upon the elements of ethos, pathos and logos. Leadership requires that one or several persons possess the ethos that is required. This person (or these persons) also needs the ability to express pathos (management of feeling) and logos (management of meaning). In this way, the construction of leadership can be linked to emotions and to cognition on the individual level. However, these dimensions are influenced by the social context. Different behaviours may then be required in different contexts in order to build ethos and to express pathos and logos.

A CEO at work – the case of the teleoperator Telia

Telia is the largest teleoperator in Sweden. It is a limited company whose objective is to provide its shareholder (the Swedish state) with a return on its investments. Telia's turnover today is around SEK 45 billion, a figure generated by its approximately 30 000 employees.

In recent years, the deregulation of the industry in Sweden has confronted Telia, which previously enjoyed a monopoly, with several changes. The number of competitors has risen fast in certain areas and foreign companies have entered the market.

Telia has taken several radical steps in order to handle the new situation. For instance, in January 1995 Telia started *Team 2001,* an organization whose purpose was to coordinate the changes at Telia. Three values, 'development, co-operation and engagement', were defined as a platform for the changes. In adopting these values, the intention was to realize *Vision 2001.* Within Telia the renewal project as a whole has often been illustrated by the metaphor of the river raft. Here, the CEO Lars Berg has emphasized the nature of the company as a united force: '*Telia. One name. One company.*'

Telia has also changed its way of working by creating teams in which people with different competencies are supposed to work together. In addition, Telia started a chain of retail stores, in order to make contact with the market and to be able to supply new products more quickly.

Top management has tried to improve overall communications in the company in order to meet the new challenges in the environment. For example, at certain times during the week employees have had direct telephone access to the CEO. Internal TV and videotapes are among the most important communication channels at Telia. The company even has a department that makes the programmes and videotapes.

We have studied eleven videotapes in order to describe how Telia's top management has been trying to persuade its staff of the need for strategic change. All the videotapes studied are concerned with this managerial task. The videotapes were analysed thematically on a basis of the dimensions of ethos, pathos and logos. The themes initially traced in the data set (i.e. the videotapes) were continuously compared with additional data. We focused on the most common themes and these are the ones that are presented below. Hence, data that were inconsistent with the common themes have been excluded.

Videotapes as a rhetorical channel

Before discussing ethos, pathos and logos, there follows a description of the overall content of the videotapes.

The purpose of one tape is to inform employees about an international alliance called *Unisource*. A 'journalist' (dressed as a foreign correspondent with hat, coat and a large microphone) wishes the observers welcome to Amsterdam. He says that a big press conference will take place in the building behind him. At this conference news will be released that will have a big impact on Telia's future.

The movie then shows various short cuts from the conference, including an interview with Unisource's CEO, and a presentation called '*A changing environment*' about the competition on the market. Lars Berg gives an 'exclusive', interview in which he discusses the alliance and introduces Vision 2001 and an action plan for implementing it.

Another tape shows a summary of a leadership conference. Lars Berg comments on his first six months as CEO in the company and his view of the future. In addition, various experts give lectures on leadership and some well-known people offer comments relating to Telia. To start with, a sad picture is painted. Telia is portrayed as a company with little self-confidence. However, by the end of the three-hour long film everyone seems to be happy and confident because of the underlying strengths that Telia possesses. The members of Team 2001 come on the scene, holding in their hands the paddles needed in the river raft. Lars Berg says: '*This is a game, you are the players, and the playground is moving. We shall be competitive!*'

In another tape, Lars Berg addresses Vision 2001 for approximately fifteen minutes in front of an audience. A tape called *Customers on Telia and staff on the team* contains short cuts in which customers and staff express their overall positive beliefs about Telia.

A leadership conference about the changes that have been implemented at Telia is shown in a further tape. The conference was located at four different places in Sweden, and included a mixture of themes. The headquarters in Stockholm is 'present' at the conference via internal TV. For instance, Lars Berg wishes everyone welcome and introduces the content of the conference. He also comments on Telia's financial situation. The main idea behind this conference was that it should be about the leaders of Telia. Even so, Lars Berg is the one who leads the discussion. At the end of the conference, Lars Berg takes out his 'leadership-card' from an inside pocket. On one side of the card it says 'Everyone together'. The text that follows proclaims that 'You personify Telia'. The other side of the card shows keywords from Vision 2001.

Ethos, pathos and logos

The explicit purpose of the tapes is to inform. There are some facts, such as how many new stores the company is going to open. Even so, the bulk of the information concerns the importance the company attaches to the various changes, and the importance of everyone working together to transform Telia into a proactive winner in the market-place. The tapes also seek to create a picture of Telia as a united force. Together we can make it! The overall impression is that the managers in charge of the changes know what they are doing, and that the CEO is safely watching over it all.

Several studies of the working atmosphere at Telia were taken into consideration during the production of the videotapes. These studies showed that a lot of people were anxious about their jobs. Hence, to a certain extent the messages in the videotapes have been aimed at reducing the uncertainty of individuals and at bolstering their self-esteem and self-confidence. This is particularly clear in the tape that introduces the international alliance. Here, a 'reporter' talks with the CEO: 'There's uncertainty in Telia. In this new alliance [. . .] people think they'll be swallowed up.' The CEO smiles, as if this was something really funny, and answers that it is the other way round. The employees can now feel calm, since with the help of the alliance Telia can cover the entire market.

The language in the tapes varies. Some words are even defined, although this is not usually the case. When the CEO presents Vision 2001 he uses several typical management terms, such as competitiveness, market leadership, and first-class. The values of the company as described above are expressed by the terms 'development, co-operation and engagement'. A lot of positive words are also connected with these terms, such as learning, creativity, respect, participation, team-work, etc.

The language is also decorated with some classical rhetorical ornaments. The most common is the metaphor. This is sometimes expressed in single words, but often in terms of a whole picture. For instance, in one of the tapes the company is portrayed as a car in motion: 'We have to change to a higher gear; everyone's getting into the car; we know where we're heading; now we're off.'

The metaphors are taken from different areas. In one of the tapes the national hockey team coach talks about team-work, and uses several sporting metaphors: 'It's time to take the offensive'; and 'The teams are like soccer-teams, where everyone's a specialist, but they know enough to cover each other.'

This vision is not only created by using modern expressions. It is also built up with the help of classical rhetorical tools. The vision statement adopts the classical disposition with a short exciting introduction, or *exordium*. This is followed by the *narratio*, a short description of facts to explain the background to the vision. This part then ends with the *proposito*, '*2001, now!*' After this, three points are presented about how the vision will be implemented; in this case, comprising the business idea, the company's values and its strategy. All this constitutes the rhetorical *argumentatio*. The vision statement culminates with a concluding repetition of the *propositio*, namely the *conclusio*. Another rhetorical tool is the *anaphora* whereby several phrases begin with the same expression. This is used particularly in the argumentative passages (e.g. 'Telia is to . . .; Telia is to . . .; Telia is to . . .; etc.').

The vision is also built up round antithesis, i.e. the placing of two opposing arguments close to each other. A threatening picture is painted of the development in Sweden and in Telia's industry. But after this scary message, the saviour is presented: the new vision that will solve the problems! Hope is aroused and a recipe for a way of saving everyone from the threat is offered. Antithesis is probably the most common rhetorical tool to appear in these tapes and in particular the antithesis of hope and fear.

Hyperbole, used to exaggerate certain effects, is another rhetorical tool often used in the videotapes. The viewers are exposed to a plethora of positive words about Telia and its chances of handling the competitive situation

Another frequent tool is the use of authority figures (or experts). By bringing in experts to make statements, the actions and character of the company and its leaders are legitimized and reinforced. One example occurs when a journalist from a well-known financial journal is asked whether he's surprised at the alliances Telia has developed. The journalist answers that he thinks they are perfect for the company.

So, in terms of ethos, pathos and logos, how does management try to persuade the employees in these tapes? Despite the explicit purpose of the tapes, i.e. to inform, the use of logos is not extensive. In one of the tapes a lot of pictures are shown looking like rational maps of the company and the changes there. Everything appears to be under control. But, the information is not in figures or hard facts. It's more a question of metaphors and other positive means of expression. Management appears here to be very competent and aware of what it is doing, setting out to win confidence.

Persuasion by pathos also appears here, mostly in the attempts to create a 'we' feeling in the company. This is effected in several ways: by telling the audience how good the company is, how important the work is that the staff is doing, and how important the staff are themselves. Apparently, management is seeking to make people proud of Telia as a company.

The ethos dimension is also used in the tapes in the cause of persuasion. Management puts a lot of effort into trying to strengthen the Telia ethos. Telia is portrayed as a strong company on its way forward, especially by exploiting its international network. The company is no longer a bureaucratic institution, but is rather a vigorous force with a large number of competent people. Taped interviews with many of these people representing different parts of the company and different professions help to make the company seem more human. Political correctness appears to have governed the choice of subjects, since both sexes, all ages and people of different looks have all been included. Anyone watching the tapes can find someone to identify with.

We also see the management ethos, represented by a small number of people, above all the CEO. The CEO is in his fifties and is always correctly dressed for business. Most of the time he wears glasses, but in the latest productions, these have gone. He is presented as The Leader. He answers all kinds of questions as though he is some kind of omnicompetent oracle. In some of the tapes, he is not present, but people talk about him and he is often cited. It is hardly surprising to find that the CEO had come from the telecom giant, Ericsson. Added to which, his recently appointed successor came from Ericsson too.

The CEO is not only presented as The Leader. He also acts like one. He is tall, talks extremely articulately and always sounds as though he is very sure of what he is saying. He stands up very straight and his gestures are expressive. When he talks, he does so with great intensity, occupying a lot of space in the discussions, which also serves to reinforce his dominance. His image is not that of a father figure, but rather that of a very competent, powerful and driven leader. The CEO receives by far the greatest exposure in the tapes.

The rhetorical construction of leadership

The rhetoric of the videotapes can be described as a rhetorical arena in which the leadership is constructed. As noted above, the tapes are adapted to the receivers' view of themselves and of the company. By emphasizing the need for teamwork with the help of numerous metaphors, the future with all its new demands appears less fearful. In addition, the CEO is portrayed as a saviour in a tough environment. This picture is evoked by using the rhetorical tool of antithesis. If the environment had been described as calm and controllable, the impact of the CEO's call for change would probably have been undermined. Alternatively, the CEO could have announced that he was not in fact in control. This approach would probably have caused more uncertainty in the organization, along with other possible disadvantages or advantages. Obviously, top management had chosen a less provocative stance towards the employees. In aesthetic terms the leadership rhetoric can be seen as romantic and beautiful.

Ethos, pathos and logos are all involved extensively in order to persuade the employees of the need and direction of change. It is interesting to note that the CEO appears as a legitimizer of change. If a change project is to be taken seriously, the visible support of the CEO seems to be vital. The CEO ethos is thus transferred to the change project itself. In addition, the CEO and other representatives of top management try to strengthen the Telia ethos in the minds of the staff. This is done partly by emphasizing that it will be more challenging and demanding to be part of the Telia team in the future. In this way, the Telia ethos is underpinned by a future rather than a present image of the company. It would probably have been easy for the employees to reject too positive a picture of the company if it had been based on the present situation.

In our view, logos is under-used relative to ethos and pathos. It's difficult to find specific information from the tapes about what is going to happen. For instance, the CEO's language is abstract, which makes it very difficult to criticize him. Moreover, the tapes contain several statements of a general nature. For instance, the importance of 'renewed leadership' is emphasized on several occasions, but no information is given about what this statement actually means.

So, the films have been made to persuade the audience, using logos to inform them. However, pathos and ethos predominate, and above all the ethos of the CEO. What kind of leadership is constructed, then, by means of the rhetoric of these tapes? In sum, the following elements can be seen in this construction process, relating to the elements of ethos, pathos and logos:

- an emphasis on one leader rather than a group of leaders;

- a confident male leader who has things under control;

- an omni-competent leader who understands most things;

- a proactive leader who encourages people to act;

- a visible present leader who observers what is happening;

- a logical leader who bases his decisions on rational choices.

Hence, to a large extent the rhetoric reproduces the traditional picture of leadership. It is a picture of the rational manager. Pathos is used as a tool in conveying this picture. This does not mean that the leader is described as an emotional person. Instead, he is portrayed as someone who has a lot of integrity. Further, the emphasis on a strong leader, who legitimizes most of the changes at Telia, somewhat contradicts the team-building metaphor being communicated within the company.

How, then, can this rational picture of a manager be constructed? It appears that this question cannot be answered by focusing on the literature concerned with the management of meaning. According to that school of thought, it is important for managers to be understood if they are to lead. However, Telia's CEO is abstract in his rhetoric. As a CEO, Lars Berg uses many modern and sophisticated expressions. In this way, he emerges as knowledgeable and dynamic. At the same time, there is a risk that people may find him difficult to understand. As a consequence, people may remember that certain issues are important since the CEO was visibly committed to them, but it will probably be difficult for them to translate his talk into action. Perhaps it is necessary for a top manager to use this kind of rhetoric in order to make things happen. If we make the bold assumption that he is not omni-competent or rational, then it would be risky for him to try to be concrete about things in logical terms. His ethos would be impaired, and thereby his legitimacy to lead.

In conclusion, we believe that the Telia videotapes reveal more 'management by pathos' than 'management by logos'. It is very difficult to know whether the managers are logical, on the basis of the information given in the tapes. Nevertheless, viewers can easily draw this conclusion since the contribution of ethos and pathos serve to reinforce it.

How feelings are managed is an interesting area of research for the future. This is important, not least because of the extensive focus on the management of meaning. And in this context it is important to study the extent to which beliefs about missions, visions, values and strategies are shared in an organization.

It is beyond the scope of this chapter to discuss the communicative distance between the strategic and operational levels in an organization. Nonetheless, this can be seen as an issue that calls for investigation.

References

Alvesson, M. (1993). The Play of Metaphors, in Hassard, I. and Parker, M. (eds.), *Postmodernism and Organizations*. Sage, London.

Aristotle. (1991). *Art of Rhetoric*. Harvard University, Cambridge, Mass.

Berger, P., and Luckmann, T. (1966). *The Social Construction of Reality: A Treatise in the Sociology of Knowledge*. Penguin Books, London

Bourne, L. E., Dominowski, R. L., Loftus, E. F., and Healy, A. F. (1986). *Cognitive Processes*. Prentice-Hall, Englewood Cliffs, NJ.

Burke, K. (1969). *The Rhetoric of Motives*. University of California Press, Berkeley.

Conger, J. A., and Kanungo, R. (1987). Toward a behavioral theory of charismatic leadership in organizational settings. *Academy of Management Review*, vol. 12, pp. 637–47.

Corbett, E. P. (1990). *Classical Rhetoric for the Modern Student*. Oxford University Press, New York.

Goldhaber, G. M. (1993). *Organizational Communication*. Brown & Benchmark, Madison, Wisc.

House, R. J. (1977). A theory of charismatic leadership. In Hunt, J. G., and Larson, L. (eds.), *Leadership: The Cutting Edge*. Southern Illinois University Press, Carondale.

Johannesson, K. (1990). *Retorik eller konsten att överyga*. Norstedts, Stockholm

Locke, E. A., and Henne, D. (1986). Work motivation theories. In Cooper, C. and Robertson, I. (eds.), *International Review of Industrial and Organizational Psychology*, pp. 1–35. John Wiley & Sons, Chichester.

Müllern, T., and Stein, J. (1999). *Övertygandets ledarskap – om retorik vid strategiska förändringar*. Studentlitteratur, Lund.

Ortony, A., Clore, G., and Collins, A. (1988). *The Cognitive Structure of Emotions*. Cambridge University Press, Cambridge.

Perelman, C. (1990). *The New Rhetoric and the Humanities*. Reidel Publishers, Dordrecht.

Pettigrew, A. (1973). *The Politics of Organizational Decision-Making*. Tavistock, London.

Polanyi, M. (1966). *Personal Knowledge: Towards a Post Critical Philosophy*. Doubleday, Garden City, NY.

Rothschild. J. (1977). Political legitimacy in contemporary Europe. In Denitch, B. (ed.), *Legitimation of Regimes*. Sage, London

Scott, R. (1981). *Organizations: Rational, Natural and Open Systems*. Prentice-Hall, Englewood Cliffs, NJ.

Sims, J. R., and Gioia, D. (1986). *The Thinking Organization*. Jossey-Bass, San Francisco.

Sjöstrand, S-E. (1985). *Samhällsorganisation*. Doxa, Lund.

Smircich, L., and Stubbart, C. (1985). Strategic management in an enacted world. *Academy of Management Review,* vol. 4, pp. 724–36.

Spender, J-C. (1989). *Industry Recipes: The Nature and Sources of Managerial Judgement.* Basil Blackwell, Oxford.

Starbuck, W. H. (1976). Organizations and their environments. In Dunnette, M. (ed.), *Handbook of Industrial and Organizational Psychology.* Rand McNally, Chicago.

Starbuck, W. H. (1983). Organizations as action generators. *American Sociological Review,* vol. 48, pp. 91–102.

Weber, M. (1947). *The Theory of Social and Economic Organizations.* The Free Press, New York.

Weick, K. (1979). *The Social Psychology of Organizing.* Addison-Wesley, Belmont.

Weick, K. (1995). *Sensemaking in Organizations.* Sage, Thousand Oaks, California.

Willner, A. R. (1984). *The Spellbinders: Charismatic Political Leadership.* Yale University Press, New York.

Yukl, G. (1994). *Leadership in Organizations.* Prentice-Hall, Englewood Cliffs, NJ.

CHAPTER FIVE

The home – a disregarded managerial arena

Annelie Karlsson Stider

This chapter deals with old family businesses and the relation between the owner families and their companies over the generations. In an attempt to get a clearer picture of how families actually manage their companies, I challenge the separation between public and private that is usually upheld in organization theory. The idea is to extend the usual scientific management discourse to include a traditionally invisible and once relatively inaccessible private arena, the home. The home is highlighted as one arena among others, not only for managers as such but also for other actors involved in company management – an arena that rational organization theory has generally overlooked. Is management really only performed in the formal public arenas of the boardrooms or head offices? And does management really only include those who have formal, public ties with a company?

The chapter begins with a discussion of the family business as an arena that challenges the traditional boundaries between private and public as usually drawn up by organizational theorists. On the basis of an in-depth study of one family's relation to its company, it illustrates the arenas and actors that comprise a central part of the family's management. It then looks at the effects of regarding 'private' as 'public', and argues that the home, like the boardroom, does constitute an arena for management. When the role of the home in management is made visible, certain important processes such as entertaining also emerge, and with them the role of wives and mothers in the management of the business.

Family business and gender

Many researchers claim that a family business involves the integration of two separate institutions – family and business – each with their own norms (e.g. Gibb Dyer, 1986; Ward, 1987; Gersick et al. 1997). Researchers have long divided our human lives into dichotomies, such as reproduction/production, private/public, and so on (e.g. Rosaldo, 1974). Production encompasses an individual's working life, while reproduction refers to the private life of the home. The former, the public sphere, has been described as a world dominated by men and governed by male logic, while home life, or the private sphere, has been described as a world dominated by women and governed accordingly by female logic (Fishburne Collier and Yanagisako, 1987; Maynes et al. 1996).

In defining a studied population, however, most researchers of family business take their point of departure in ownership and in the company itself, i.e. in the public sphere and in production. Some (e.g. Rosenblatt et al., 1985; Gibb Dyer, 1986) claim that a family business is a company whose ownership is dominated by one family (domination meaning anything from 25 per cent to 100 per cent of the vote). Others claim that in a family business the family can or should also be represented in operative leadership positions (Handler, 1989). Yet others believe that the family can or should also be represented at other levels of employment in the company (Ward, 1987).

The problem with these definitions is that they are all based on a traditional and narrow conception of what ownership influence and management are, and where they are exercised and by whom (cf. the development of Hirschman's [1970] ownership strategies 'exit' and 'voice', cited in Hedlund et al., 1985). The various definitions and theories focus above all on *formal* arenas (the shareholders' meeting, the board and company management), *formal* actors (board members and management groups) and *formal* processes (the appointment of management, and strategic decision-making).

Thus the descriptions of family businesses offered in corporate biographies (Olsson, 1986; de Geer, 1995) and in other more theoretical writings on family business (Rosenblatt et al., 1985; Neubauer and Lank, 1998) all assume the dichotomy whereby home, the feminine sphere, is subordinate, while business, the masculine sphere, is dominant. There is an obvious lack of observations, interpretations and theory about the way the two are integrated in the construction of family business management, and what effects any interaction between the two may have.

Feminist theory implies adopting the fundamental view that what happens in the home does have significance at work, and what transpires at work also has a bearing on life at home (Wahl et al., 1998, p. 35). A gender-aware approach stresses the impact on public managing of arenas traditionally seen as private (Fishburne Collier and Yanagisako, 1987, p. 24). The adoption of such an approach – in which the inter-gender relation is regarded as socially constructed – can be a way of exploiting the potential of the family business in the context of theory building.

It is argued that by bridging the boundaries between family and business, home and public, private life and work, the family business enables us to challenge the traditional conceptions of management. By opening the door to the home and what has traditionally been private life, the chapter aims to show how private and public, family and company are integrated. A descriptive study of the Bonnier family's almost 200-year-old business allows us to observe how family and firm, and thus also the relation between the two, are constructed differently over time and from generation to generation. Constructions of the family's relation to the company depend among other things on what arena we are considering, and at what time, as well as on the gender and age of the individual actors concerned and their kinship status within the family.

The influence of different actors also varies over time. (Major ownership does not always imply great influence, nor does little or no ownership always mean little or no influence.) It should be noted that using the Bonnier family residence in the empirical study to render visible the importance of women in a family business does not imply any statement about women's unusual invisibility in this particular family or in their business. If anything, the opposite applies. As a researcher, I place myself among those who recognize the importance of gender: in society, in organizations, in business, in family businesses and in families. In pursuing this line of study, by looking at the role of women in the Bonnier family business, I hope that not only will the reader learn something about family businesses or the Bonnier family per se, but also that more can be discovered about management and leadership in general.

Using an interpretive research approach (Ödman, 1977; Alvesson and Sköldberg, 1994), the chapter presents one story of the Bonnier family business, focusing on the family's relation to the firm. It is a story based on biographies and books written by men and women belonging to the family (Albert Bonnier Jr, Jytte Bonnier, Tor Bonnier and Åke Bonnier), and in-depth interviews with many members of the Bonnier family today. The idea has been to include a traditionally invisible and previously inaccessible private arena, the home, in the scientific discourse on management.

This chapter presents the home as an arena of management, thus demonstrating the involvement of this arena's actors in the management of the business, in a way that gender-blind organization theory has not usually done. When the door to the home is opened, the family women emerge as actors in company management and in the reproduction of the family's relation to the company, albeit from a subordinate position relative to that of the family men.

It should be noted that the following exposition makes no claim to be an exhaustive account of the Bonnier women's relation to the firm; rather, it is an initial interpretation of their importance in the family business. A more extensive presentation and interpretation of the women's, and the whole Bonnier family's, relation to the company is offered in my doctoral thesis, *Family and Firm* (Karlsson Stider, 2000). The presentation is also testimony to the relation of family owners to their companies – a group of business managers often overlooked today.

Bonniers – the History of a family business [1]

Albert Bonniers Förlag, a publishing company, was founded in Sweden in 1837 by Albert Bonnier, who had emigrated from Denmark. The media family of today, however, can trace its origins right back to 1804, when Albert's father Gerhard Bonnier opened a small bookshop in Copenhagen. Gerhard Bonnier himself was a German immigrant (born Gutkind Hirschel), who had moved to Denmark to seek his fortune. Little information exists on the wives of Gerhard or Albert Bonnier, other than that Albert's wife Betty gave birth to three children: Jenny, Karl Otto and Eva. Karl Otto's son Åke writes of his father:

> 'He was the only son of Albert and Betty, and the given heir to the publishing business, which, at the time of his birth (1856), had already become one of the most influential in the country.'
>
> (Å. Bonnier 1974, p. 96)

It was thus never even considered that Karl Otto's sisters, Jenny and Eva, might succeed their father. So, while Karl Otto was not the *only* heir, he was the only *given* one. Nevertheless, the sisters were to play an important role in the company's work. When their mother Betty died, Jenny took over the role of hostess for her father.

> 'For many years we would go to grandfather Bonnier's every other week for Sunday dinner. It was unbearable! We weren't allowed to talk at the table [...]. As soon as dinner was over, grandfather would take father into his study and close the door. It wasn't until the last few years of the [18]90s that I was occasionally allowed to

accompany them. They would continue with the day's work in there, usually going through the foreign publications to see if there was anything that could be translated [...]. After grandmother died, the house was run by the eldest daughter Jenny, first the house on the corner of Norrmalmstorg-Berzeliipark, and then the one at Hamngatan 2.'

(Tor Bonnier on the home of his grandfather Albert Bonnier, 1972, p. 18–19)

Both sisters also helped Albert more directly with the publishing work. For example, he once sought his daughters' opinion on whether a couple of sketches by the author August Strindberg were worth publishing (Å. Bonnier 1974, p. 103). With the death of their father, the influence of Albert Bonnier's daughters diminished. Since he had left them no shares in the firm, their main channel of influence to a formal manager inside the company, their father, had gone. In their place, Karl Otto's wife Lisen now took over the work that the sisters had done before, and she came to play an important role in the vigorous social life that she and Karl Otto ran together, with its many literary contacts and social engagements. While Albert's relations with some of his authors had naturally been close, his involvement on this count had been far less than that of his son and his family. Moreover, most of Albert's socializing had taken place in public venues. In his time authors were not invited home nearly as often as they were after Karl Otto and Lisen took over.

This social life in the home became much easier to manage after 1910, when Karl Otto and Lisen moved to Nedre Manilla, a property on the small island of Djurgården in Stockholm, which became and still remains an important family meeting-place. Karl Otto's eldest son describes his vivid memories of his father and the love he felt for Nedre Manilla.

'Perhaps our fondest memory is of him standing, on a summer's day, on the terrace outside his library at Manilla singing life's praises. "I count myself lucky," he said, "that my grandfather went to Copenhagen, my father came to Stockholm, and I came to Djurgården." Yes, we all remember him, from so many different occasions, in his great home on Djurgården, where he collected portraits of his authors. Maybe it's because we choose to remember those days, when our mother would ring round to us all and say "Papa has something he wants to read," and we would gather to hear him read yet another new chapter from his great portrait of our bookselling family.'

(Tor Bonnier, 1972, p. 247–48)

Nedre Manilla, on the island of Djurgården over the water from a school for the deaf and dumb, has been the family's home ever since, and has always been open to friends and acquaintances. Karl Otto and Lisen spent a great deal of time socializing with the great names in the cultural circles of the time, often at Manilla. Manilla was built for entertaining, as if this were an obligation that came with the house. Most dinner parties had a purpose, a reason for inviting just those particular guests. For the guests, the identity of their fellow-guests was also a matter of great significance (J. Bonnier, 1993, p. 68). And all this entertaining affected the children of the house, who on some occasions were permitted to be present.

> 'As children, we weren't allowed to be there at dinner, but would stand together outside the glass doors separating the hall from the dining room, watching and doing our best to eavesdrop. The serious business would begin after the meal and the coffee. Ellen Key [a famous Swedish author] or my father would read something of current interest at the time. Much of what was read was *inédit* [unpublished], as the French say, pieces from some new manuscript or the proofs of a book still being typeset – the prerogative of the publisher trade and pretty exciting. For most of the great literature of the [18]90s, this was its first audience.
>
> [...] As we grew older, roughly in our teens, we were allowed – or *had to* – attend these readings. It wasn't always that much fun and I remember trying to sneak out sometimes. Afterwards, my father would say: "Of course, it's silly to give bread to the baker's child."'
>
> (Tor Bonnier, 1972, p. 24–25)

Dinners were held with close friends and business acquaintances in the new wings that were added to Nedre Manilla. Karl Otto was interested in art and had begun to collect portraits of authors he had worked with. At the time of the move to Manilla, he already had quite a grand collection of portraits of the family and its friends and business associates, who were often the same people.

The parents' social circle of artists and writers prepared the family's younger generation early on for a life in this sort of world. They acquired a feeling for what their own work would be like and learned to relate to it. Tor, the eldest of Karl Otto and Lisen's sons, talks about what his home meant to him. The first chapter of his book *Längesen* (1972) deals with 'The Office', the second deals with 'The Home'.

> 'It [art and literature] was part of our life at home [...]. After all, our father brought all the company's new books home with him – and

you have to remember that at that time, in the 1890s, almost all new Swedish literature was published by Albert Bonniers förlag – and our parents' social circle consisted almost entirely of writers and artists.'

(Tor Bonnier, 1972, p. 24)

Tor's mother Lisen also recognized the importance of the younger generation's early acquaintance with the company and the writers in its ambit. Thus she made sure that her sons, as the next generation of publishers, should get to know some of these authors. Albert Bonnier Jr writes of his grandmother Lisen:

'Grandmother Lisen had arranged for my youngest uncle, Kaj, to eat lunch with the [Hjalmar] Söderberg [a famous Swedish author] family [. . .]. For a year or so I also had to attend these repasts. Once a week or so we would drop by to visit "uncle" Hjalle. The idea was to give the young Bonniers an opportunity to establish a personal link with this great and famous writer [. . .].'

(Albert Bonnier, 1985, p. 64–5)

Another grandchild, Lukas, tells as an adult of the uncertainty he felt about who really was the publisher – his grandfather or his grandmother. As a child Lukas would sit on the floor and listen while Karl Otto read new manuscripts to Lisen. This memory is an example of how in practice the wife acted as a valuable sounding board, no doubt also often helping to decide whether or not a book should be published. Even if she was never recognized as having any formal ties with company management, she did have an influence on company activities. Tor, the eldest son of Karl Otto and Lisen, explains how difficult it was to separate home and firm.

'I was once asked if I would like to jot down a few memories of my father, a miniature portrait as it were, and the first thing I thought of was – proofs. He was always reading proofs. He wasn't allowed to bring them to the dinner table, but the table wouldn't have been cleared for long before he would sit down with a set of proofs – either at home or, if that was too noisy, back at the office. Sometimes we were asked to help, perhaps with the check-reading of proofs, or maybe the whole family would gather round the dining-room table and sort the notes for the index of the *Handelskalendern* (The Swedish Commercial Directory). Home was almost as much a workplace as the office.'

(Tor Bonnier, 1972, p. 237)

Another more specific arena for company talks was the study. Here, the men of the family would gather after dinner to drink cognac and hold important business discussions (T. Bonnier, 1972, p. 22; J. Bonnier, 1993, p. 15). Neither wives nor daughters knew what was said at these meetings, apart from what their husbands chose to tell them.

Karl Otto had been the sole owner of the firm. Lisen and Karl Otto had six children: Tor, Åke, Greta, Elin, Gert and Kaj. When Karl Otto died in 1941 the inheritance principle was that only children who wanted to take an active part in the firm, i.e. to be employed there, were to inherit their father's shares. According to the unspoken rule that had applied before, no Bonnier daughters would work in the company. In other words, it was only the sons who were active in the firm who stood to inherit it. The other three children inherited real estate and other financial assets. Any insight into company affairs or any influence over them would therefore be very limited for the Bonnier daughters in future. As the sisters married, they also moved away from Manilla and henceforth were simply guest on a par with other non-owners at the company functions and family gatherings in the home they had grown up in. Thus, the daughters also lost the day-to-day contact with the authors associated with the firm, that they had previously enjoyed.

When Karl Otto and Lisen had both died, Tor decided in agreement with his two brothers in the company, Åke and Kaj, that ownership of the house and the collection of author portraits adorning its walls should be transferred to the company. The ground floor would continue to be used for entertaining and big family gatherings, while the upper floor would be used by Tor and his new family. Manilla became the possession of the firm (J. Bonnier, 1993, p. 33) In a sense it could be said that from that moment the members of the family no longer connected with the firm – the two sisters and Gert – became 'homeless'.

> 'So long as Karl Otto and Lisen were alive, everyone was kept up to date with news of the firm and the family. However, after their deaths, things changed. Manilla had been part of the firm and the firm part of the family. When the firm was passed on to the company men alone [...] the sisters and their children slipped slowly out of the picture – even with respect to Manilla.'
>
> (Jytte Bonnier, 1993, p. 16–17)

Wife involvement in company management

The involvement of the firm in the family's private and social life had various effects. The position of the women of the family and their importance to the company became more visible than before. Lisen not only opened her house to business associates but she also took part to a great extent in the company discourse. Friends of the family included several couples such as Hanna and Georg Pauli, where both husband and wife were artists. The Paulis, together with Ellen Key and Richard and Gerda Berg among others, formed a group that came to be known as the *Junta*. Ellen Key had been Lisen Bonnier's teacher and their friendship deepened over the years.

The women, and particularly Ellen Key, were the unifying force of the Junta. The women-dominated group was a contributory factor in the status enjoyed by Bonniers as the country's leading publisher in the first half of the 1900s. The family's cultural capital, built on its affiliations with other well-known cultural figures, attracted authors to the company, which in turn helped to support the development of a strong financial position (Sundin, 1996).

The wives took part in daily discussions with their husbands round the dinner table, not only on private but also on more festive occasions, and socialized regularly with the population of the publishing world. These women, who had married into the family, thus knew much more about the company – although they had no formal positions in it – than the women who had been born into the family. One of today's Bonnier daughters describes how the really powerful Bonnier women were those who came in from outside, and who recognized the expectations that faced them.

The women of Manilla not only acted as hostesses for company parties and literary evenings, but family gatherings too were arranged at the house. In her time Lisen was the central figure, holding together this big family of six children and numerous grandchildren, arranging the great Christmas parties that were the highlight of the year, especially for the children. Jytte Bonnier, third wife of Tor, offers a slightly less harmonious picture of these big family get-togethers, however.

'A family gathering might be a purely family affair or a combined company-family party. In the second case, on the really grand occasions, the family was in its element. In the first case though, there were undercurrents of competition and uncertainty. In a big family the competition between the various branches can either bring people together or drive them apart. Little groups form, and the reigning clique begrudges the intrusion of outsiders and becomes suspicious of them. The ladder of hierarchy seemed to be open to anyone at first, but it soon became clear that not everyone would be permitted to climb it. The last women to marry into the family were among those to whom the steps were closed. In fact, the big company parties were actually less stressful than the smaller family get-togethers. At family gatherings, it was so easy for people to gang up on each other, perhaps by placement at the table or by forming a clique.'

(Jytte Bonnier, 1993, p. 81)

One advantage that women marrying into the family did have, however, and that daughters of the family did not, was the Bonnier name – a universally recognized and visible symbol to all of belonging to the publishing family. On the other hand, some of those marrying in – Åke's wife Eva (in the third generation) being one of them – could also further augment the influence of their husbands and children by bringing substantial fortunes into the family. And the fortune left by her father to Betty, wife of Albert Bonnier the founder of the company, also enabled Albert to expand activities (Å. Bonnier, 1974, p. 63).

'[...] women who married into the family were made privy to every development, cultural or financial. They entertained on behalf of the company and might even be lucky enough to produce a son, thereby further strengthening their positions.'

(Jytte Bonnier, 1993, p. 16)

During the children's early years it was their mother who did most to instill into them the values of management. Karl Otto's wife Lisen, Tor's mother, was much influenced by Ellen Key's ideas on child rearing, and she made sure that Tor and his siblings were raised according to these values. However, as the children (which in these generations meant the sons) approached their teens, the father became more involved in their upbringing and education, which often included gaining practical experience through staying with other families in the international publishing and press world (K. O. Bonnier, 1930–31; T. Bonnier, 1972; Å. Bonnier, 1974; A. Bonnier, 1985). When the sons married, they would be sent abroad with their wives so that *both* could benefit from this experience (A. Bonnier, 1985). Even the current generation of Bonniers (i.e. those interviewed for the present study) remarked on the difference between being 'just' a wife and being a mother – especially a mother of sons.

The indirect influence of the wives-mothers through their children is exemplified in various accounts of Tor Bonnier's first wife, Greta Lindberg, of whom it is said by the family today that she 'took the family business with her' when she and Tor were divorced in the 1920s. This is a reference to her insistence as part of the divorce settlement, that her three sons (Albert Jr, Johan and Lukas) were to share the inheritance of the family business. The shares in the business for Tor's other three sons, Simon, Karl-Adam and Mikael from subsequent marriages, were therefore much smaller than their older brothers'. Greta is also described as one of the few people who Albert Bonnier Jr really listened to (Sigfridsson, 1995, p. 9). Thus, one interpretation of this is that, as a mother, Greta retained an influence on the family business even after her divorce from Tor, primarily through the sons whose interests she had so strategically protected. If nothing else, her influence on the distribution of company shares for coming generations is indisputable.

The wives of the next, or fifth, generation never worked actively in the company, but as in earlier generations their social lives revolved round their husbands' business associates. Albert Bonnier Jr (or Abbe as he was sometimes called) and his cousin Gerard Bonnier, were now the family's managers. Abbe's responsibility was the constantly growing Bonnier Group, while Gerard was the publisher of the family. During this period the Manilla estate became less important to the Group, since Abbe – the family's current patriarch – did not live there. But because it still housed the collection of author portraits, Manilla still played a central role in the life of the publishing company. For the Group it was now Albert and Birgit's home, and as such it came to play a major role in the company's development.

As already noted, the wives of this generation did not work in the company, but they still organized the entertaining and the social events. Legendary among these happenings were Albert and Birgit's midsummer parties on Dalarö, to which many of the Group's business associates were invited (see Strömstedt, 1994). Their daughters remember well how their two homes (Manilla and Dalarö) were subject to a constant stream of visiting journalists and editors. One of their memories is of Carl-Adam Nycop and their father Abbe kneeling on the floor amidst a sea of paper, trying to come up with a name for a new evening paper (*Expressen*). Another of the sisters' vivid memories is of a visit by Walt Disney to their summer house on Dalarö.

According to his daughters, Abbe's wife Birgit was one of her husband's most important discussion partners. Their father listened to her and took her advice. When Abbe went on business trips all over the world, she accompanied him. Olle Måberg, the Group's former chairman, testifies to Birgit's frequent presence at board meetings. In addition, Abbe would invite potential employees to his home – invitations that always included the wives, as this was seen as an important factor in getting a complete picture of the person in question. Birgit's opinion weighed heavily, the daughters recall, when it came to the final decision to appoint a candidate.

When they were interviewed for this study, the children of Gerard Bonnier told how they would meet the company's authors and other friends from the big Swedish daily newspaper *Dagens Nyheter*, either in Stockholm or at the family's summer house on Dalarö – a tradition they still keep up.

> 'In my childhood home, socializing with the authors was a bit more formal. There were rather grand dinners. I think perhaps I have a more relaxed relationship with my authors, and socialize with some of them privately. My children have become quite close to some of them, and have seen their less-than-great sides as well!'
>
> (Eva Bonnier, CEO, Albert Bonniers Förlag)

Bo Strömstedt offers several accounts of conversations with Abbe and Gerard about *Expressen*, during his time as editor-in-chief on the paper (Strömstedt, 1994). He also tells how he and his wife Margareta became friends with Gerard and his wife Peggy during their summer stays at Dalarö. The wives are described as participating to the greatest possible extent in discussions, both at Dalarö and elsewhere.

The company home

Manilla and its collection of portraits of well-known Swedish authors and artists and of various members of the family – most of them painted by Carl Larsson or Hanna or Georg Pauli – is regarded by the Bonnier family of today as a particularly valuable possession, even though they did not grow up there themselves. In particular they refer to Manilla and its collection as a symbol of their family tradition. After Tor's death in 1976, Gerard Bonnier (1917–87) took over responsibility for adding to the portrait collection. Gerard Bonnier was the publisher of the family, and is said to have been the one to establish a bridge between the cultural obligations of the family on the one hand and its commercial responsibilities on the other. Gerard was the leader of the publishing house, Albert Bonniers Förlag, and as a result of his knowledge and interest in art in general, he came to know most of the influential literary figures and artists of his time.

Today the home is no longer owned by the firm, but belongs to a newly established family trust. One of the reasons for setting up this foundation was the family's wish to separate home and business, so that the home would remain in the hands of the family, should future generations decide to sell the company. Manilla was to belong not to the firm but to the family. Responsibility for adding to the great portrait collection has been taken over by the family trust. In addition to maintaining the collection, the Foundation also manages the upkeep of Manilla. It is also responsible for more family-oriented activities such as scholarship funds for members of the family, administration of the journalism prize (Stora Journalistpriset) and of a newly established education programme (Gutkind and Co.) for the younger generation of owners in the Bonnier family.

Major events are still held at Manilla, such as luncheons for Nobel laureates and the award ceremonies for the journalism prize. One of the family's daughters, Charlotte Bonnier, has resumed Lisen's tradition of big Christmas parties. Manilla is also the venue for the annual shareholders meeting each spring, and family members are able to rent the house for such occasions as wedding receptions and birthday celebrations. Manilla also continues to be used for entertaining and similar events, and dinner parties are held there for Swedish and international guests. The programme for the younger generation owners of Bonnier is also held here. For most present-day members of the Bonnier family, however, Manilla has not retained its old atmosphere, although all agree that it represents the historical family home and is a symbol of the family's past in Swedish business.

As family and firm have both grown enormously in the fifth and sixth generations, the role of the wives has changed. And since daughters of the family are now able to inherit shares and are allowed to work in the firm, they have also taken on many of the jobs traditionally performed by Bonnier wives. Today, a daughter holds the family together and arranges the traditional Christmas festivities. Moreover, many of the daughters retain the Bonnier name upon marriage, thus continuing to be visible representatives of the family.

The home – a managerial arena

This historical account of the Bonnier family has led us through a series of events demonstrating just how fluid the line between home and company has been in this family. The formal has merged with the informal, the public with the private. Proofs were read aloud at home to a critical audience of wives and children. Products were packaged at home, with the children's help. Corporate entertaining was conducted at home at Manilla, where Swedish and foreign representatives of the world of culture were received. The business arena was not restricted to the formal business premises, nor were discussion partners restricted to the formally employed.

The family home was owned by the firm for close on fifty years, and although Manilla is now in the hands of the family trust the boundaries between home and firm have not been as clear as earlier organization theorists have claimed them to be. The Bonnier home used to serve not only as a private arena for intimate family life but also as a public arena. Today Manilla, the corporate family home, has become public, while the homes of individual family members remain more private, implying that a distinction has been made between public and private homes.

In her studies of families and kinship, Boholm (1983) has described how, in the course of time, objects and houses and places all become imbued with symbolic value. Old family homes serve as symbols, passing on knowledge about the family and strengthening the ties between present-day family members. They serve as the venue for special family events or celebrations, and symbolize the family's permanence and integrality.

Today, the corporate house Manilla serves as a family heirloom, an arena in which family belongingness and the family's relation to the firm are reproduced. The house is used as an arena for transmitting knowledge of the family history. At family gatherings and company parties, the Bonnier family and its relations with the Swedish cultural world are constructed. Before, this was done by maintaining close relations with writers in the family setting. Today, it is done by using the home for training and large-scale corporate entertaining.

The home is accordingly an arena where, in the past and today, it is possible to exercise owner influence. It is not therefore possible to distinguish between production and reproduction or between public and private. Instead, production and reproduction can be seen as more coordinated in time and space. Thus, the home becomes an arena for management.

Further leadership processes

However, visiting this corporate family home has not only served to expose arenas in which the family, the firm and the relations between them are constructed. The visit has also brought other processes out into the open – processes not traditionally included in management, but affecting the management of the Bonnier family and business just as significantly.

This gender-aware depiction of the family's relation to the firm shows that any real understanding of the way the 'managing' family is constructed must take account of the distribution of the inheritance.

Who may inherit shares and who may not affects the composition of the family and, consequently, the family's relation to the firm. But the family who runs the firm is not constructed on an ownership basis alone. The empirical data clearly shows that even non-owners – wives, for example – partake in management. This is particularly obvious in the early generations, when the wives were part of the 'management family'. The relation of the wives to the firm is different today. Earlier, they undertook certain tasks without holding any formal position. Today some of them are also employed by the company (e.g. Kerstin Bonnier of Svensk Filmindustri). In earlier generations, only the sons-in-law – never the daughters-in-law – were formally involved in the firm. Yngve Larsson, city commissioner in Stockholm and married to Karl Otto's daughter Elin, was for several decades in the mid-1900s the only non-Bonnier on the board of Dagens Nyheter. For a number of years, Abbe's son-in-law, Göran Forsell, previously married to Abbe's daughter Charlotte, was in charge of the mill at Billingsfors, a subsidiary of the Bonnier Group. Thus, the construction of the family emerges as a parallel process, with a strong influence on the firm.

Another traditionally neglected management process to emerge from the empirical data is the corporate dinner. The following excerpt provides yet another illustration of the direct impact of entertaining on management – in this case, the management of the Wallenberg family.

'To lay a solid foundation for developing operations, the Wallenberg family, rather like the Bonniers, began with something that in modern colloquial terms could be called "driving the big wedge". In order to gain the social recognition of the ruling strata of society, the Wallenbergs took to throwing the city's biggest parties, to which were invited diplomats and political dignitaries, scholars, rich people in general, popular artists and writers, and the like. The main thing was that they were, or were on their way to becoming, influential. It didn't take long before it was the "in" thing to attend these parties. The parties created a broad contact network and were a way of gathering information and gossip that was meticulously noted. The activity led to [the Wallenbergs] getting a lot of assignments to administrate fortunes and trusts [...].'

(Ångström, 1990, p. 49)

Bourdieu (1996, p. 273) describes the importance of families establishing and maintaining social relations and contacts, such as can be mobilized and drawn upon when needed. The construction of a network of favours and return favours, obligations and dues between a family and its associates, must be a conscious process. Entertaining and other social events are part of this social reproduction of the relation between family and firm. Socializing with company employees, customers and suppliers converts commercial relations into another type of relations – the more private and genuine – between family members and 'business associates' (see Sjöstrand, 1993, 1997). In the case of the Bonniers, it also reproduces the position of the family in Sweden's cultural world. And, finally, it serves to reproduce the family's professional know-how by versing the coming generations of the family in the social ways of the Bonnier trade – publishing.

Thus entertaining and business parties are not just a private affair; they are a way of reproducing contacts with other people in the business. They are an important element in company management, something that becomes increasingly apparent when we open the door to the home – the arena where much of the entertaining takes place.

The invisible managers[2]

Once the home is recognized as a business management arena, we discover actors, women, who have not been visible to historians of family business. These women – wives, mothers and hostesses – have been active participants in the construction and reconstruction of the family's relation to the firm. They can therefore be regarded as having a management role, although admittedly a role performed from a subordinate position relative to that of the family men (Karlsson Stider, 1999).

The wives of the first generations had access to the management arenas and processes of the home. They were not owners and were not employed by the firm, but despite this they associated with its leading men. They made their home Manilla, the great meeting-place for family and company. They also bore the Bonnier name, and were thus perceived by outsiders as members of the Bonnier family.

The role of the wives can be interpreted by referring to Kanter's discussion on wives' relations to the companies in which their husbands are employed (Kanter, 1977, p. 104). Kanter describes how marriage is not merely a matter of a man and a woman, but also of a woman and her husband's company. A woman's position and status are dependent on the stage that her husband has reached in his career and his position in the company. The demands made on the wife increase in relation to her husband's social networking, and it is her job to deal with any tension between private and public – a diplomatic balancing act of the utmost importance both to the firm and to her husband's career. In entertaining, for example, she must combine the role of hostess with that of a public relations person for the company.

We have seen how the daughters of Albert Bonnier, founder of the Bonnier empire, and the wives of the following generations helped their husbands to perform tasks of a purely publishing nature (e.g. assessing manuscripts). They also bore the ultimate responsibility for the upbring-ing of the heirs in their early years. At the same time, they gave dinners for company associates in their homes. In later generations, now that the company has become a cultural as well as a financial institution in Swedish society (Sundin, 1996, p. 460), most of these associates are also friends, as business relations are now closely intertwined with social relations. The wife's role is to give business meetings a personal – even a private – air, and to strengthen the family's personal ties with potential customers and business associates.

I have demonstrated here the existence of further actors who take part in constructing the family–firm relation, and thus also in the production and reproduction of the family's corporate management. Both family men *and* women influence the management of the company, albeit in the women's case from subordinate positions. To disregard the home and the wives in the management process is to present an incomplete picture of management.

Managers of the home

Due to its varied conceptual blend – family and business, home and public workplace, private life and work life – the family business provides a constellation conducive to a questioning of our traditional conceptions of management. To extend the study of management beyond the actors in the formal, public arenas is clearly justified. Even such arenas and actors and processes as are traditionally perceived as private, have a bearing on management constructions. The home is one arena in which management is constructed (see Holgersson and Höök, 1997). Wives are actors who participate in the construction of management in this arena. And entertaining is a management process in which management is constructed. Consequently, in studying management a conscious effort to bring the home out into the open not only adds to our understanding of the family business itself, but also promotes a better understanding of management in general.

What management constructions do the Bonnier women help to (re)produce? Do they merely reproduce the reigning male construction of man as the dominant corporate manager and wife as the subordinate hostess whose only skills are social, or do they contribute to some other acts of construction?

Several researchers have claimed that management is effected by means of talk, both consciously in formal speech and in the more informal type of daily conversation (see Gustafsson, 1994; Ekman 1999). However, these scholars have been speaking primarily of talk in formal organizational arenas. This depiction of the Bonnier family shows that the family business and various business activities are also dealt with in the family home, where the wives of company managers actively partake – to varying degrees, depending on their generation – in the discussion of company business. The Bonnier family wives played a crucial role in the history of the management of the family business, by way of such traditional management processes as operative decision-making (e.g. on the publication of books), recruitment or quality control (e.g. proof-reading).

They have also served as the financiers of company operations, and have participated in management processes not traditionally associated with management such as entertaining, biological reproduction and teaching the necessary arts to coming generations of owners. In doing so, the wives have contributed to the company's management planning and development by bringing forth and educating future leaders of the family and the family business. And, finally, the wives must also be seen as the ones who have taken upon themselves the responsibility for organizing the owners, since it is the wives and mothers who have held the family – or the owners – together. When the business is handed on from one generation to the next, it is not only ownership of company shares and formal management positions that is being passed on. The role of family organizer also needs to be brought out into the open and recast. In some American family businesses, this owner-organizer role has been institu-tionalized in a position entitled 'director of shareholder relations'. Where it has been established, this position is often associated with the management of a special department within the company whose responsibility extends to organizing and implementing activities relating primarily to the family ownership – the 'family office'.

Mention was made above of the family home Manilla in its role as a family heirloom. Following Bourdieu's conception of capital (Bourdieu, 1984, 1996), we can also look at family business as composed of a series of different assets. When one generation takes over from another, it is not only a financial inheritance of the ownership, the company, and various products or services that must be passed on to the next generation. There are also social, cultural and symbolic aspects to be considered. The social inheritance is made up of the genuine relations of blood, marriage and friendship established by the family over the generations. The symbolic inheritance is on the one hand a cultural heritage made up of the family's knowledge of its trade and its values, i.e. the family's perception of *what* the business does, how it does it and why, and, on the other, a heritage symbolized by heirlooms denoting family belongingness, e.g. the family name and its properties and estates (Karlsson, 1996).

The historical family home and symbolic capital – Manilla – is used to engender what Bourdieu (1984, p. 228) calls 'profits of distinction'. The family's collective assets of a particular capital and their position in society are used to increase their ownership of other types of capital. By exploiting this family heirloom and social and cultural capital, the family also gains financial advantages. This is the tradition of both past and present. Entertaining is thus not only a private affair or a way of reproducing contacts with business associates. It is a strategy for converting social and cultural capital into financial gain. It is also a significant part of the management of the company, as becomes apparent when the door to the home – the arena where the entertainment most often occurs – is opened. In this arena, the women of the family emerge as the actors bearing the ultimate responsibility for making these profits of distinction possible. It is they who bear the responsibility for the reproduction of the family's heirlooms and its social and cultural capital, so that these in turn may contribute to the reproduction of financial capital.

Perhaps the undeniable power that the women of the Bonnier family wield over the company management is due to the type of business in which the family is involved. A common conception of our world is that it is 'easier' for women to be visible in the arts. On the other hand, Chadwick (1990) shows how female artists have been made invisible over time, and have not been considered a part of the artistic discourse. The fact that several of the strong cultural figures in the family's social circle were women was certainly important. Ellen Key's efforts in the campaign for equality for women were considerable, albeit of rather an essentialist nature. And certainly women like Hanna Pauli, Karin Larsson and Sigrid Hjertén became recognized artists although remaining subordinate to their well-known husbands (both Karin and Sigrid gave up their careers for their husbands – Carl Larsson and Isaac Grünewald respectively).

More than the specific type of business, it is the strength and intimacy of the relation between family and firm that makes possible, and visible, the participation of the family women in the construction of management. I have displayed the owners' relation to the company and have shown how our everyday conceptions of management are often limited: we tend to see it as a quality attaching to a professional person, a formally employed manager, who leads a company (cf. Chandler 1977, 1990). Perhaps the form of the ownership plays a major role in a woman's influence on management, although probably only because it's easier to demonstrate the influence of women in a family business. Can it be that their presence and influence is more legitimate in the management of a family business than in other companies?

Thus the Bonnier women's contribution is not really a question of a 'new' construction of management. Rather, this exposure of the home, the women and their entertaining activities as an active part of the management processes challenges the basis for the traditional masculine construction proclaimed by organization theory. In this way, I myself am serving as a constructor of an alternative construction of management, and one that is more composite and complex.

It would thus be reasonable to assume that the arenas, the actors and the processes made visible in this study of a corporate family empire, namely the home, the wives and the entertaining, also exist in the case of the publicly owned companies. Thus, in any future study of the processes of management, let us open the door not only to family business managers, but also to the homes of the managers of other big corporations.

Notes

1 The terms *family business*, *company* and *firm* have been used interchangeably, partly with a view to reflecting the different references to the family business made by the family members interviewed.
2 This discussion is based on an essay on the situation of daughters, wives and mothers in family business, presented in *Kvinnovetenskaplig Tidskrift*, March/April 1999. See Karlsson Stider, 1999.

References

Alvesson, M., and Sköldberg, K. (1994). Tolkning och reflektion. Vetenskaps-filosofi och kvalitativ metod Studentlitteratur, Lund.
Ångström, L.-J. (1990). *Därför mördades Ivar Kreuger*. Sellin & Blomquist, Stockholm.
Boholm, Å. (1983). *Swedish Kinship: An Exploration into Cultural Processes of Belonging and Continuity* Acta Universitatis Goethoburgensis, Goteborg.
Bonnier, Å. (1974). *Bonniers. En släktkrönika 1778–1941*. Albert Bonniers Förlag, Stockholm.
Bonnier, A. (1985). *Personligt*. Albert Bonniers Förlag, Stockholm.

Bonnier, J. (1993). *Manilla. Innanför murarna*. Trevi, Stockholm.

Bonnier, K. O. (1930–31). *Bonniers. En bokhandlarefamilj*. Anteckningar ur gamla papper och ur minnet av Karl Otto Bonnier, vols. I–IV. Albert Bonniers Förlag, Stockholm.

Bonnier, T. (1972). *Längesedan. Sammanklippta minnesbilder*. Albert Bonniers Förlag, Stockholm.

Bourdieu, P. (1984). *Distinction: A Social Critique of the Judgement of Taste*. Harvard University Press, Cambridge.

Bourdieu, P. (1996). *State Nobility. Elite Schools in the Field of Power*. Stanford University Press, Stanford.

Chadwick, W. (1990). *Women, Art and Society*. Thames and Hudson, London.

Chandler, A. (1977). *The Visible Hand*. Harvard University Press, Cambridge.

Chandler, A. (1990). *Scale and Scope. The Dynamics of Industrial Capitalism*. Harvard University Press, Cambridge.

Ekman, G. (1999). *Från text till batong*. EFI, Stockholm.

Fishburne Collier, J., and Junko Yanagisako, S. (eds.) (1987). *Gender and Kinship. Essays Toward a Unified Analysis*. Stanford University Press, Stanford.

Gibb Dyer, W. (1986). *Cultural Change in Family Firms: Anticipating and Managing Business and Family Transitions*. Jossey Bass, San Francisco.

de Geer, H. (1995). *Axel Johnson Inc. 1920–1995*. Bokförlaget Atlantis, Stockholm.

Gersick K., Davis J., McCollom Hampton M., and Lansberg, I. (1997). *Generation to Generation. Life Cycles of the Family Business*. Harvard Business School Press, Harvard.

Gustafsson, C. (1994). *Produktion av allvar*. Nerenius & Santérus, Stockholm.

Handler, W. (1989). Methodological Issues and Considerations in Studying Family Businesses. *Family Business Review*, vol. 3, Autumn, pp. 257–77.

Hedlund G., Hägg I., Hörnell E., and Ryden B. (1985). *Institutionerna som aktieägare. Förvaltare? Industrialister? Klippare?* Studieförbundet Näringsliv och Samhälle (SNS), Stockholm.

Hirschman, A. O. (1970). *Exit, Voice and Loyalty*. Harvard University Press, Cambridge, Mass.

Holgersson, C., and Höök, P. (1997). Chefsrekrytering och ledarutveckling som arenor för konstruktion av ledarskap och kön. In Nyberg, A., and Sundin, E. (eds.). *Ledare, makt och kön*. SOU 1997:135, pp. 17–45.

Karlsson, A. (1996). *The Family Tradition: A Social Capital Sustaining Growth Throughout Generational Transition*. Award-winning paper presented at the Family Business Network Conference in Edinburgh, Scotland.

Karlsson Stider, A. (1999). Hemma hos firmafamiljen. *Kvinnovetenskaplig Tidskrift*, vol. 1, pp. 21–31.

Kanter, R. M. (1977). *Men and Women of the Corporation*. Harper Collins, New York.

Lindqvist, M. (1996). *Herrarna i näringslivet. Om kapitalistisk kultur och mentalitet*. Natur och Kultur, Stockholm.

Maynes, M. J., Waltner, A., Soland, B., and Strasser, U. (1996). *Gender, Kinship, Power. A Comparative and Interdisciplinary History*. Routledge, London.

Neubauer, F., and Lank, A. (1998). *The Family Business. Its Governance for Sustainability*. Maximiliam Business, London.

Ödman, P. J. (1977). *Tolkning, förståelse och vetande*. Almqvist & Wicksell, Stockholm.

Olsson, U. (1986). *Bank, familj och företagande. Stockholm Enskilda Bank 1946–1971.* Institutet för Ekonomisk Historisk Forskning, Stockholm.

Rosaldo, M. Z. (1974). Woman, Culture and Society: A Theoretical Overview. In Rosaldo M. Z., and Lampher, L. (eds.), *Woman, Culture and Society.* Stanford University Press, Stanford.

Rosenblatt, T. C., de Mik, L., Anderson, R. M., and Johnson, P. A. (1985). *The Family in Business.* Jossey Bass, San Francisco.

Sigfridsson, S. (1995). *Boken om Bonniers.* Wiking & Johnsson, Stockholm.

Sjöstrand, S-E. (1993). *Om företagsformer.* EFI, Stockholm.

Sjöstrand, S-E. (1997). *The Two Faces of Management. The Janus Factor.* Thomson, London.

Strömstedt, B. (1994). *Löpsedeln och insidan. En bok om tidningen och livet.* Albert Bonniers Förlag, Stockholm.

Sundin, S. (1996). *Från bokförlag till mediekoncern. Huset Bonnier 1909–1929.* Meddelanden från ekonomisk-historiska institutionen vid Göteborgs Universitet.

Wahl, A., Holgersson, C., and Höök, P. (eds.) (1998). *Ironi och Sexualitet.* Carlssons, Stockholm.

Ward, J. (1987). *Keeping the Family Business Healthy.* Jossey-Bass, San Francisco.

CHAPTER SIX

The social construction of top executives

Charlotte Holgersson

Introduction

This chapter addresses the question of the recruitment of top executives. The point of departure is an interview study in which board chairmen of large Swedish companies were asked about the way in which chief executive officers are recruited in Swedish business. The procedure and criteria for selection and assessment are described and discussed. In the final section of the chapter, the concept of co-option is introduced in an attempt to improve our understanding of how the construction of top executives is produced and reproduced in the recruitment process.

Considering the importance we attribute to top managers as decision-makers and role models in companies and society, there is surprisingly little theory concerning top executive recruitment. Research on top managers is abundant although it has not specifically focused on the recruitment process (Vancil, 1987; Hollenbeck, 1994; Sessa and Campbell, 1997). Instead, it has dealt with issues such as the qualities a manager or leader should possess (e.g. Stodgill, 1974; Kirkpatrick and Locke, 1991) and the demands and requirements of executive positions (e.g. Stewart, 1976; Rock, 1977; Hambrick, 1988). Research on top managers has also addressed the issue of executive selection, mainly examining links between the organization's characteristics and the characteristics of the individuals selected as CEOs (see e.g. Guthrie and Datta, 1997). The causes, consequences and effects of CEO successions (see e.g. Furtado and Karan, 1990; Cannella and Lubatkin, 1993) have also been studied. Most of this research is based on Anglo-Saxon cases.

Few of these studies employ a social constructionist perspective (see Chapter 2) but are more concerned with the statistical testing of various models. These studies can be interesting from an empirical standpoint, but they leave us with few descriptions of the actual process and little knowledge of how the perception of top executives is developed and used in the process, or how the process itself shapes the construction of leadership and top executives. How the construction of leadership and top executives is produced and reproduced in the recruitment process is still a fairly unexplored topic.

In this chapter, however, the recruitment of CEOs is regarded as an arena in which the perception of the characteristics and requirements of a CEO are constructed. The purpose is to throw some light on the mechanisms involved in the production and reproduction of the construction of the CEO in the recruitment process, and how this affects who is actually selected. Attention is drawn to an interesting paradox: the recruitment of CEOs is described as involving the careful selection of a person who matches the company's specific needs, although it is apparent at the same time that with regards to such factors as age, background, education and gender, top managers are in fact a homogeneous group.

Presentation of the empirical study

The material was gathered as part of an ongoing study of top executive recruitment. The empirical study, on which this chapter is based, focused on company chairmen, since these people are usually considered to be key persons in the recruitment process (Holmberg, 1986).

The nine board chairmen selected and interviewed are all highly regarded figures in the Swedish business world, with extensive experience of corporate management. The companies of which they were chairmen were listed companies, representing a variety of industries and owners. The majority of the industries were male-dominated, and all the boards were male-dominated, with seven of the nine being all-male. All companies had a male CEO. These figures are not surprising, considering that women represent four per cent of board members of Swedish listed companies and six per cent of the members of management in privately owned companies (Höök, 1995). In 1998 only three companies out of 307 listed companies had a woman as chair (Sundin and Sundqvist, 1998).

The interviews were semi-structured and the respondents were asked to describe the procedure adopted when a CEO was to be recruited, and to illustrate this with cases from their own experience. Questions were also asked about what was required of a CEO and about the experience and qualities that were felt to be important. Moreover, respondents were asked to discuss characteristics or actions that would probably disqualify a candidate. Finally, as far as time allowed, the respondents were asked to discuss why few women are recruited to CEO positions. Six out of nine chairmen had this opportunity.

The analysis of the interviews consisted of identifying recurrent themes as well as issues that were not recurrent, but interesting in relation to the study's underlying theoretical framework. An extensive account of the results from the interviews has been published in Swedish in the research report *Styrelseordförandes utsagor om vd-rekrytering* (Holgersson, 1998).

The board and the CEO in Swedish listed companies

In order to understand the relationship between the CEO and the board in Sweden, a brief introduction to the formal hierarchy of Swedish listed companies, adapted from Hultbom (1997), will be given. The three top levels of hierarchy in Swedish listed companies comprise the owners, represented by the shareholders' general meeting, the board of directors that represents the shareholders, and the CEO. The owners generally voice their opinion once a year only, at the shareholders' general meeting. A listed company is by law required to have a CEO, who is responsible for the execution of company operations. In most companies, the CEO is also a board member (Hultbom, 1997).

A listed company is also required to have a board of directors, with a minimum of three board members,[1] and it is customary to include representatives of owners with large shareholdings. According to Hultbom (1997), one of the primary duties of the board is to represent the shareholders' interests, usually defined as increasing shareholder values, and to appoint, and when necessary dismiss, the CEO. In order to execute its duties, the board must direct and control company operations, i.e. be involved in strategic processes and decision-making. Further, the board is responsible for supervising the CEO and has the legal backing to intervene if necessary (Rhode, 1987).

The board appoints its chairman, and the duties of the chairman are regulated to a very limited extent by law. In practice, however, the chairman is by far the most important person on the board. The chairman chairs board meetings, represents the company externally together with the CEO, and is often perceived as the foremost representative of the company. The relationship between the CEO and chairman is therefore considered very important.

Researchers have often discussed whether the CEO or the board is the most influential body (Hultbom, 1997). The CEO is formally subordinate to the board, but is at the same time generally the person on the board with most knowledge of the company. The tasks of the CEO include managing and allocating the company's activities. The CEO also has the formal responsibility to inform the board about company operations. Brodin et al. (1995) write that board members often have limited time, and are generally less informed about the company than the CEO. As a result, the relationship between the board and the CEO relies heavily on mutual trust.

An outline of the procedure

'[...] one involves [the members of the board] in order to get viewpoints but also to get a consensus. Consensus, business as usual, is highly valued and the chairman usually works informally with this.'
(Chairman on the recruiting procedure, in Holgersson, 1998)

'You create an occasion. You invite them home for a late supper and you drink beer and you talk [...] very informally!'
(Chairman describing occasions when the recruitment of a CEO is discussed, in Holgersson, 1998)

In a typical recruitment procedure, the board will request the chairman and a small team to find one or more candidates. This is sometimes done together with an executive-search consultant. The use of executive-search consultants when recruiting a CEO seems to vary. The majority of the respondents claim that they consulted executive-search firms. Nevertheless, a few asserted that executive-search consultants were never involved in recruitment at the CEO level.[2] The executive-search consultants would typically help the chairman to identify the company's needs, draft a profile and provide names of possible candidates.

The majority of chairmen claimed that they usually draft a profile of the ideal candidate, specifying characteristics, knowledge and experience, according to what they consider necessary to fulfil the needs of the company (this will be discussed in greater detail later). Once a number of candidates have been selected, the board will meet with them in order to decide who is the most suited to the assignment. The board may be presented with only one candidate, although there are cases where the owner or chairman single-handedly appoints a new CEO without having consulted the board prior to the decision. In a typical case, however, the chairman discusses the matter with different members of the board. This is often done in a certain order, according to several factors such as share of stock, seniority, commitment and knowledge. Although union representatives have a formal role in the recruitment process, since they are members of the board, according to the interviews they are not always consulted.[3] This indicates that there is a hierarchy within the board that the chairman takes into account when managing the recruitment process.

The role of the incumbent CEO in the process seems to vary. A few chairmen were very sceptical as to whether the incumbent should have any say in the matter at all. Nevertheless, several chairmen mentioned that they often want to hear the opinion of the incumbent CEO, but that it is ultimately the chairman's prerogative to choose the candidates. Some respondents, however, maintained that the CEO has a responsibility to provide a number of candidates from within the organization. A couple of chairmen also recalled cases where the CEO was to become the new chairman and searched for his own replacement in collaboration with the resigning chairman. We can therefore conclude that resigning CEOs can be either directly or indirectly involved in the recruitment of their successor.

Although the chairmen's descriptions focus mainly on the board and executive-search consultants, we cannot exclude the possibility that potential candidates are also actively involved in the process. The CEO position is seldom advertised and there are very few opportunities to apply or even gain knowledge about the position being available.

In addition, the legitimacy of someone submitting an application would appear to be questionable, as some of the interviewed chairmen commented that this would make them suspicious of such an applicant, and one respondent remarked that a person's career planning should be left to their superiors. Nevertheless, some respondents said that potential candidates could act in other more discreet ways to make the superiors aware of their aspirations.

The arenas in which the CEO profile and candidates are discussed are often informal ones. According to the interviews, such discussion seldom takes place at formal board meetings but rather before or after meetings or other events and over the telephone. Recruitment can also be discussed at more informal or even private events, such as hunts, lunches or dinners. The majority of the chairmen felt that the decision process was swifter when conducted more informally. One chairman mentioned that speaking informally with each board member individually was a good way to unite the board and create strong support for a candidate. According to several of the interviewed chairmen, by the time the issue appears on the agenda, the matter should already have been settled.

Another reason for having informal arenas of discussion was that the chairmen were concerned about discretion, not only for the sake of a dismissed CEO's reputation, but also in order to give the employees, clients, contractors and the market as a whole, the impression of stability. Similarly, Hannan and Freeman (1984) observed that it was of paramount interest to organizational stakeholders to send out signals of stability and control to external constituents. Vancil (1987) has also described how directors and executives go to great lengths to smooth the transition of power, thus minimizing disruption and sending a message of stability to outside constituents.

Although the respondents pointed out that the recruiting process varies between cases, it was nonetheless possible to discern a pattern depending on the motives behind the recruitment, that is, whether the company had to recruit a new CEO because the present CEO was retiring, resigning, being dismissed or had died. Most respondents spoke primarily about two of these cases: when a CEO retires and when a CEO is dismissed. When a CEO retires, the board can prepare the recruitment in advance and the process is therefore not judged as complicated. However, when a CEO is dismissed it is more difficult to handle, since the process has to be swift and discreet.

Most chairmen argued that in order to choose the best man for the job, it was important that the search procedure was very structured. (The respondents referred almost exclusively to CEOs and candidates as 'he' or 'him'.) However, several respondents claimed that not all recruitment procedures included a thorough analysis of the company's needs, and that the candidates were not properly screened because board members would start deleting different names from their personal lists right away. Sorcher (1985) concludes that the CEO selection decisions he observed were subjective and to a large extent based on personal observations. Similar observations have also been made in other empirical studies of manager selection and assessment, both Swedish and Anglo-Saxon (e.g. Dalton, 1959; Rock, 1977; Barlow, 1989; Hollenbeck, 1994; Tengblad, 1997) and by executive-search consultants (e.g. Nilsson, 1993). Barlow (1989) concluded, in a study of systems for executive evaluation, that informal activities could be so influential that formalized activities would legitimize the informal activities. The system for executive evaluation that Barlow studied had very little impact on the final appointments made. The system, although conveying an image of an effective, fair and objective procedure, did not hinder executives from appointing managers according to their own personal preferences.

Selecting the candidates

'It is a sign of poverty or at least a sign of poor planning if one has to go outside the company and recruit.'
(Chairman on insiders; in Holgersson, 1998)

'You simply can't come from nowhere and be a manager. You can't just take anybody from an academic career and make this person operating manager of a company.'
(Chairman on why women are not recruited to CEO positions;
in Holgersson, 1998)

'When a CEO or member of the board is to be appointed, you want someone with 20–25 years of experience.'
(Chairman on why women are not recruited to CEO positions;
in Holgersson, 1998)

'Track record is usually decisive for an appointment.'
(Chairman on the candidate's track record; in Holgersson, 1998)

The chairmen described how they often search for candidates in their own network and how they keep a list of people they find interesting. These lists would typically be composed of people they have found promising upon meeting them in various more or less professional settings, ranging from business meetings to conferences or dinners. The respondents preferred to search for candidates in circles close to them, such as within the company or the corporate group, or in other companies owned by the same owner or in the same industry. Several respondents mentioned that in certain corporate groups there are pools of up-and-coming younger managers being groomed for future top executive positions.

As mentioned above, the majority of chairmen claimed that they usually drafted a profile of the ideal candidate. Several chairmen mentioned, however, that in most cases the final candidate does not match the profile perfectly. In a study of top executives' mandates, Holmberg (1986) observed that the profiles were only roughly defined. Certain criteria developed while the candidates were being reviewed, and this opened the door to changes in the profile as well as further detailing. According to Holmberg, the profile is shaped in such a way because the people who represent possible choices are already regarded as possessing the necessary skills.

The respondents maintained that when drafting the profile, it was important to pinpoint the needs of the company, taking into account the company's current phase as identified by the board and the direction in which the company was headed. The task was then to identify the type of manager who would be able to manage the company, that is to say to specify the characteristics, knowledge and experience that were considered necessary to fulfil the needs of the company.

Most respondents claimed that there are certain types of manager who fit certain types of situation. Several respondents referred to different well-known businessmen, both in Swedish and international business, to illustrate these types. The perception that it is possible to match leadership need and manager profile is also found in management research (e.g. Chandler, 1962; Porter, 1980; Leontidades, 1982; Gupta, 1986). According to Guthrie and Datta (1997), the resource dependence perspective (e.g. Pfeffer and Salancik, 1978) and the strategic staffing perceptive (e.g. Guthrie and Olian, 1991) contend that a firm's critical contingencies or contextual conditions will result in the hiring of executives with particular types of experience. Several researchers, however, have argued that attaining a perfect match is probably very difficult (e.g. Szilagyi and Schweiger, 1984; Holmberg, 1986).

The chairmen seemed to focus on factors such as previous functions, track record and age. Similar observations have been made by researchers such as Guthrie and Datta (1997), who claim that there is a generally held notion that observable CEO experience characteristics, e.g. function, tenure and age, interact with organizational factors to signal the relative 'fit' of a person with the requirements of the position. The chairmen tended to classify management types; a manager was either good at marketing or good at finance, etc. Furthermore, these types were perceived as fairly static. A candidate seemed to be expected to address the same problems as in previous functions. These expectations have been confirmed by research suggesting that functional backgrounds do in fact influence the identification and processing of problems (see e.g. March and Simon, 1958; Gupta, 1984; Thomas et al., 1991).

The majority of the respondents reported that they preferred recruiting 'insiders', i.e. candidates who had worked within the company for a certain number of years. They felt that they were better able to assess a candidate who they had seen in action over a fairly long period of time. They could also be sure that the insider was well acquainted with the company and the industry. Knowledge and experience of the industry seemed to be of great importance to the majority of the chairmen, both because they thought different industries required different types of leaders due to the varied nature of the businesses, and because of the authority such qualities entail. However, recruiting an outsider was justified if the company needed a radical change in strategy, e.g. in case of a crisis. The theme of 'insider vs. outsider' can also be found in management research (for a review, see Kesner and Sebora, 1994). However, Guthrie and Datta (1997) point out that the results of such research are difficult to interpret since it often pays very little attention to other factors related to experience, and to the idiosyncrasies in the definitions of 'insider' and 'outsider' depending on company and industry.

Further, certain managerial functions such as personnel and information were not seen as relevant to a CEO position. This is confirmed by a study in which Swedish companies stated that the areas of responsibility that offer the most substantial opportunities for promotion to a CEO position, apart from functions specific to the industry, are technology/production, marketing and finance (Höök, 1995). Interestingly, personnel and information are the functions most typically held by women, and some respondents saw this as an indication that women were not interested in positions that lead to the top. According to research, however, this could also be attributed to the change and decline in the status of the position in general, and the subsequent feminization of the position (Legge, 1987). It has also been suggested that women are allowed to have these positions because they are not seen as stepping-stones to a CEO position (Cockburn, 1991).

As mentioned above, in addition to functional background and track record, age was also an element that the chairmen took into consideration. A certain age was often considered to lead to a certain strategy. A younger candidate was often perceived as more dynamic than an older candidate, who was perceived as less energetic but more experienced and well connected. Several chairmen mentioned that it is a custom in Sweden not to hire a CEO over the age of 50, if the person concerned has not already held a CEO position. A similar line of reasoning can be found in past research, (e.g. Vancil, 1987; Hambrick et al., 1993). However, other research has also questioned the link between age and strategy (e.g. Rosen and Jerdee, 1976; Guthrie and Datta, 1997).

Assessing the candidates

'You have to do your job well, but if you have a job which can't be measured, well then that person, regardless of whether it is a man or a woman, has a great disadvantage.'
(Chairman explains why women are not recruited to CEO positions;
in Holgersson, 1998)

'You can't be considered an unreliable person if you are to be part of this lot [...] one must be considered to be reliable [...] they have to be able to trust you, in business at least.'

(Chairman on honesty and reliability; in Holgersson, 1998)

'[...] if you start a family, women must *a priori* be off duty for a number of years and are simply not able to accumulate the experience and knowledge necessary to be able to apply for these big jobs.'

(Chairman explaining the small number of women CEOs; in Holgersson, 1998)

When assessing the type of manager a candidate represents, the chairmen looked at the candidate's track record, what they have achieved previously in their careers and how well they have achieved it. A spotless track record was extremely important to the respondents. The candidate had to have had a successful career without any mishaps or failures. Some chairmen said that one had to bear in mind that some failures were due to factors beyond the control of a candidate. Nevertheless, a candidate with an immaculate track record was to be preferred. Several respondents argued that it was important to be able to measure a candidate's performance, since it was difficult to evaluate his or her abilities. It was therefore important for candidates to have held positions with some sort of profit and loss responsibility. Staff positions were not seen as stepping-stones since it was difficult to measure the achievements in such positions in terms of profit. There was consequently a strong preference for line-management functions.

Jackall (1988) points out that the distance between a person and the actual tasks where crucial mistakes can be made increases, as the person rises higher in a management hierarchy. This makes it even more important not to be associated with failure. Success and failure thus appear as a question of interpretation rather than objectivity. Similarly, Barlow (1989) argues that, in practice, an individual may have little control over variables that can influence his performance. (Barlow (1989) refers to managers and individuals exclusively as 'he' or 'him'.) Both appraiser and appraised are part of organizational contexts subject to the caprice of technological and socio-economic forces and influenced by political considerations. The strength of an individual is likely to reflect his alignment with – and prosecution of – the interests of relevant power groups, at least as much as his innate ability.

A candidate's style, in both appearance and behaviour, is also of significance. The overall impression of the CEO is not to be conspicuous in any way. Clothes and hair should not be loud. Moreover, the candidate should be able to behave well and to socialize with people in different settings. Pleasing behaviour is important. Some chairmen mentioned that there were a number of unwritten rules of conduct in Swedish business that one had to conform to.

According to one respondent, however, many of the rules did not apply to women, since they had been created by, and were meant to apply to, men. The respondent expressed his dislike of women who did conform to these rules and adopted a behaviour he identified as male or masculine. A majority of the respondents perceived women as different from men, and maintained that the difference should be preserved. This can be seen as an example of the contradictory expectations, discussed by Cockburn (1991), that face women in management positions. Women are seen as lacking authority and are not therefore promoted to management positions. However, women who are selected are often chosen because they display masculine characteristics (which are in accordance with the dominant culture), and are then 'de-feminized' in the promotion process. Subsequent authoritarian behaviour on the part of these women managers is often condemned, however, because it is perceived as masculine.

A stable social situation was also a good sign. Several chairmen claimed that they preferred a candidate to have a stable and happy family, since it was felt that this was important in enabling the CEO to do a good job. Some respondents mentioned that the wife of the CEO could also play an important role, for example by entertaining clients and other people of importance to the company. Devoting time to the family, however, was not regarded as a merit. For example, most chairmen explained that one of the reasons why women were not recruited to top positions concerned their family situation. Women did not have as much work experience as men, mainly due to the bearing and rearing of children, which set them back a number of years relative to their male peers. Several respondents commented that it was difficult to be a CEO while also having responsibility for children and the home. The CEO position demands a high degree of commitment, requiring long hours and a family life allowing for this. At the same time, some chairmen thought women should have children, and that they should also take care of them, since they were best suited to that task. Paradoxically, it was considered a drawback for women to have children, and not to have them.

When asked about virtues in the world of managers, several chairmen mentioned the importance of honesty, in the sense of not having committed any crime. Trustworthiness was also a trait that the chairmen considered significant. Showing loyalty towards the company and the shareholders and deserving their trust was also important. This is not just because the CEO is supposed to act as a role model within the company, but it is also seen as vital because the relationship between the CEO and the board is based on trust.

Parallels can be drawn with what Jackall (1988) calls a person's public face. A person's appearance, their way of carrying themselves and of interacting with others, their general attitude – all are part of their public face. Managers must shape and enforce the social rules that employees are to follow, while at the same time personifying the company's public image. Consequently, they are compelled to rationalize their public faces in order to conform to the social criteria that exist within the company. Managers are generally expected to reflect a seriousness and sobriety befitting those responsible for the weighty affairs of industry, finance and commerce. Business organizations try to epitomize social normality, and managers are expected to be attentive to the norms prevailing in society. A person who cannot 'read' the most obvious social norms, won't be considered capable of reading more ambiguous cues and will therefore be regarded as unsuitable for any higher position. Consequently a manager will not be promoted on the basis of achievement alone; he or she must also have the desirable traits (Jackall, 1988).

A good reputation and a certain degree of visibility in society are also considered favourable attributes in a candidate. The candidate should be known in circles that are considered to be relevant, such as the Federation of Swedish Industries or the Swedish Employers' Confederation. A majority of the respondents also thought it important that candidates should have a wide contact network if they were to be recruited, and if they were to do to recruiting themselves in the future. Some respondents explained that because the opportunities to make formal applications are few, it is crucial for a person to be visible, in particular to the board and the chairman, in order to become a candidate. Some chairmen claimed that one reason why there were so few women in CEO positions lay in women's lack of contacts.

Similarly, the empirical findings reported in Barlow (1989) and Jackall (1988) suggest that in order to become a candidate it is essential to build alliances with key people in the higher echelons and with other managers. These alliances guarantee a stable political base and make the aspiring candidate attractive in the eyes of their superiors. Possession of a patron, who could give aspiring candidates opportunities to show off their talents, was important.

Co-option and the construction of top executives

'[...]the way [to the CEO position] is by building the recruitment from below over several years, by building a hierarchy.'
(Chairman on why women are not recruited to CEO positions; in Holgersson, 1998)

'I think it [top management] is quite common that it is a uniform group, they are of the same age, have the same experience, same sex, same background and are therefore likely to choose copies of themselves, and that is not so good.'
(Chairman on why women are not recruited to CEO positions; in Holgersson, 1998)

'There is only one type of career planning that works. Do your job as well as you can. You should never do your own career planning. But when you become a manager you can do it for others.'
(Chairman on applying for a CEO position; in Holgersson, 1998)

The process of recruiting a CEO is described above as the careful selection of a person and the matching of that person's skills and experience with a number of requirements based on an analysis of the company's situation. At the same time, however, CEOs are a fairly homogeneous group in terms of gender, background, education and experience (Affärsvärlden, 1994; Collin, 1994). A survey conducted by Collin (1994) shows that the average top executive in Sweden is a 50-year-old man from a middle or upper class background, who has studied business or engineering at one of the élite schools in Sweden such as the Stockholm School of Economics, the Royal Institute of Technology, Lund University or the Chalmers Institute of Technology. According to another survey conducted by the business magazine *Affärsvärlden* (1994), the top management teams of the 70 largest companies in Sweden are composed of men with an average age of 50.

How can we explain this paradox? A common – almost self-evident – explanation is that the CEO position requires this type of education and experience, and that at the present time only men with a certain background have the necessary competence even to be able to aspire to such a position. However, this explanation is insufficient from a social constructionist perspective. It does not give us answers to questions such as: Why does it seem natural and unproblematic that a CEO is a man of a certain age with a certain background and experience? Why is there a contradiction between being the CEO of a listed company and, for example, being a woman, having a foreign background, or holding a degree from a non-élite school?

In order to find an alternative and more fruitful explanation of the paradox, the concept of co-option is introduced here. Co-option has been used to elucidate the mechanisms that produce and reproduce élite groups in society (e.g. Bourdieu, 1984). Selznick (1949) has used the related concept of co-öptation to describe the mechanisms whereby the organization absorbs new elements as a means of legitimizing and securing its existence. In the following discussion, however, the concept of co-option will be used in the spirit of Bourdieu (1984) and Lindgren (1992).

To co-opt means 'to appoint to membership of a body by invitation' (*The Oxford American Desk Dictionary*, 1998), and consists in carrying out a selection that conforms to an existing order or format (Lindgren, 1992). Recruitment based on co-option designates not only formal criteria but also certain informal criteria i.e. secondary qualities, which have to be present for a presumptive member to be elected. Hence, the members of groups based on co-option have more common characteristics than those explicitly required (Bourdieu, 1984; Lindgren, 1992). These secondary characteristics can include age, gender, and social or ethnic background. Such requirements will more or less overtly affect co-opting decisions. The system is generally subtle, translating privilege into merit by treating everybody as if they were equal when, in fact, the competitors all begin with different handicaps based on cultural endowment (Jenkins, 1992).

The formal requirement at the beginning of a career is to have some sort of basic competence, such as a certain diploma or some particular experience. Companies usually rely on other institutions such as schools to establish these competence hurdles (Jackall, 1988). During the early years of their careers, promising young managers undergo a number of probationary tests. Who is regarded as promising depends not only on performance, however, but also on the person's ability to meet the social criteria that signal potential success. Furthermore, not only do the promotional strategies and structures produce particular types of managers, they also provide those who have already displayed characteristics that indicate potential success in one environment with opportunities of demonstrating success in others (Barlow, 1989). As a result, the system becomes self-fulfilling.

Women's careers in management can help to illustrate the mechanisms involved. Although women may have the necessary education for a management career, they are not usually considered as potential leaders. As this material and other studies of perceptions of women and management in a Swedish context have shown, male managers often see family and women's alleged lack of self-confidence as explanations of women's subordinate positions in organizations (Asplund, 1988; Franzén, 1995). It is nevertheless clear that the terms of an executive career are shaped according to a traditional male pattern of life. According to this pattern, the man is primarily loyal to the organization, and work and career are both structured as if he were married to a homemaker (Andersson, 1997). Moreover, women are perceived as lacking the right experience, the right contacts or the right style, since the constructions of leadership and masculinity are closely linked. This in turn creates a contradiction in the very idea of being a woman and a manager (Wahl, 1998). Since women do not signal potential success, they are consequently not given the opportunity to demonstrate their ability to perform. If they are promoted to higher positions, it is only to those that are considered suitable and that in most cases do not lead to the very top. Naturally the recruitment system does not only exclude women: it also excludes men who do not match the prevailing construction of leadership.

Studying perceptions of management and the CEO-ship of the actors involved is not enough, however, to show us how CEO candidates are produced and reproduced or how the construction of the CEO is shaped. Recruitment procedures are also important. Drawing on empirical findings regarding the recruitment processes in five industrial sectors in the UK, which did not specifically focus on the CEO levels, Collinson, Knights and Collinson (1990) identified the informality of the channels, the criteria and the procedures of recruitment as one of the key factors in promoting the reproduction of job segregation between the sexes. As the present material has shown, the CEO recruitment process is highly informal. The discussions between the recruiters are informal, the recruitment settings are informal and the way in which the criteria and evaluation activities are designed also seem to be rather informal. This informality in the recruitment process paves the way for the mechanisms of co-option.

Firstly, the group of people involved in the recruitment is very small, and the informality of the process also gives them control over it. Further, the practices are seldom questioned, since they are designed by those who have the prerogative of interpretation in the organization, i.e. whose prerogative it is to define reality (Smircich and Morgan, 1982; Barlow, 1989; Wahl, 1995). Accordingly, these people's construction of leadership is regarded as objective. Moreover, to a large extent the respondents share the same perception of the considerations that are important in designing a profile, and of the characteristics that a CEO should possess, i.e. they share more or less the same construction of leadership. This construction of leadership is also dominant in the literature dealing with top managers, both in academic research and in more popular publications, which indicates that the chairmen interviewed are active in the production and reproduction of a more general discourse on leadership and management. This in turn secures the respondent's prerogative of interpretation even more firmly, and the procedures and criteria are reproduced.

Secondly, the informality of the process also amplifies the importance of the relations between the people involved in the process. Relations between managers are homosocial, that is to say, managers tend to surround themselves with people resembling themselves (Kanter, 1977). This means that male managers will prefer to work together with other men who resemble themselves. Thus, female candidates do not have the same access to information and have less opportunity to do people favours and to influence important decisions, which makes it more difficult for them to establish themselves as credible actors in the organization. The system does not only exclude women, however; it also excludes men who do not conform to the dominant construction of leadership, since homosociality is created not only through gender, but also through factors such as race, education and class (Avotie, 1998).

In studies of male groups Lindgren (1996) has shown the importance of analysing the social processes in order to understand the homosocial reproduction of the group. Lindgren observed among other things that in order to become a member of a group, i.e. to be co-opted, a person must contribute to that group in some way, thus engaging in various rituals of confirmation and acknowledgement. It is important to respect the rules of the hierarchy and to show commitment and loyalty to the group. The chairmen's expectations that candidates should work long hours, should give priority to work rather than family, and should not promote themselves too much by signalling their ambitions too clearly but should let their superiors handle their career planning – all these can be interpreted as rituals or codes that confirm and signal loyalty.

An important ritual observed by Lindgren (1996) involves engaging in a particular jargon or small talk. Her observations of homosocial groups suggest that small talk is an important mechanism for shaping and preserving a group. The jargon observed among men consisted of their telling the same type of heroic stories that the members of the group could relate to, stories which often involved glorifying men and putting women down. Lindgren noted that the bond was broken if a story did not fit the pattern. It was therefore difficult for women, or for men with another type of experience, to engage in this ritual. Consequently they were not co-opted. The disparagement and exclusion of women was more a result of men's struggle for power and recognition than an explicit wish to dominate women.

Moreover, in telling their heroic tales the men were creating a phantom, an ideal man that each one of them wanted to – or felt obliged to – compare himself with. This phantom assumed different characteristics regarding such things as class or lifestyle, depending on the composition of the relevant group. All phantoms, however, were related to the hegemonic masculinity of present-day society, that is to say to the construction of masculinity that is associated with men who hold positions of power and that serves as a benchmark for other masculinities (Connell, 1995). It is not unlikely that the phantom created among board members and the construction of leadership, and more specifically, CEO competence, are all closely linked and thus call for further study.

The need for commitment, trust and loyalty from which conformity and homogeneity both spring, is often explained – both in this interview material and in other research (e.g. Kanter, 1977; Jackall, 1988; Sjöstrand, 1997) – by the uncertainty that informs the world of managers. It has been suggested that this uncertainty is a result of the managers' inability to grapple with the complexity of the world, and the lack of full information. Moreover, the relationship between the CEO and the board is seen as being imbued with uncertainty, since the board has little opportunity to control or influence the CEO. Trust between the CEO and the board is therefore regarded as vital (Brodin et al., 1995).

The uncertainty felt by managers may also stem from the uncertainty of the manager's position and power. Bonding rituals can be interpreted as a way of ensuring that everyone respects the rules of the game and preserves a stable and predictable hierarchy, thus guaranteeing each one's own power position. However, the relations between co-option and the need for trust calls for further exploration. Does the system of co-option promote the building of trust, and if so, how? More specifically, what cues inspire trust in different kinds of organization? As noted above, the interaction and rituals such as small talk among the actors in the process, also need to be studied. Attention should be paid to the features that characterize the interaction between actors and to the arenas in which this interaction takes place.

As we can see, powerful forces foster homogeneity and conformity among managers. This perpetuates a certain construction of leadership, shaping our perception of what attributes a manager should have. It is therefore not surprising that the CEO candidate group appears homogeneous. At the same time, the recruitment of every CEO is described as the careful matching of an individual to a company's needs. A possible explanation of this apparent paradox is that a more specific construction is shaped in the course of the actual selection process. The idea of matching a certain type of manager to a certain strategic need on the part of the company, the perception of the requirements of the industry and of the CEO job – all these factors come into play in the construction of a specific profile. The frame for the construction in any specific situation is set by the characteristics that the candidates already possess and by the recruiters' perceptions of the company's management needs and of leadership in general.

The present study suggests that the recruitment of a CEO and even of managers at lower levels follows the principle of co-option. More descriptions of CEO recruitment are necessary, however, so that the phenomenon of co-option and its use can be further explored. Does the system of co-option vary in different cases and, if so, what factors influence these variations? Are there differences within the company, the group and the industry? The accounts of the chairmen have unveiled some of the tacit rules and requirements. These need to be analysed more closely in case studies, to enhance our understanding of the meaning of the different criteria. The focus should include not only such things as the culture within an organization, a group or an industry, but also the relations within the board and between the board and the candidates or other actors. Structures such as social background, education, class and gender should also be taken into account.

The aim here has been exploratory and, despite numerous limitations, the findings nonetheless stress the need for more in-depth studies of the recruitment process, focusing not only on the perceptions of the actors involved but also on the social processes. Lastly, it is worth noting that further knowledge about recruitment as an arena for the construction of leadership is interesting not only from a theoretical point of view but also from a more practical and political perspective, since it also creates opportunities for change among managers and for altering the dominant leadership perceptions.

Notes

1 However, the number of board members varies considerably. In 1998, the average number of board members was six (Sundin and Sundqvist, 1998). The turnover of board members is fairly low and a common explanation of this is that there are few people with the necessary competence (Hultbom, 1997).
2 When executive-search consultants were referred to in the interviews, they were always referred to as 'he', which indicates that the consultant is generally a man.
3 It is also interesting to note that in Swedish companies today, if a board does have female members, they are usually union representatives (Höök, 1995).

References

Affärsvärlden (1994). *Ledningen kartlagd. Håkan, 53, styr svenskt näringsliv*. No. 15, pp. 28–31.

Andersson, G. (1997). Karriär, kön, familj, in SOU 1997:135, Nyberg, A. and Sundin, E. (eds.). *Ledare, makt och kön*, pp. 68–108, Fritzes, Stockholm.

Asplund, G. (1988). *Women Managers. Changing Organizational Cultures*. Wiley, Chichester and New York.

Avotie, L. (1998). *Chefer ur ett genuskulturellt perspektiv*. Department of Business Studies, Uppsala University, Uppsala.

Barlow, G. (1989). Deficiencies and the Perpetuation of Power: Latent Functions in Management Appraisal. *Journal of Management Studies*, vol. 26, no. 5, pp. 499–517.

Bourdieu, P. (1984). *Distinction: A Social Critique of the Judgment of Taste*. Harvard University Press, Cambridge, MA.

Broady, D., and Palme, M. (1993). *Pierre Bourdieu. Kultursociologiska texter*. Brutus Östlings Bokförlag Symposion, Stockholm.

Brodin, B., Lundkvist, L., Sjöstrand, S-E., and Östman, L. (1995). *Styrelsearbete i koncerner*. EFI/IFL, Stockholm.

Cannella, A. A. Jr, and Lubatkin, M. (1993). Succession as a Sociopolitical Process: Internal Impediments to Outsider Selection. *Academy of Management Journal*, vol. 36, no. 4, pp. 736–93.

Chandler, A. D. Jr. (1962). *Strategy and Structure*. Doubleday & Co., New York.

Cockburn, C. (1991). *In the Way of Women*. Macmillan, London.

Collin, S-O. (1994). *Företagsledares rekrytering och karriär*. Research Paper, University of Lund, Lund.

Collinson, D. L., Knights, D., and Collinson, M. (1990). *Managing to Discriminate*. Routledge, London.

Connell, R. W. (1995). *Masculinities*. Polity Press, Cambridge, UK.

Dalton, D. R., and Kesner, I. F. (1983). Inside/Outside Succession and Organizational Size: The Pragmatics of Executive Replacement. *Academy of Management Journal*, vol. 26, no. 4, pp. 736–42.

Dalton, M. (1959). *Men Who Manage. Fusions of Feeling and Theory in Administration*. Wiley, New York.

Franzén, C. (1995). How the perceptions of male and female executives differ, in Wahl, A. (ed.). *Men's Perceptions of Women and Management*, pp. 55–77, Fritzes, Stockholm.

Furtado, E. P. H., and Karan, V. (1990). Causes, Consequences, and Shareholder Wealth Effects of Management Turnover. *Financial Management*, vol. 19, no. 2, pp. 60–75.

Gupta, A. K. (1984). Contingency Linkages Between Strategy and General Managers Characteristics: A Conceptual Examination. *Academy of Management Review*, vol. 9, no. 3, pp. 399–412.

Gupta, A. K. (1986). Matching Managers to Strategies: Point and Counterpoint. *Human Resource Management*, vol. 25, no. 2, pp. 215–34.

Guthrie, J. P., and Datta, D. K. (1997). Contextual Influences on Executive Selection: Firm Characteristics and CEO Experience. *Journal of Management Studies*, vol. 43, no. 4, pp. 537–60.

Guthrie, J. P., and Olian, J. D. (1991). Does Context Affect Staffing? The Case of General Managers. *Personnel Psychology*, vol. 44, pp. 262–92.

Hambrick, D. C. (ed.) (1988). *The Executive Effect: Concepts and Methods for Studying Top Managers*. JAI Press, Greenwich, CT.

Hambrick, D. C., Geletkanycz M. A., and Fredrickson, J. W. (1993). Top Executive Commitment to the Status Quo: Some Tests of its Determinants. *Strategic Management Journal*, vol. 14, no. 6, pp. 401–18.

Hannan, M. T., and Freeman, J. (1984). Structural Inertia and Organizational Change. *Administrative Science Quarterly*, vol. 49, pp. 149–64.

Holgersson, C. (1998). *Styrelseordförandes utsagor om vd-rekrytering*. EFI and Näringslivets LedarskapsAkademi, Stockholm.

Holgersson, C., and Höök P. (1997). Chefsrekrytering och ledarutveckling som arenor för konstruktion av ledarskap och kön. In SOU 1997:135, Nyberg, A., and Sundin, E. (eds.), *Ledare, makt och kön*, pp. 17–45, Fritzes, Stockholm.

Hollenbeck, G. P. (1994). *CEO Selection. A Street-smart Review*. Center for Creative Leadership, Greensboro, NC.

Holmberg, I. (1986). *Företagsledares mandat*. Studentlitteratur, Lund.

Höök, P. (1995). Women at the top – a survey of Swedish industry, in Wahl, A. (ed.). *Men's perceptions of women and management*, pp. 33–53, Fritzes, Stockholm.

Hultbom, C. (1997). Makt och ledarskap i börsbolagen. In SOU 1997:135, Nyberg, A., and Sundin, E. (eds.), *Ledare, makt och kön*, pp. 46–67, Fritzes, Stockholm.

Jackall, R. (1988). *Moral Mazes – The World of Corporate Managers*. Oxford University Press, Oxford.

Jenkins, R. (1992). *Pierre Bourdieu*. Routledge, London.

Kanter, R. M. (1977). *Men and Women of the Corporation*. Basic Books, New York.

Kesner, I. F., and Sebora, T. C. (1994). Executive Succession: Past, Present and Future. *Journal of Management*, vol. 20, pp. 527–72.

Kirkpatrick, S. A., and Locke, E. A. (1991). Leadership: Do Traits Matter? *Academy of Management Executive*, vol. 5, no. 2, pp. 48–60.

Legge, K. (1987). Women in personnel management: Uphill climb or downhill slide? In Spencer, A. and Podmore, D. (eds.). *In a Man's World: Esssays on Women in Male Dominated Professions*. Tavistock, London.

Leontiades, M. (1982). Choosing the Right Manager to Fit the Strategy. *Journal of Business Strategy*, vol. 3, no. 2, pp. 58–69.

Lindgren, G. (1992). *Doktorer, systrar och flickor*. Carlsons, Stockholm.

Lindgren, G. (1996). Broderskapets Logik. *Kvinnovetenskaplig Tidskrift*, vol. 17, no. 1, pp. 4–14.

March, J., and Simon, H. (1958). *Organizations*. Wiley, New York.

Nilsson, B. (1993). Ledarurvalets svåra konst. In *Vandringsleder. Till Calle Mannerfelt*, pp. 269–81, Norstedts, Stockholm.

Pfeffer, J., and Salancik, G. R. (1978). *The External Control of Organizations: A Resource Dependence Perspective*. Harper & Row, New York.

Porter, M. E. (1980). *Competitive Strategy*. Free Press, New York.

Rock, R. H. (1977). *The Chief Executive Officer*. Heath, Lexington, MA.

Rosen, B., and Jerdee, T. (1976). The Influence of Age Stereotypes on Managerial Decisions. *Journal of Applied Psychology*, vol. 61, pp. 428–32.

Selznick, P. (1949). *TVA and the Grass Roots. A Study in the Sociology of Formal Organization.* University of California Press, Berkeley and Los Angeles.

Sessa, V. I., and Campbell, R. J. (1997). *Selection at the Top. An Annotated Bibliography.* Center for Creative Leadership, Greensboro, NC.

Sjöstrand, S-E. (1997). *The Two Faces of Management. The Janus Factor.* Thomson, London.

Smircich, L. and Morgan, G. (1982). Leadership: The Management of Meaning. *Journal of Applied Behavioral Science*, vol. 18, no. 3, pp. 257–73.

Sorcher, M. (1985). *Predicting executive success: What it takes to make it to senior management.* Wiley, New York.

Stewart, R. (1976). *Contrasts in Management.* McGraw-Hill, Maidenhead.

Stogdill, R. M. (1974). *Handbook of Leadership: A Survey of the Literature.* Free Press, New York.

Sundin, A., and Sundqvist, S.-I. (1998). *Styrelser och revisorer i Sveriges börsbolag 1998–99.* Dagens Nyheter, Stockholm.

Szilagyi, A. D., and Schweiger, D. M. (1984). Matching Managers to Strategies: A Review and Suggested Framework. *Academy of Management Review*, vol. 9, no. 4, pp. 626–37.

Tengblad, S. (1997). *Chefsförsörjning. Mötet mellan mostridiga ideal.* BAS, Göteborg.

Thomas, A., Litschert, R. J., and Ramaswamy, K. (1991). The Performance Impact of Strategy-manager Co-alignment: An Empirical Examination. *Strategic Management Journal*, vol. 12, pp. 509–22.

Vancil, R. F. (1987). *Passing the Baton: Managing the Process of CEO Succession.* Harvard Business School Press, Boston, MA.

Wahl, A. (1995). Concluding Comments, in Wahl, A. (ed.). *Men's Perceptions of Women and Management*, pp. 99–108, Fritzes, Stockholm.

Wahl, A. (1998). Deconstructing Women and Leadership. *International Review of Women and Leadership*, vol. 4, no. 2, pp. 46–60.

CHAPTER SEVEN

From lack to surplus

Anna Wahl

Introduction

Leadership has been described in management and leadership studies as being gender-neutral, a claim that has been criticized from a feminist perspective (Hearn and Parkin, 1983; Mills, 1988; Wahl, 1992). Rather, the concept of management is gendered, both in theory and in organizational practice. There is a clear connection between constructions of management and constructions of masculinities (Wahl, 1992; Collinson and Hearn, 1996).

The gender structures in organizations are constructed in relation to the gender order in society, where men's dominance and women's subordination is central. The fact that men dominate in the leading positions of organizations is regarded as normal, even natural. Male top managers attribute their dominance in these positions in Swedish industry not to sex/gender, but to their own competence. They describe their leadership style as 'what it takes', not because they are men, but because they are competent individuals (Wahl, 1995), with the result that the connection between masculinities and leadership is 'hidden' in these 'neutral' constructions.

Starting from the results of an empirical case study, this chapter focuses on the relationship between gender and leadership in relation to power. Leadership discourse in general will not be directly addressed, although prevailing perceptions of what leadership is, as a whole, are embedded in the empirical results. Thus, even the general 'neutral' leadership discourse is gendered. Behind 'normal' leadership constructions masculinity lurks, while femininity is 'invisible' and subordinate. Nor will the general discourse of gender differences be explored here. Managers have their perceptions of what leadership is, of what male and female are, in other words of gender, but these will not be specifically focused.

What will be analysed, however, is the *relationship* between the two concepts, and the analysis will proceed in relation to the dominant notion of women's inadequacy in leading positions (Wahl, 1996, 1998).

Women as 'lacking'

Research on women in management often exposes an idea, prevalent in organizations, that women are inadequate and lacking in leadership qualities. In fact, this lack on the part of women is commonly quoted as the reason why there are so few women in leading positions, and is sometimes even reproduced in research as the 'true' explanation (for a critical review of the field, see Marshall, 1984; Wahl, 1995, 1998).

Women are described as lacking in will, competence, self-confidence and other desirable leadership qualities (Wahl, 1995; Holgersson and Höök, 1997). In the absence of a power – i.e. a feminist – perspective on gender relations, the notion that women lack these qualities is often related to the dichotomy of sameness and difference (for feminist theorizing on sameness and difference in general, see Bacchi, 1990). Constructions of leadership as far as women are concerned, emanate from the dominant perception and consist of ideas about what women are like – and what they ought to be like – as managers. This is often expressed in terms of the perception of women as an unexploited or different kind of resource in organizations (Wahl, 1996, 1998):

- Women are inadequate but can compensate for this, thus representing an unexploited resource in the organization ('sameness').

- Women are inadequate but have other qualities and experiences compared with men, and can thus represent a different resource in the organization (difference).

In both cases, women managers are being compared to the norm, i.e. to male managers, and they emerge as deviant and, consequently, as lacking. Theories of gender order in society and in organizations enable us to move beyond sameness/difference, and make other interpretations possible.

Two kinds of power context are related to gendered leadership in this chapter:

- the position of women in the gender order of society – gender order as an institution;

- the power position of women in the organization – gender order in the specific organization.

The organizational context is the gender distribution of top management in a specific company (i.e. the case study). This means that on the organizational level gender order is represented by the number of women and men, and by their positions. In referring to gender order in society this chapter draws on current theoretical understandings.

From lack to surplus

This chapter aims to show that the gender order in organizations (i.e. the numbers and positions of women) affects the constructions of gendered leadership. However, there is a constant (inter)action with gender order in society, which is itself characterized by male domination and female subordination. The question that will be raised and analysed here is simply this: what happens to gendered constructions of leadership when the minority situation typical of women managers is replaced by a majority situation?

It will be argued that the gender distribution of a management group has an impact on gender relations and on constructions of leadership. As a result women change, men change, and in turn even the constructions of leadership change. By confronting the dominant notion of women leaders as lacking, the same or different, the study contributes to our understanding of constructions of leadership in relation to power.

- Surplus replaces lack in the construction of leadership relating to women managers.

- Sameness replaces difference, relative to the leadership style of male managers.

- New constructions replace sameness, relative to the dominant leadership discourse based on dominant masculinity and subordinate femininity.

Management and gender

In organizational theory it is still often necessary to justify taking up the gender issue at all, to argue that it is important. The problem of women as an invisible or marginalized category in organizations, in theory and in practice, still has to be dealt with. In the popular discourse of 'women in management', essentialist definitions of gender are often used in practice to explain differences between men and women managers. This discourse is also present in everyday talk in organizations. Gender studies thus help to demonstrate the significance of gender in management, and to problematize the meanings of gender.

If gender is regarded as socially constructed then the meaning of femininity and masculinity is seen as neither absolute nor true. Rather, the concepts vary in their content, depending on the particular point in history or the geographical location. Gender can be studied on two levels: as a thought construct and as a social relation. Gender can thus be understood by examining the meaning of 'male' and 'female' and of the consequences assigned to these meanings in concrete social practices (Flax, 1990, p. 46). Perceptions of gender in empirical research may appear contradictory or ambiguous. The concepts of 'women' and 'leadership' are used in different ways in different situations, which makes it difficult to understand them unless a power perspective is adopted in the analysis.

Gender order in society and in organizations

We have already noted that in order to move beyond the concept of sameness/difference, theories of gender order in society and in organizations are crucial. The power relations between women and men greatly affect the ways in which femininity and masculinity are constructed (Connell, 1987; Flax, 1990; Eduards, 1992). The focus on gender relations in feminist theorizing is closely associated with assumptions of a gender order in society based on power asymmetries. On a structural level, this gender order is based on male domination and female subordination. The concept of gender order is related to the concept of gender, as socially and culturally constructed.

The gender order of society is reproduced in the gender order of organizations, and vice versa. Every organization has a gender order that reflects the power relation between men and women. In organizations, meanings of gender are expressed through perceptions, structures and processes (Kanter, 1977; Baude, 1992; Acker, 1992; Wahl et al., 1998). Gender structures in organizations can differ when it comes to gender distribution, with respect to both professions and positions, and to power and influence (Wahl, 1992). An organization's gender order is related in several ways to that of society, and cannot thus be separated from the more general context of gender relations. One aspect of this connection is the paradox of gender, that organizations are basically gendered and at the same time that is being denied (Acker, 1992; Wahl et al., 1998). In this way, gender-blind descriptions of society are reproduced in organizations.

Women managers as 'lacking', 'the same' and 'different' in minority positions

Numerous investigations regarding the leadership style of women were carried out in the 1970s and 1980s (Hennig and Jardim, 1976; Harragan, 1977; Loden, 1986). Did women behave differently from men when they became managers? A majority of these studies showed that this was not the case (Bartol, 1978; Marshall, 1984; Eagly and Johnson, 1990). In general, women displayed behaviour and leadership styles similar to those of men.

In many of these early studies, the aim was to show that women were just as competent as men. However, there was rarely any reference to theories about gender and gender order, and explanations focused instead on women as individuals. Women were described as acting in almost the same way as men in management positions, albeit lacking certain qualities of leadership. Girls were not raised in the same way as boys, women were not properly socialized into the management culture, etc. (Hennig and Jardim, 1976; Harragan, 1977). This analysis, inadequate from a gender perspective, was succeeded by a popular market for success manuals for women who aspired to management positions. The message was that women, as individuals, could compensate for the leadership qualities they lacked.

In the discussion on sameness/difference, women managers are compared with the norm: they are either like or unlike men. In the business world, female and male leadership are both discussed as related to inherent qualities rather than being based on experience. Women who aspire to managerial posts are often criticized for their lack of authority. The conclusion is then that the small number of female managers can be attributed to the fact that women lack the authority needed to be managers. At the same time, women managers are criticized for being too masculine, also a quality that makes them less suitable for management work (Cockburn, 1991). In both cases, the judgement of sameness/difference is made from a male perspective, due to the gender order obtaining in organizations. Women are thus caught in men's interpretations, and the fact remains that, regardless of their similarity or dissimilarity relative to men, women in influential posts are still in a minority.

A number of studies from Kanter onwards, have shown that the significant minority representation of women in managerial posts does affect structure (Kanter, 1977; Morrison, White and Van Velsor, 1987; Wahl, 1992). To understand the constructed gender differences that prevail in the field of leadership, it is necessary to analyse women's conditions in organizations. The minority position of women managers is central to our understanding of women as leaders. One of the consequences experienced by the members of a minority group is that since they are the ones who are different, they must adapt to the norm, which in management means to a typically male managerial behaviour. Many researchers claim that it is impossible to say whether women in managerial posts are the same as, or different from, men. Women are quite simply too few to develop their 'own' leadership (Marshall, 1984; Bayes, 1987; Cockburn, 1991).

Leadership and masculinity

Understanding the gendered nature of leadership also helps our understanding of leadership as socially constructed. Mainstream research on leadership, however, is typically gender-blind, and male managers are studied as managers, leaders, decision-makers, individuals, people, human beings, etc., but not as men in the sense of belonging to a certain gender category (Connell, 1995). In recent years this approach has been criticized and identified as a problem in feminist and gender theories. Critical studies on men and masculinities have also indicated a dialectic relationship between constructions of masculinities and constructions of leadership (Collinson and Hearn, 1996). Masculinities and femininities are often constructed as each other's opposites. Since they belong to the 'wrong' sex, women are confronted with problems at the management level. This is sometimes visible indirectly in the dilemma that women face. There is a set of appropriate male behaviours for men in clearly identifiable leadership situations, such as giving a talk or presenting a topic at a meeting. This behaviour is so self-evident, however, that it only becomes visible when a woman imitates it, since it then looks wrong (Sheppard, 1989).

Critical studies on men have offered other explanations for the dominance of men at the executive level. Theories about men's homosocial behaviour (Lipman-Blumen, 1976) and men's homosocial desire (Roper, 1996) describe the importance of men confirming other men in organizations. The male dominance among managers can thus be understood as a question of men choosing men, rather than of men rejecting – or at least actively rejecting – women (Lindgren, 1996).

Women adapt to the norm in minority positions

In order to gain credibility as competent and businesslike individuals, and to show their willingness to melt into the organization, female managers often deny the importance of gender. The gender-neutral strategy is adopted in order to blend in with the majority, and to establish a distance relative to other women. It becomes a way of showing loyalty toward the majority, the men (Kanter, 1977; Lindgren, 1985; Sheppard, 1989; Wahl, 1992). If the gender order becomes too apparent, women in minority positions often change their approach, adopting a positive strategy in which the advantages of being a woman are stressed (Wahl, 1992). This positive strategy is also an expression of women's adaptation to the norm, and to the subordinate position of women in the gender order. Sometimes women in minority positions react by moving on to a more typical woman's position, or by leaving the organization altogether (Lindgren, 1985).

Women in a majority in top management

The connections between the gender structures in organizations and the constructions of leadership made by men and women managers have been analysed in a research project. What significance do men and women attribute to gender in their constructions of management? The project included two case studies involving a total of 32 interviews with managers on three different levels.

The data referred to below represents a limited portion of the interview material obtained in the study, namely the data concerning the top management group of one of the companies. This included tape-recorded interviews with five women and three men, interviewed separately for 1.5 to 2 hours. The interviews were held in the offices of the interviewees, and were semi-structured around questions concerning the manager's own leadership, and possible ideal leadership, in their organization. The interviews thus focused on leadership not gender. At the end of every interview, however, the manager was asked to reflect on whether the fact that the management group included a majority of women had any influence on leadership in the organization. The interviews have been analysed thematically.

The interviews presented in this chapter were conducted in a private-sector service company. The organization as a whole is dominated by women, with approximately 97 per cent of its employees being women. What is unusual here is not the high percentage of female employees, however, but the fact that women are also in the majority at the management level. The company's managing director is a woman, and the management group consists of five women and three men.

In some ways it is difficult, as usual, to compare these female and male managers, because they do actually *do* different things as managers. The women are responsible for operations, while two of the three men hold staff positions. It is typical that positions tend to be gendered, but it is the division of positions that is unusual in this organization. The fact that women dominate in number and are actually in charge of operations turns out to have significance for the way in which they describe their leadership.

Those parts of the empirical data have been used that serve the aims of the present article, namely, to illustrate the relationship between gender order, the relative power-position of women, and style of leadership. The questions raised here deal with the way in which the respondents described their own style of leadership, and whether they felt that the predominance of women in management positions affected the leadership style prevailing in the organization.

Personal leadership style: women and men are the same

The women managers in the organization offer similar descriptions of their leadership. They describe themselves as enterprising, quick, clear and to the point. They all say they manage by delegating responsibility. They have no desire to manage things in detail. They prefer to communicate ideas, which can be taken up by others. Several of the women say they expect a great deal from their subordinates, they expect independence and results. This type of leadership is based on their own role as good listeners and communicators, and their ability to get others to develop.

Of the male managers, only one has anyone working under him. He describes himself as a pleasant person, 'soft-hearted'. Like his female colleagues, he emphasizes the importance of being able to listen and of being humble. The other two men function as discussion partners for the operative managers, and in this way have considerable influence over operations. They describe the importance of gaining the confidence of the managers, so that their own views will be listened to. Their colleagues' confidence in them is the basis of their influence, and they also emphasize the importance of having a sensitive ear.

The descriptions of leadership style in this organization are largely concordant. The description of one manager is confirmed to a large degree by the others. When they want to describe the dominant style of leadership in the organization – that is, among managers at all levels – the image of the enterprising, quick and attentive manager, who can also delegate, keeps recurring.

Men and women managers thus provide very similar descriptions of personal leadership styles. They also say that the same leader-style is the one that dominates among the managers in the organization, men or women.

In speaking of the ideal manager, both men and women say that personality is more important than educational background. The ideal manager is able to communicate, she or he has an entrepreneurial spirit, and so on. The management group is currently working on a manager profile, in which they are trying to capture this ideal.

Several of the managers interviewed mention the importance of changing the time-input that is expected of management work. When it comes to managers' working hours it is necessary to set limits and this has been a problem. There used to be a culture of 'we don't work full-time, we work all the time'. Two of the managers, both women, hope to see more respect for a manager's private time, children, and so on, in the new company policy. Both these managers have small children.

The women managers all point out the importance of the managing director: as a role model, as a woman, and as a support in the day-to-day work. Two of the male managers say that they have good working relations with her on a daily basis, while one of the men looks instead to the managing director of the Group (a man) as the role model for the managers. *'He sets the standard'*, he says. This interviewee has himself learned to be a good leader from the example of this man. *'He has this softer way of leading.'*

It is clear that the leadership style adopted by the women and the men is the same. In this organization gender differences in relation to leadership are not stressed in practice or as an ideal. So, rather than 'difference', it is 'sameness' that is dominant in constructions of leadership here. But opinions differ when it comes to the managers' role models. All the women refer to the importance of the female managing director as a role model, while this emerges less clearly from the interviews with the men. One of them specifically mentions the managing director of the Group, a man, as the role model for *all* top managers. This can be seen as an example of gender order from 'outside' the organization interacting with, and influencing, the constructions of leadership within it.

All the managers interviewed were also encouraged to reflect on whether the style of leadership in the organization as a whole was affected by the fact that women were in the majority. The answers to this question were not as unequivocal as the responses to the questions on personal leadership style and on leadership style within the organization. Firstly, there is a certain disparity between what the women and what the men say on this point, and secondly there is a greater tendency towards contradiction and ambiguity in the answers.

The men's views

Two of the three men interviewed were somewhat dubious as to whether or not the female majority has influenced the formation of the leadership style in the organization. One of them voiced the following reflections:

'I've not thought about it much. It's leadership qualities that count in our organization irrespective of whether the leader is a man or a woman. Though it's difficult to say, of course, since there is no male divisional manager here.'

The same interviewee, asked whether as a manager he had experienced any personal consequences, answered:

'No, I can't say I have. In my previous job there were also a great many women in management posts, so I suppose in this case I'd have noticed the differences long ago [laughs], if there were any. I can't say I see any at present. Perhaps it's easier being a sounding board for ideas with women managers, since to some degree they find it easier to accept advice. This might be the case, though I'm only speculating here. Perhaps I would feel obliged [laughs], to a certain extent, to show a bit more authority towards male managers. But I believe that basically you have to show that you are competent, since the advice is in fact worth taking. In which case it doesn't really matter.'

Thus, he considers discussions between himself and the women managers to be influenced to some extent by the existence of the female majority, citing as the cause of this women's possibly lower degree of prestige. However, he points out that a good ear is necessary in this particular service business. This, he deduces, is why bigger differences between female-dominated and male-dominated organizations may be more noticeable in other types of business, such as manufacturing or computers. He has never worked in an organization with a majority of male managers himself, however.

Another male manager also considers the part played by type of business in relation to gender. However, in his view the fact that his company was expansive and creative meant more in the context of leadership style:

'It's difficult to say whether it's [the leadership style] due to the women or to the company. We are very informal, spontaneous and keen on ad hoc solutions here, in a different way from the other companies [in the group]. Not to mention company X [a male-dominated company where he was previously employed], which of course was completely different! [laughs] I don't know whether this has anything to do with women and men, or whether it's to do with the company experiencing growth and innovation. Perhaps it would be the same if men were in the majority.'

He goes on to comment that women are perhaps less formal in their way of working. But he thinks it is mainly a question of different personalities, and these can occur among men or women. He thinks that growth in itself leads to better opportunities for women. *'In a stable system, it's easier to get stuck in old patterns when recruiting managers'*, he says.

Both of these male managers are very positive about the company managers, that is to say, the women managers, and they emphasize the sound knowledge of the business that these managers possess. They consider them to have a good leadership style, but do not describe it as particularly feminine.

The third man in the management group was also very positive with regard to the women managers, and describes the management group as dominated by women. He feels there is a 'womanish atmosphere' in the management group, an atmosphere that he defines as 'pretty chatty'. He appreciates the softer style of leadership and compares it to other similar businesses he is acquainted with:

'It's nice not to have to concentrate exclusively on results. The only disadvantage is that things can become rather long-drawn-out. For me it feels good not to have a tough tone. Of course, I haven't been in a male-dominated management group, but I do meet people from companies Y and Z [similar business firms] and there's an awful lot of shouting and screaming going on! It's nice not to have all that aggressiveness.'

He says he thinks it's right to have a female domination in management in this kind of woman-dominated company. He prefers the leadership that they represent, and thinks it's a positive thing. However, he feels that the men in the organization adapt themselves to a more 'feminine' style of leadership:

'The disadvantage is that men tend to become more womanly, just like women in male-dominated organizations tend to become manly. So the men who have been around a long time have become a bit feminine [laughs]. As for me, I'm not especially macho, well a bit, I feel I have to be a bit more macho than usual, so that there's some testosterone in there as well [laughs]. But there's a good atmosphere in the group. There is room for manoeuvres, they quite like it, the men. But they get more womanly, softer, in a group like this.'

He relates this to the story of an earlier male manager who did not fit in, he had no 'feminine characteristics', he was too 'aggressive' and 'blunt', in comparison to the man who succeeded him, who was '... *a bit more feminine and perfectly suited*'. He reflects on this particular story during the interview, and asks himself what it is all about:

'When you're appealing to the people you're talking to, looking for agreement, then you send out various signals. There are masculine and feminine signals. This nodding and agreeing, what a difference there is depending on whether it's a more feminine type of man talking to the management group rather than a more masculine type. Though no one would grasp this on the stock exchange, for example.'

Before presenting the women's points of view, a few reflections on the men's views can be summarized. Two of the men put no stress on gender as being important in relation to leadership. One of these men has previous experience from male-dominated organizations. He sees differences in types of leadership, and finds the leadership in this organization to be more informal, spontaneous and creative. However, he attributes this not to gender but to other factors, namely growth and innovation, but he concludes that women are perhaps more informal. It is not self-evident, though, to connect growth and innovation with better conditions for women the way he does. The two men express neither 'lack' nor 'surplus' when it comes to women as managers, as they do not directly connect leadership with gender.

The third man does make a connection between leadership and femininity. He thinks the women are 'pretty chatty', and says that '*things can become rather long-drawn-out*', which can be described as a surplus rather than a lack of something. He explicitly states his appreciation and preference for this kind of leadership, as compared with that in other male-dominated organizations. *'This is the kind of leadership that works'*, he concludes, referring to communicative signals (nodding and agreeing) in the meetings. It is obviously something learned, and something that men can adapt to in contexts such as this.

He also quotes the example of a male manager whose leadership style was of a more traditionally masculine and dominant (towards women) kind, who did not fit in and had to be replaced, and he compares a typically male-dominated organization to his own current company where women are in a majority. He says that the kind of leadership that works – and indeed is required – in his own management group, would not even be understood elsewhere, that is to say in 'normal' male-dominated organizations. And he takes the opportunity to describe *men* as either more masculine or more feminine, instead of describing women – as is more usual – in that way.

The women's views

The women interviewed also described the company's leadership style as the same for men and women. But in their responses they were more inclined to use women as the norm for this style of leadership. The men in the organization fit in or have adapted themselves in order to do so. Several of the women managers emphasize that the language used by the management group has changed as a result – or simply that there are language differences between women and men in general. There is a common understanding that women talk more and that this has consequences, not least for the men.

One of the woman managers compares the men in her current company with men in her previous jobs:

> 'I think that there's a special type of man who gets into women-dominated jobs. If you choose health care, irrespective of whether it's practical work or management, then I think there's a really special type of man there. He has to be able to cope with working with a lot of women, because it is rather different. But I've not had that much experience with men in management positions around me, not since I came here. I can't make any concrete comparison. But I've had male bosses before, and I guess they have a lot of advantages just because they happen to be men. But I don't mean they're bad at what they do when I say that.'

The women managers seem to be more aware of gender order in society, and they also reflect more upon the influence of women in the organization than the men do. This particular woman talks about there being a 'special type of man' who can 'cope with working with a lot of women'. She declares that another kind of leadership is required to adjust to a context like this one. Her reflections on the advantages and competence of men are interesting, as they imply that because a man gets special treatment he is not necessarily incompetent. Competence and positive discrimination need not be mutually exclusive as is often thought when women are the subjects of it (Wahl, 1995).

The women managers are careful to point out that they prefer to see 'mixed' groups of women and men. The goal is not female dominance but 'balance'. When women dominate, there can be too much femininity. And although this is not a problem for women, women managers believe that it can be for men. One woman put it as follows:

'I think that it's easier to bring out the softer side of things. I've never worked in a male-dominated organization so I don't really know what the difference is. But I think it may be so. The most equal work situation I have been in is the current one, in the management group. I am very pleased with it. I would not like it if there were only women. God forbid! Sometimes I'm so fed up with women – including myself – you just can't believe it. You get stuck in a woman's way of thinking. You need someone to cut in and see things from a different angle.'

She favours letting these differences influence the work, continuing:

'I think women are more inclined to stray towards emotional considerations. While men have a more concrete way of thinking. Women are always ready to tackle several things at once. Men make a project out of every little thing they do ... with them there's a beginning and an end. Whereas we make a start now and a start then, a start here and a start there. Then suddenly we have more than enough on our plates, and are left wondering what to do about it. This is when it can be useful to have the input of a man's way of thinking: I think it's about time we gave all this a bit of structure!'

She describes clearly the precedence given to women's views, and the unquestioning acceptance of the space they perceive for themselves as women managers, because of their numbers. It's the women who assume the traditionally male role of being active, enterprising, and dynamic. While the men, in contrast to their traditional role, play the part of slowing things down and keeping everything in order.

One of the women tells how she recruited the management group for her own division. It consists of four women and one man. She was determined to find a man for one particular position, as she thought this would be good for the group. Many women applied for the post, but she waited until the right person – a man – turned up. She explains:

> 'We wanted a man to give the management team a bit of balance. But, strangely enough – and this must sound terrible – it was also because when you're out visiting clients and customers men still carry extra weight even nowadays. What a male manager says carries more clout than if a female manager says the same thing. This one's also a man of experience who's seen a lot and is used to meeting people. And really clever. It's reassuring when you're out and something happens, you listen to him. I think it was a good move. I usually tell him that he's worth his weight in gold.'

This description shows her awareness of society's gender order. The male managers add 'extra weight' and legitimacy to her management group. It is *not* his explicit competence or leadership qualities that make him 'worth his weight in gold', but his position as a man in the gender order. However, this does not exclude acknowledgement of the fact that he is 'really clever'. Comments such as these, that managers are explicitly described as being competent, are often made in connection with female managers, to meet the organization's expectations of the qualities lacking in women (Cockburn, 1991; Wahl, 1992, 1996; Höök, 1998).

She comments on the weekly meetings of her management group, with five women (including herself) and one man as described above, in the following way:

> 'He thinks it's great working in a woman-dominated group. He's used to working with just men in the past and says: "There's not much difference, really, because you act just like men!" He says the only time it fails is when we're finishing our weekly meetings. Then we go into this womanly thing, socializing and talking about everything in general. Then he disappears. The agenda's been dealt with.'

For women managers to 'act like men' is considered a compliment in the gender order. But the surplus of femininity, the small talk, 'when it fails', is only a problem to him (as this interviewee sees it), not connected with the way the work is being done ('the agenda has been dealt with').

One other woman in the management group reflects about the male managers' situation as being part of a minority:

> 'We've got some men here as well, of course. I don't know what they think. [laughs] Sometimes I think, heavens, this is a real pain for

them! I can see it. [laughs] [a long silence] Sometimes I think you can't take them quite seriously. I don't know if this is because they are men, or whether it's just certain people. There's a risk that you don't quite count them in. It [management] is harder for them. In other organizations that I've worked for in the past, the management thing was so firmly rooted: "this is what a manager is like". They do not fit in here.'

The construction of leadership in the organization is compared here to the 'normal', 'firmly rooted' construction in male-dominated organizations. She concludes, in line with the male manager above, '*they don't fit in here.*' She also assumes responsibility for the men in the group, and is uncertain whether or not they have problems with women being in the majority. The male managers themselves do not describe these problems in the interviews.

Another example showing the precedence given to the women's opinions is that of the *inverse comparison*, whereby women managers represent the norm with which the male managers are compared. One of the women managers puts this in the following way, as regards language differences:

'I think the management qualities required are the same for everybody. What can be different is the language used by men, since men have a different language compared with us women. We are a whole lot more emotive and in this way unlike men. Yet, on the other hand, I cannot see any difference in leadership. I've met many men in management positions, and I usually say that when you really get to know them, they are in fact just like us women. Women managers may of course giggle and have a great laugh about certain things, it's just that it takes a bit more time to really get to know men. Or men in management positions.'

This is an example in which women's way of talking and laughing is not described as a problem (a surplus) at all, but is seen only in positive terms. The women managers have fun, as a part of their leadership.

When the woman quoted above is asked whether this environment has been important to her leadership style, she is less sure:

'It may have been affected. There's plenty of latitude here. I've not thought much about it. We work exceptionally hard and get a lot of enjoyment out of it! We share both our joys and our sorrows with each other, and run a company at the same time. Otherwise, I don't know. This kind of company is very much dominated by women, so it would be a bit strange if there were a crowd of men here selling this kind of service.'

However, she agrees that male top managers in women-dominated organizations are common in many other places. *'Having a woman appointed as managing director has been very important'*, she claims. *'She has acted as a role model for women in the organization.'* This is mentioned by all the women. The scope and the enjoyment of being a manager are also remarked on in the interviews with the women. They describe management as fun. Though there are days like this:

> 'It's a great job. There is both responsibility and freedom. But some days I would just like to sit behind the till at the local Co-op. Not often, but now and again, when I'm fed up with people and don't want to make any decisions. And I try to concentrate on something else instead. Just one real vision: give me a greenhouse and let me talk to the flowers!'

Another woman offers another example of the ambiguity that surrounds the question of language. She claims that women's language can cause problems for men, but not for women. While at the same time she believes that men who are used to working with women adapt themselves to women's language. Upon further reflection over what it was like working in a male-dominated organization, she says she had to adapt herself to the language that was dominant:

> 'Without beating about the bush, I admit that I sometimes think: *blasted women's prattle*! That sometimes it's a bit much. That they go on and on. Men talk a different language compared to women, they are more explicit. Men can find women's language a problem. Though it is no problem for women, since they understand it when you write something like "it would be great if you could" instead of "please do this". But men ... but there again, I think the men in our organization are actually so used to working with women that – I think they've changed as men. They listen in a different way. X [a male] is occasionally asked what it's like to work with so many women. He doesn't consider it a problem. He usually just grins and says they're just like men, all of them.'

'Sometimes it's a bit much.' Here this interviewee's voice holds a note of suggestion that women's way of talking is somehow not quite right. But in practice, it still works well, *'... it's no problem for women'*. She describes men's language as generally clearer than women's, while at the same time describing herself and her female colleagues in the management group as

very clear in their leadership style. The social construction of leadership in relation to gender is well illustrated by her description of how the male managers have adapted to the situation, *'they've changed as men'*. As regards leadership, both masculinity and femininity are open to change. However, it is still a compliment, in interaction with the gender order as institution, for women managers to be said to act 'just like men'. This is also evident from her description of how language develops from the immediate context, and how those forming the minority or those of lower rank adapt themselves. She continues:

'I also feel that when we get together and meet now, our language is different from what I remember of the time I spent with company Q [large male-dominated manufacturing firm]. There, it was rather a case, as a woman, of adapting your own language. When you work just with men, I think you adapt yourself a little ... .'

The other women interviewed, like their colleague quoted above, make comparisons with the male-dominated organizations they have previously worked for, or else with 'normal' organizations. This is a way of referring to gender order in society in general, and marking a contrast. The following are examples of how this is put:

'I really enjoy working with this many women. It's a challenge. It's fun. You get confirmation that in fact women can also succeed. Not just men.'

'When I started in this management position, I had three male managers and two female managers below me. So there was a male majority in my area. So I went to a consultant, to try and find out what made the men tick. I don't think they work any differently as managers, they are the same. But they say things in a different way. I was the youngest in the group and had not been with the company for as long as the men who now had me as their manager. That was incredibly difficult for them to accept. In the sessions with the consultant, I got help with ways of gaining their confidence, men who had seen me – a younger woman – being promoted above them. I don't pull rank, they don't have to come to my office, I can go to theirs. Simple things like that made it work. On the other hand, I made it clear how our division was going to operate. It was my responsibility and they had to work within the same framework as everybody else.'

'It's much easier for women to work in this kind of organization. We are the ones who give it shape. Of course, there are problems but somehow there is a completely different kind of understanding. You build up your self-confidence. You get the time you need to develop in your role, to feel more and more sure of yourself . . . . We feel that we've done something that has turned out well. We are very flexible, if a change is necessary then it happens very quickly. I think it's much easier to change an organization run by women than one run by men. In our organization, we think a great deal more about the business rather than about our own careers. There again, I am so involved in it all that I find it difficult to remember how it was [laughs]. But as I remember it, in company W there was an element of hopelessness . . . for women. Women found it hard to develop as managers, they didn't get the time they needed to develop in peace and quiet. That must have been how it was, there was a lot of pressure.'

The woman in the second quoted passage is aware of the gender order and ready to accept its consequences. She seeks help from a consultant to enable her to handle a situation where men are confronted by a younger woman as their superior. She 'uses' the gender order by acting less formally, a strategy that has been described before by women in management positions (Wahl, 1992). And, combined with using her power position to show them that 'they had to work within the same framework as everybody else' (i.e. as women), it worked.

The third quotation is the one that most explicitly identifies the importance of power in giving the organization 'shape'. '*It is much easier for women to work in this kind of organization*', she explains. Above all, she underlines the importance of being given time to construct her leadership: '*. . . you get the time you need to develop*', in contrast to '*. . . they didn't get the time they needed*'. Here the relation between gender and leadership power is clearly being socially constructed over time, and by way of a position of power. The majority situation is crucial to this kind of process.

Surplus femininity

The gender distribution in the management group studied here could be said to be unusually well balanced, with a distribution of five and three – if the men had been five in number and the women three. The fact that the group instead is perceived as being composed of a majority of women reflects the gender order. The feeling of surplus femininity does not presuppose a dominance of women. A fairly well balanced group is enough – at least – to allow women to 'excuse' their majority numbers as if it were dominant. Only one of the three men remarks on this, while at the same he clearly acknowledges the advantages of the type of leadership adopted in the organization.

The enjoyment and self-confirmation that the women experienced from their leadership stands in sharp contrast to the adaptation, pressure and hopelessness that they describe in 'normal' organizations. The idea that women talk more shows the unquestioning acceptance of the amount of time and space they occupy at the management group meetings, and probably tells us something that is important as regards the way women are viewed in the organization. Women and men both describe the women managers as very capable and competent. The ideal manager is described as being a skilled entrepreneur and a listener, an ideal that goes for both men and women. Women and men actually describe the men's and women's leadership in the organization as being alike.

There is no talk of women lacking the right leadership qualities. On the contrary, there seems to be an understanding among the women managers that at times there is a surplus of femininity. Some men, according to the women interviewed, and one of the interviewed men, share this view. Women talk too much, talk too long, take more time to make decisions, and socialize more, are some of the comments. This could be understood as a surplus of femininity in power positions. However, it is not perceived as a problem, at least for the women. Instead, it is described as a problem mainly for men, but expressed mainly by women. One can also interpret the described 'surplus' in terms of new constructions of leadership, where informal talk takes place in both formal and informal arenas.

The surplus femininity is created in contrast to the 'normal' gender order in organizations and in society as a whole, and in contrast to claims concerning women's lack of the right leadership qualities. The description of women as lacking in leadership qualities is a feature of the minority position. Surplus femininity is a result of the majority position, which reinforces women's competence as legitimate. The gender order in society, expressed by way of language, mental perceptions, structures and processes, can have a slightly negative effect, however – a feeling that all this femininity is 'a bit much'.

The idea of an ideal balance, as advanced by the women managers, can be understood in relation to this as being a more desirable way of changing the gender order of organizations. This can be interpreted as women's way of:

- being aware of a gender order in society;

- visualizing the gender order; and

- accepting the consequences of this gender order.

Envisioning 'balance' as an ideal does not originate in any idea that men are more competent or better leaders, but is rather a way of acknowledging the importance of power, and of men's position in the gender order. Having men in the management group helps to legitimize its work. A mixed group offers better conditions for women managers than a male-dominated one would do – and without creating a surplus of femininity that could be perceived as problematic for men. Recruiting men 'as men' for management positions, does not exclude the idea of recruiting someone competent.

The majority position of women can sometimes imply the idea of women as the norm for leadership. This is illustrated by the use of inverse comparison in the interviews. Men's language is considered 'different' and men are described as being more, or less, masculine or feminine, and so on. It is also illustrated by the use of inverse adaptation: men adapt to the situation, or fit in to it. But there is no basis for the idea of different styles of leadership for women and men; as leaders, they are described as being the same.

The gender distribution in the management group does impact on gender relations. It is not possible to apply a dominant masculine leadership style that treats women as subordinate. It simply does not work. Gender relations based on equality, in numbers *and* position, must be built into new constructions of leadership. Women change and men change in their leadership, in other words there are changes in the constructions of leadership.

Concluding remarks

This chapter is based on rather a small number (eight) of interviews, but the interviews were extensive. The analysis must therefore be interpreted in light of this. The results cited touch on tendencies that can be seen in connection with many studies on women managers in minority positions. Finding a management group consisting of five women and three men in the private sector is not easy, so the empirical study is in itself a contribution to the research in the field. The study also contributes by drawing attention to the idea of women managers being seen as lacking, the same or different, in the dominant discourse of leadership.

The results are sometimes ambiguous. According to the managers interviewed, the female majority has made an impact on some aspects of leadership style, but has not affected others. On some issues, female and male managers agree. On others, they do not. Beyond the dichotomy of sameness/difference, however, lies the possibility of describing and understanding gendered leadership in a power perspective. Regarding 'women's leadership' as different is of little interest. But it is interesting to see that it makes a difference in the organization when women are in the majority at the management level.

Gender order in society affects the interpretation of femininity in leadership. New constructions may appear in an interaction with the gender order in society, by way of language, mental perceptions, structures and processes. The 'surplus femininity' is here interpreted as an effect of gender orders in conflict.

The gender relation of male domination and female subordination can be changed in organizations, and such change will have an effect on the way leadership is constructed. New constructions, built not necessarily on difference but on mutual respect, could serve to change the perception and reality of women's and men's leadership.

References

Acker, J. (1992). Gendering Organizational Theory, in Mills, A., and Tancred, P. (eds.), *Gendering Organizational Analysis*, pp. 248–60, Sage, London.

Bacchi, C. L. (1990). *Same Difference: Feminism Sexual Difference*. Allen & Unwin, Sydney.

Bartol, K. (1978). The Sex Structuring of Organizations: A Search for Possible Causes. *Academy of Management Review*, vol. 3, no. 2, pp. 805–15.

Baude, A. (1992). *Kvinnans plats på jobbet*. SNS, Stockholm.

Bayes, J. (1987). *Do Female Managers in Public Bureaucracies Manage with a Different Voice?* Paper presented at the Third International Congress on Women, July 6–10. Trinity College, Dublin.

Cockburn, C. (1991). *In The Way of Women*. Macmillan, London.

Collinson, D., and Hearn, J. (eds.). (1996). *Men as Managers, Managers as Men*. Sage, London.

Connell, R. W. (1987). *Gender and Power: Society, the Person and Sexual Politics*. Polity Press, Cambridge.

Connell, R. W. (1995). *Masculinities*. Polity Press, Cambridge.

Eagly, A., and Johnson, B. (1990). Gender and Leadership Style: a Meta-analysis. *Psychological Bulletin*, vol. 108, no. 2, pp. 233–56.

Eduards, M. (1992). Den feministiska utmaningen – kvinnors kollektiva handlande, in Åström, G., and Hirdman, Y. (eds.), *Kontrakt i kris*, pp. 237–69, Carlssons, Stockholm.

Flax, J. (1990). Postmodernism and Gender Relations in Feminist Theory, in Nicholson, L. J. (ed.), *Feminism/Postmodernism*, pp. 39–62, Routledge, New York.

Harragan, B. L. (1977). *Games Mother Never Taught You*. Warner Books, New York.

Hearn, J. and Parkin, W. (1983). Gender and Organizations: A Selective Review and a Critique of a Neglected Area. *Organization Studies*, vol. 4, no. 3, pp. 219–42.

Hennig, M., and Jardim, A. (1976). *The Managerial Woman*. Pocket Books, New York.

Holgersson, C., and Höök, P. (1997). Chefsrekrytering och ledarutveckling, in Nyberg, A., and Sundin, E. (eds.), *Ledare, makt och kön*, (SOU 1997:135), pp. 17–45, Fritzes, Stockholm.

Höök, P. (1998). Kvinnligt ledarskap – en helt hysterisk historia, in Wahl, A. et al., *Ironi och sexualitet – om ledarskap och kön*, pp. 87–106, Carlssons, Stockholm.

Kanter, R. M. (1977). *Men and Women of the Corporation*. Basic Books, New York.

Lindgren, G. (1985). *Kamrater, kollegor och kvinnor*. Umeå universitet, Umeå.

Lindgren, G. (1996). Broderskapets logik. *Kvinnovetenskaplig tidskrift*, vol. 17, no. 1, pp. 4–14.

Lipman-Blumen, J. (1976). Toward a Homosocial Theory of Sex Roles: An Explanation of the Sex Segregation of Social Institutions. *Signs*, vol. 1, no. 3, pp. 15–31.

Loden, M. (1986). *Feminine Leadership or How to Succeed in Business Without Being One of the Boys*. Times Books, New York.

Marshall, J. (1984). *Women Managers. Travellers in a Male World*. Wiley, Chichester.

Mills, A. (1988). Organization, Gender and Culture. *Organization Studies*, vol. 9, no. 3, pp. 351–69.

Morrison, A., White R., and Van Velsor, E. (1987). *Breaking the Glass Ceiling*. Addison-Wesley, Reading.

Roper, M. (1996). Seduction and Succession: Circuits of Homosocial Desire in Management, in Collinson, D., and Hearn, J. (eds.), *Men as Managers, Managers as Men*, pp. 210–26, Sage, London.

Sheppard, D. (1989). Organizations, Power and Sexuality: the Image and Self-image of Women Managers, in Hearn, J. et al (eds.), *The Sexuality of Organization*, pp. 139–57, Sage, London.

SOU 1994:3. *Mäns föreställningar om kvinnor och chefsskap*. Fritzes, Stockholm.

Wahl, A. (1992). *Könsstrukturer i organisationer*. EFI, Stockholm.

Wahl, A. (1994). Sammanfattande kommentarer, in *Mäns föreställningar om kvinnor och chefskap*, (SOU 1994:3), pp. 125–39, Fritzes, Stockholm.

Wahl, A. (ed.) (1995). *Men's Perceptions of Women and Management*. Fritzes, Stockholm.

Wahl, A. (1996). Företagsledning som konstruktion av manlighet. *Kvinnovetenskaplig tidskrift*, vol. 17, no. 1, pp. 15–29.

Wahl, A. (1998). Deconstructing Women and Leadership. *International Review of Women and Leadership*, vol. 4, no. 2, pp. 46–60.

Wahl, A., Holgersson, C., and Höök, P. (1998). *Ironi och sexualitet – om ledarskap och kön*. Carlssons, Stockholm.

CHAPTER EIGHT

Management as uncontrollable sexuality

Pia Höök

Introduction

The title of this chapter signals two topics – managerial leadership and sexuality – each of which attracts a good deal of attention in our society. How the two are interrelated, however, is seldom taken up in traditional research on organization and management as a subject calling for attention in its own right. Instead they are typically seen as separate, as having (almost) nothing to do with one another. This chapter draws attention to this 'blind spot' in traditional organization and management studies, by discussing the way constructions of sexuality affect the constructions of managerial leadership.

There are two reasons for the invisibility of sexuality in traditional organization and leadership studies (Hearn and Parkin, 1987; Wahl, 1998). Firstly, traditional organization and leadership studies have been gender-blind, and just as gender has remained invisible and unproblematized, so too has sexuality. The second reason lies in the dichotomization of private and public that has characterized most major social and political theories and movements (ibid.).

Among these modern social and political movements, and in contrast to most of them, feminism is a prime example of an attempt to relate the personal and the political (Burell and Hearn, 1989, p. 13; Wendt Höjer and Åse, 1996, p. 10). And in doing so feminism has problematized sexuality (e.g. Jackson and Scott, 1996). Zita (1990) labels the different perspectives adopted in feminist research on sexuality as the explanatory perspective, the topographical perspective and the normative perspective. In the explanatory perspective, the origin of sexuality is problematized by asking how sexuality is constructed socially, and what are its cultural and biological limits. The topographical perspective problematizes the localization of sexuality, by asking where sexuality is to be found. Finally, the normative perspective problematizes the political consequences of sexuality, by asking how sexuality reproduces the subordination of women.

This chapter has both a topographical and a normative purpose. From a topographical standpoint, it will show the presence of sexuality in arenas where it has traditionally been unseen, i.e. in organizations in general and in the upper echelons of organizational hierarchies in particular. The normative purpose stems from problematizing the political consequences of sexuality in organizations.

Like the other texts in this anthology, this one falls within a social constructionist tradition. The point of departure is thus that what people perceive as the objective reality 'out there' is in fact socially constructed through their interactions with each other. Reality is not given once and for all, but is the result of negotiations, power interests and people's actions. Social constructions vary in time and space and are dependent on who has the prerogative of interpretation, i.e. the power to name them, define them and give them meaning, and the context in which this takes place (see Chapter 2 in this book).

This chapter is about three conceptually distinct but simultaneously interrelated constructions: managerial leadership (management), sexuality and gender. The interrelatedness becomes visible if we try to imagine one without the other. It is difficult, for instance, to imagine sexuality without gender, gender without sexuality and leadership without gender (e.g. Calàs and Smircich, 1992; Collinson and Hearn, 1996; Wahl et al., 1998; Weeks, 1986). The nature of the relationship between the three, however, is contested.

Method

The fact that sexuality is open to many different interpretations makes it difficult to study with the help of traditional research methods (Hearn and Parkin, 1987). The elusiveness of sexuality has meant that researchers have constantly had to contend with ambiguity, subtlety, collusion, rumour, gossip, joking, innuendo and allusion, as well as using these as research resources (ibid., p. 123).

The empirical material of this chapter consists of quotations from interviews with eleven CEOs, four executive research consultants (Franzén, 1994) and nine board chairmen (Holgersson, 1998a) – all of them men. The interviews with chairmen were held in connection with a study on CEO recruitment, while the interviews with CEOs and executive search consultants were part of a study of the low proportions of women at management level. None of the interviews were conducted with the specific aim of exploring conceptions of sexuality in organizations (i.e. the men were not asked explicit questions relating to sexuality). Nor, until now, has the interview material been interpreted in this way.[1]

This chapter contrasts some selected quotations from these studies with existing theories on organization, leadership and sexuality, in order to explore new ways of interpreting them. In doing so, it hopes to show that *how* the material is interpreted depends on the theoretical framework that is used to interpret it. Inspired by Martin (1990), where prominence is given to deconstructing as a method in revealing taboos and 'hidden' power structures, I argue that my (re)interpretation of these quotations is one of many that would be possible, and that it thus undermines any claim to 'objective truth'.

There are two reasons for using these specific studies. Firstly, they are studies with which I am familiar. The interviews with CEOs and executive search consultants (Franzén, 1994) were conducted as part of a research project in which I was involved (SOU 94:3). The study on board chairmen (Holgersson, 1998a) was conducted by my colleague, working in the same research programme. So although I did not personally conduct the interviews myself, they represent material with which I am familiar.

The second reason for choosing these studies is the fact that all the men interviewed held powerful positions. This implies that they have a prerogative of interpretation in their organizations. What they say may thus be seen as a reflection of the dominant discourses on sexuality, gender and management in these organizations. This does not mean, however, that these men are cut off from the rest of the society. Their conceptions are just as socially constructed as anybody else's. But because of their prerogative of interpretation, their constructions have a wider audience and a tendency to become the 'truth' in their organizations. More simply put, these men are interesting because what they say matters.

Sexuality in organizations

In discussing some social constructions of sexuality that appear to exist in organizations, this chapter begins by looking at how sexuality is constructed in terms of its location and expressions. It then discusses how men and women managers are socially constructed in terms of sexuality. Some of these constructions correspond to each other, while others contradict each other. In other words, the picture I paint of sexuality in organizations retains an element of ambiguity.

Sexuality as opposed to organizational rationality

As mentioned in the introduction to this chapter, all modern social and political movements, except feminism, have taken the division and dichotomization of private and public for granted (Burell and Hearn, 1989, p. 13). Feminist theories, on the other hand, have problematized the fact that the dichotomy of private/public is highly gendered: the private sphere is the sphere of women, the public sphere is the sphere of men (see Chapter 5 in this book). How the private/public dichotomy interacts with, produces, and is reproduced by other dichotomies such as production/reproduction, sense/sensibility, mind/body, rationality/ emotionality etc. has also been problematized (Glennon, 1983).

The fact that all divisions listed above are gendered is not a coincidence, but an expression of how crucial the logic of dichotomization is in the social construction of gender and gender order (Hirdman, 1988). Turning to sexuality, we find that, like emotions and reproduction, it is socially constructed as something 'private', i.e. it is believed to take place in the sphere of women.

Defined in the private sphere, sexuality is constructed in opposition to concepts that are crucial to traditional understandings of organizing and organizations: (paid) work, production, rationality, etc. Quotations from interviews with CEOs (Franzén, 1994) indicate the prevalence in Swedish business of the belief that sexuality does not – and should not – exist in the public sphere.

While commenting on the small numbers of women managers, one CEO described sexuality as something 'unknown' and something 'to be feared'. Sexuality appears to be associated with uncontrollable emotions, and as such is in opposition to organizational order (control, rationality and efficiency). According to this particular CEO, the low number of women in top management is a consequence of desexualizing organization by maintaining same-sex groups. A similar kind of reasoning is expressed by an executive search consultant who argues that '. . . *women are different – sexual tension will arise'*.

> 'Yes, it's easier that way [for men to choose men]. When men and women come together, emotions are aroused. It's basically a fear of the unknown, of emotional relations between the sexes.'
> (Male CEO on the low number of women in top management; Franzén, 1994, p. 65)

> 'Women are different – sexual tensions may arise.'
> (Male executive search consultant on why women are not recruited to top management positions; Franzén, 1994, p. 89)

Moreover, both these quotations seem to rest on the assumption that heterosexuality is the only kind of sexuality there is, and that sexuality arises when male managers are confronted with a female peer.

Women as sexual, with no sexuality of their own

As mentioned above, researchers have pointed out that the dichotomization of what is considered 'proper, natural maleness' and what is considered to be 'proper, natural femaleness' is critical to the social construction of gender. Masculinity and femininity are constructed in relation to each other and as each other's opposites (Rubin, 1975; Hirdman, 1988). Moreover, there is a hierarchical relation between constructions of femininity and masculinity: what men are believed to be like, what they do and what they represent, are all assigned higher value than what women are believed to be like, what they do and what they represent. In terms of the dichotomy of private and public, this implies that the private sphere is subordinate to the public sphere.

In simple terms, the social construction of masculinity could be said to consist of concepts like rationality, reason, intellect, action, productivity and competition. And as rational, intellectual, active, competitive and productive beings, men become, as Gutek (1989) puts it, the natural inhabitants of organizations, i.e. of the public sphere. Women, on the other hand, are seen as the opposite: emotional, passive, caring, reproductive, and as such are the natural inhabitants of the private sphere (Kanter, 1977; Pringle, 1988). The belief that women lack the proper competence, and that this explains why there are so few women in top positions, could be interpreted as an expression of this dichotomy.

> 'I have been looking for a woman to recruit to my board, since a lot of people have said that not having one makes us look bad, but I haven't found a woman with sufficient competence.'
> (Male CEO on the low number of women in top management;
> Franzén, 1994, p. 67)

Fearing that a woman will be unable to perform as well as a man and that she will not make it in a demanding environment, men hesitate to recruit a woman. A woman's lack of competence (however defined) might influence the performance of the group as a whole. The CEO quoted, who asks what a woman might be exposing herself and her male peers to, is probably referring to this assumed lack of competence.

> 'What is she going to expose herself to, and, even more, what is she
> going to expose us to?'
>> (Male CEO on the low number of women in top management;
>> Franzén[2])

As regards sexuality, I have argued that this is associated with the private
sphere, both in terms of its perceived location and those who 'bear' it (i.e.
women). Together with the social construction of femininity as something emotional, passive, caring and reproductive, comes the conception
of women as sexual. The man quoted above, who explained the shortage
of women executives by the fact that their presence could cause sexual
tension, was constructing women in this way. In line with what has been
said about the dichotomization of private/public and femininity/
masculinity, women are socially constructed as sexually attractive *instead*
of competent, or at the expense of their competence – at least according
to one chairman whose explanation of why women are not recruited for
CEO positions was that men find it difficult to see women's competence
(and consequently women as competent), because they see women as
sexually attractive.

> 'They [men] don't see women. How the hell could a man of that age
> see women unless they're a lot younger, and then he would look at
> her for other [reasons].'
>> (Male board chairman on why women are not recruited as CEOs;
>> Holgersson, 1998a, p. 34)

It can be argued that the above quotation reflects a view of women as
sexual objects. The construction of women as (sexual) objects is not
unique to this man, but reflects a widely held view of women in society as
a whole. The objectification of women can be understood as an
expression of a patriarchal gender order. MacKinnon (1979) argues from
a radical feminist point of view that a woman is a being who identifies
and is identified, as one whose sexuality exists for a someone else who is
socially male. Women's sexuality is the capacity to arouse desire in that
someone. Thus, women are socially constructed as sexual beings, but with
no sexuality of their own.

One could go on to argue that as sexual beings women are believed
to disturb the organizational order by introducing the element of
sexuality. And since their own sexuality is socially constructed as lacking,
or non-existent, it is not their own but men's sexuality that they bring
into the organization (Gutek, 1989).

But, let us also take a look at men, to see how they are socially
constructed in terms of sexuality.

Men as asexual with an uncontrollable sexuality

It was argued above that women are socially constructed as sexual, but without having a sexuality of their own. According to the dichotomization of gender, this would imply that men are asexual. This has also been shown to be the case. Hearn and Parkin (1987) and Gutek (1989) have pointed out how the conception of men as asexual – together with the conception of men as active and work-orientated – are important in the construction of men as organizational beings. In the words of Hearn and Parkin (1987), the male manager is more dedicated to his job than to his gender or his sexuality. However, if men do happen to be dedicated to their sexuality this is not a problem, since there is a correspondence between the construction of valued labour and hierarchy on the one hand, and men's sexuality on the other. Thus, men's sexuality is associated with things like control, activeness, physical power, freedom from constraint, intellectualism, and coolness (ibid., p. 92).

This chapter argues, however, that the image of the organizational male as asexual and men's sexuality as controllable (or in some cases even non-existent), is too narrow. Parallel with these notions of men in organizations is a view of men's sexuality as uncontrollable. This is not a concept unique to the world of business or management. Rather it is a widely held belief about men in general. According to Birke (1992), men are believed to be above biology – except in the case of sexuality. Women, on the other hand, are typically viewed as victims of their biology. A similar argument is put forward by Rich (1983), who refers to a study on adolescents' conceptions of sexuality by Barry (1979), showing that men's sexuality is perceived as uncontrollable: a force that not even men themselves are able to control completely.

Looking more specifically at men in organizations, Hollway (1984) found that men in organizations, in powerful or subordinate positions, invested in what Hollway has termed the male sex drive and female have/hold discourses. The notion of the male sex drive takes for granted that men's sexuality is biologically driven, natural and uncontrolled. According to Hollway, men are seen as sexually incontinent, while women are seen as objects of sexuality who arouse men's natural urges.

A study of officers in the Swedish army, an organization highly dominated by men, revealed the same conception of male sexuality. When asked how they liked having women peers, some male officers voiced concern: they apparently felt that in stressful situations they might either have to defend their colleague or find themselves raping her (Johnsson, 1992). The first of these reactions is based on the conception of women as insufficiently competent: they cannot be counted on to do their jobs. The second is based on the conception of their own – i.e. men's – sexuality as uncontrollable. Stressful situations imply reduced control, which paves the way for women to trigger – and become the target of – men's uncontrollable sexuality.

Turning back to private industry, we find that the idea of the uncontrollable nature of men's sexuality allows for another interpretation of the quotations above. For example, the CEO who wondered what a woman entering his all-male executive group would be 'exposing herself to' (see p. 184) may well have been referring to sexuality as well as competence. The social construction of male sexuality as something unpredictable, means that by their very appearance women are able to release this 'force' and thus to cause organizational disorder. And if the woman is not careful, she may become the target of this force herself. Perhaps this particular CEO fears that the presence of a woman would trigger the sexuality of the men in his executive group, and that she would become its target. I do not wish to suggest that male executives actually believe that they might rape their female counterparts, but simply that there is an obvious uncertainty about what would actually happen if a woman joined the group in terms of sexuality. How would they respond to her presence? How would they deal with her, and the sexual attraction they might feel?

Women as able to use sexuality

The second part of this CEO's statement concerns what the woman would be exposing the men to. This part of his statement, too, can be interpreted in terms of sexuality, since the CEO could well be asking what a woman would expose the men to in this sense. According to this interpretation, the woman is socially constructed as the sexual subject, while the men become sexual objects. This construction seems to build on the assumption that women have the ability to use sexuality.

Gutek (1989) points out that the stereotype of the woman who uses her sexuality to advance her career is quite common. In this context, women's sexuality becomes a (power) resource. According to Gutek, this is not a true reflection of real life, since few women use sexuality to achieve organizational goals. On the contrary, men appear to be the ones who use sexuality more often than women and in a variety of ways. What intrigues Gutek is that almost everyone who believes that women use their sexuality to get ahead, also lays the blame on women for offering sex rather than men for accepting it (ibid., p. 63).

I argue that the construction of women as able to use their sexuality corresponds to the construction of men's sexuality as uncontrollable. If men are really seen as asexual, how can a woman use her sexuality? How would she go about it? Thus the conception of women using their sexuality to rise in organizations, is based on the assumption that men's sexuality is, at least potentially, uncontrollable. Referring back to Gutek on how men are not blamed for accepting the sexuality offered by a woman, we could say that men are excused because nobody expects them to be able to say no. How could they be expected to control the uncontrollable? After all – men! They have 'natural urges'!

Consequently, the social construction of women as able to use sexuality gives rise to the social construction of men as vulnerable. Men become subject to women's wishes. This line of reasoning can be discerned in the following quotation, where one CEO for example seems to think that if a woman joined his all-male executive group, she would turn her (sexual) attention to one of the men. This, in turn, would make it difficult for those who do not receive her attention. The quotation exemplifies the way women are seen above all as sexual, and as having the ability to use sexuality.

> 'If a woman were to join the senior management group and turn to one of the men, it will be tough on the men she didn't choose.'
> (Male CEO on the low number of women in top management;
> Franzén, 1994, p. 65)

In attributing to the woman manager the ability to use sexuality (as a sexual subject), men seem to be afraid that she will give rise to new forms of gender confirmation, since being a woman she has the ability to confirm the masculinity of certain men. According to this line of argument, a woman in a powerful position has the prerogative of interpretation and, since this can be perceived as disruptive to the predominating power relations, she becomes a source of uncertainty among men.

> 'Many are afraid of women in higher positions, partly because of the competition, partly because women are different. My position as ruling the roost might be questioned, and this could divide the group.'
> (Male executive search consultant on the low number of women
> in top management; Franzén, 1994, p. 89)

> 'I dislike women who use their sex appeal. It really leaves a bad taste in your mouth.'
> (Male CEO on the low number of women in top management;
> Franzén, 1994, p. 65)

Controlling the uncontrollable – a heterosexist management culture

In the above discussion I have argued that sexuality is socially constructed as being opposed to organizational order, that is to say to rationality and efficiency. Further, men are socially constructed as asexual and possessing uncontrollable sexuality. And finally, women are socially constructed as sexual beings with no sexuality of their own (sexual objects) and as being able to use sexuality (sexual subjects).

This chapter goes on to discuss the manifestations of what I call a heterosexist management culture, seen as the *reproducer* of the diverse constructions of sexuality, gender and management discussed above. In other words, as representing the process of (re)construction. Further, while the constructions and (re)construction processes are mutually dependent on each other, I also argue not only that the heterosexist management culture reproduces the constructions of sexuality, management and gender, but that it is also a construction itself. As such, it is socially constructed as functional in its ambition to desexualize and organize sexuality in organizations.

Desexualizing through exclusion

One way of organizing sexuality is to see that management groups consist of men only, since this is believed to rule out the possibility of sexual relations between group members. This line of argument can be found in Burell (1984), where it is suggested that the segregation of men and women at work has been justified by some managers on the grounds that it would eliminate the possibility of 'hanky-panky' between employees. Some of the quotations above could be interpreted in the same way. For instance, the CEO who stated that it was easier for men to recruit other men as managers, since this prevented arousal of 'feared' and 'unknown' sexuality. One vital aspect of this culture is thus the exclusion of women, since they are the ones who are believed to bring sexuality into the organization.

In one sense, however, it is wrong to speak of all-male settings or groups consisting of men only. Men *do* work with women. There *are* women around, but these women are in subordinate positions, as secretaries for instance (Kanter, 1977). Although the manager–secretary relation as such can be seen as sexualized, this is not regarded as a problem according to the dominant discourse in organizations (Pringle,

1988), perhaps because men as managers and women as secretaries correspond to the gender order of our society as a whole. Thus, in speaking of exclusion, we have to remember that it is not women in general that are being excluded, but women as managers. Thus, to put it bluntly, as long as the woman remains in a subordinate position, the organizational order is not threatened by men's uncontrollable sexuality. That women suffer more sexual discrimination the higher they climb in the organizational hierarchy, the fewer women peers they have and the more they commit themselves to the pursuit of a management career (Wahl, 1992) – can all be seen as consequences of a heterosexist management culture.

But women are not the sole bearers of sexuality in organizations. They are accompanied in this by homosexual men (Connell, 1995). The fact that most male-dominated organizations are also highly homophobic,[3] could be understood as an expression of this heterosexist management culture (Butler, 1997; Segal, 1990). The calculated risk of sexuality at work is probably even more stigmatized in the case of homosexual men, since they are socially constructed as being *more* sexual than heterosexual men (Segal, 1990).

According to Burell and Hearn (1989), the existence of homophobia in all-male settings is ambiguous. Most organizations, they write, maintain highly complicated and embedded structures of heterosexuality and heterosexism. Most organizations are dominated by groups of men who may be socially defined as heterosexual, yet who are at the least homosocial and possibly even homoerotic in their relations with each other: there is a characteristic routine homosexuality among heterosexual men in organizational situations (ibid., p. 23).

A culture that is strongly homophobic – at least on the surface and according to what is said – renders it possible for heterosexual men to reproduce their power in an all-male, homosocial and potentially homoerotic setting. Homophobia is also a prerequisite for the exclusion of women, since the conception that women would disturb the order by bringing in sexuality is based on the assumption that all men are heterosexual. It is thus suggested that homophobia and sexism are co-dependent.

Desexualizing through the symbolism of marriage

Kanter (1977) suggests that management can be understood in terms of uncertainty, communication and total commitment. She sees the working conditions of managers as characterized by uncertainty that is reduced by communication and a total commitment to the work. In line with this, Cockburn (1991) argues that a management career is often synonymous with long working hours, mobility and continuity.[4] This, she says, could be seen as a cultural expression of management (ibid.). Spending as much time as possible at work is one way of demonstrating that no other commitments in life are as important as work. Or in other words, that the private sphere is subordinate relative to the public sphere. One board chairman (Holgersson, 1998a) puts it like this:

> 'He is supposed to give his work higher priority than his family [...] of course, he must take care of his family, but the family must be extremely tolerant.'
>
> (Male board chairman on what a CEO should be like; Holgersson, 1998a, p. 34).

Management is thus socially constructed as very time-consuming. Because of this, Kanter (1977) continues, a manager requires the emotional and practical work contributions of a wife. Thus management consists of the work contribution of two people, one of whom is paid and visible (the manager) while the other is unpaid and invisible (the wife). The working hours and career path mean that a (male) manager spends all his days (and late nights) with male colleagues. He is exposed to, is a part of, and reproduces homosociality and homoeroticism.

> 'Men are men, and they like to socialize with other men!'
> (Male board chairman on the low proportion of women managers in management; Holgersson, 1998a, p. 34)

In this context, marriage assumes a symbolic function. Having a wife indicates that the male manager, despite opting to spend most of his time with other men, is still attracted to women. His sexual drive is directed towards women and, furthermore, is 'under control' (as far as is possible) by his being married. Having a wife proves that he is 'normal', i.e. heterosexual.

In her interviews with company chairmen on the question of what a CEO should be like, the respondents emphasized the importance of a CEO having a wife (Holgersson, 1998a). One director declared that without a wife when he entertains, a man could be suspected of being either a homosexual or a womanizer, neither of which was desirable.

A further indication of the preference for married (read, heterosexual) men in Swedish industry, is that married men command higher salaries than unmarried men (Edin and Richardson, 1997). Could this marital bonus be a monetary reward to a man for showing that he is heterosexual and that he is trying to control the uncontrollable?

Desexualization through the symbolism of fatherhood

It has been discussed how the social construction of marriage interacts with the social constructions of sexuality, gender and management. This line of argument is continued here by problematizing the social construction of parenthood.[5] Like marriage, parenthood can be understood as a form of desexualizing – at least for men. And, like marriage, fatherhood can be seen as a guarantee of heterosexuality in all male, homosocial and potentially homoerotic surroundings (Lipman-Blumen, 1976; Butler, 1997; Roper, 1996; Sedgewick, 1985). In this way fatherhood is thought to desexualize business life in general and executive groups in particular. Thus, although (biological) fatherhood originates in a sexual act, it is perceived as a desexualizing factor in organizations.

As indicated above, however, the construction of parenthood varies, depending on gender. In the following quotations, we can see how motherhood is constructed as a biological process. To have children is something that concerns women only. Fatherhood, on the other hand, is socially constructed as a one-time event (insemination). In comparison with the mother, the father is not believed to be affected by any of the practical or emotional consequences of parenthood (Andersson, 1997; Bekkengen, 1999; Franzén et al., 1998).

> 'It all comes down to market forces; it's a race. You can't take part if you're off having a baby. You've got to be there at work.'
> (Male CEO on the low number of women in top management;
> Franzén, 1994, p. 61)

> 'You have to make your presence felt when you're between 25 and 32, and put all your energy into your work. And that's the time when women have children.'
> (Male CEO on the low number of women in top management;
> Franzén, 1994, p. 64)

> 'You can't forbid women to become pregnant.'
> (Male CEO on how to increase the number of women managers;
> Franzén, 1994, p. 63)

The implications of this are that a woman who has children and who also wants to pursue a professional career, is seen as doing so at the expense of her children.[6] A father, on the other hand, is seen as pursuing his career for the sake of the children, since it is believed that this will guarantee their material welfare.[7] The constructions of fatherhood and management are mutually reinforcing, while the constructions of motherhood and management undermine each other.

It can also be suggested that fatherhood has an important symbolic function for the manager, since it constructs him as a 'real man': a potent, executive he-man who can make women pregnant. The social construction of men's sexuality and that of fatherhood confirm the father's ability and competence as a manager. Parallels can be drawn here with the argument in Burell and Hearn (1989), namely that there is a correspondence between the social construction of men's sexuality and the social construction of valued labour and hierarchy.

Desexualizing through heterosexist activities

In addition, constructions of sexuality, gender and management are reproduced through different forms of heterosexist group activities, such as visits to sex clubs and/or the use of prostitutes. According to Holgersson (1998b), such activities can be seen as a way of testing male managers, both in terms of sexuality and in a wider context: Are you in or out? Do you accept the rules of the game? Can you take it? Are you a wimp or a 'real man'? It can also be seen as a way of testing a woman's loyalty to the group and a way of intimidating her by exposing her to an objectified and demeaning view of women as a category (Dworkin, 1981; Holgersson, 1998b).

A culture that views women as sex objects undermines a woman's credibility as men's equal as well as strengthening the male homosociality. Power differences between men and women increase, and men orientate themselves towards the dominant group, i.e. towards each other (Kanter, 1977; Lipman-Blumen, 1976). This is believed this to be the case not only in the relationship between men and their female peers, but also in the relationship between men and their wives.[8] Sexist group activities can be seen as a means of perpetuating that a man's loyalty to the management group is stronger than his loyalty to his wife. In other words, there is a subordination of the private sphere relative to the public one.

Sexist group activities can thus be interpreted as a form of male bonding. A group or culture that encourages people to do something more or less 'forbidden' strengthens the loyalty between the members of that group. Managers come to know little secrets about one another (visits to strip clubs, adultery, sexual harassment, etc.), which can be seen as cultural loyalty deposits (cf. Williamson, 1983). In such contexts, a subordinate woman, e.g. a stripper or prostitute,[9] enables men to socialize and develop a liking for each other without being suspected of homosexuality. The woman becomes both the symbolic guardian of heterosexuality and, at the same time, the mediator of homosociality and potential homoeroticism.

Closing remarks

In this chapter I have discussed how constructions of sexuality, gender and managerial leadership (management) interact with each other. The purpose of the chapter has been to show how sexuality can be found where people can be found – irrespective of their sex (woman or man), their sexuality (homo-, bi-, or heterosexuality) or the surrounding context (the private or the public sphere).

I have discussed the following constructions: sexuality as opposed to organizational order, men as asexual with an uncontrollable sexuality, women as sexual with no sexuality (sexual objects) or with an ability to use sexuality (sexual subjects). I have also discussed how these constructions are reproduced through a heterosexist management culture.

The fact that the constructions are contradictory is in itself intriguing. It contradicts perceptions of management, gender and sexuality as 'natural' or part of a 'natural order'. Instead, this implies that their meanings are dependent on where the prerogative of interpretation is located. *Whose* sexuality (women's or men's), and *which* sexuality (homosexuality or heterosexuality) is defined as problematic, is a matter of power. Since traditional management discourse is dominated by heterosexual men (both in terms of numbers and power), it has a tendency to preserve the privileges of these very men. Organizations are characterized by the norm of compulsory heterosexuality, as Pringle (1988) puts it. According to this norm, men's heterosexuality dominates women's heterosexuality, and all other forms of sexuality are suppressed.

One indication of heterosexual men's prerogative of interpretation in organizations, is the fact that women's sexual preferences are seldom visible or problematized. The possibility that women might not be (sexually) interested in men at all does not seem to exist. Homosexual women are, unlike homosexual men, invisible in the reasoning of these men. Another indication of men's prerogative of interpretation is their ability to define themselves as *powerless* – in relation both to their own sexuality and to women, who are assumed to have the ability to use sexuality – without changing the discourse. The 'blame' is still put on women and homosexual men for triggering heterosexual men's sexuality, not on heterosexual men for being unable to control their sexuality. And, therefore, women and homosexual men are excluded in the name of rationality, efficiency and holy profit!

Notes

1 However, in *International Review of Women and Leadership*, 'Deconstructing Women and Leadership', Wahl (1998) does partly interpret Franzén's interviews in terms of sexuality.
2 Unlike the other statements taken from Franzén (cf. 1994) this one has not been published before. She has approved of my publishing it here.
3 Homophobia means fear of homosexuality (Svenska Akademiens Ordlista, 1998) Homophobia is sometimes interpreted as an expression of men's wish to repress anything feminine within themselves (Hopkins, 1992).
4 The concept of continuity refers to 'the idea of an added career' (Cockburn, 1991, p. 99), which means a career with no breaks. Parental leave is consequently not possible.
5 (S)exuality is constructed, among other things, in relation to motherhood and fatherhood (Keller, 1987, p. 8).
6 Cf. Hays's (1996) discussion on the ideology of intensive mothering.
7 Ferree (1993), referring to Hunt and Hunt (1982), states that the link between masculinity and the provider role is significant for two-income families today.
8 Sharing the provider role can be threatening to men who have constructed their ideal of masculinity on this economic foundation.
9 Holgersson (1998b) calls these women the necessary periphery.

References

Andersson, G. (1997). Karriär, kön och familj, in Nyberg, A., and Sundin, E. (eds.), *Ledare, makt och kön* (SOU 1997:135), pp. 68–108, Fritzes, Stockholm.
Barry, K. (1979). *Female Sexual Slavery*. Prentice Hall, Englewood Cliffs, N.J.
Bekkengen, L. (1999). Män som pappor och kvinnor som föräldrar – den könsfördelade föräldraledigheten. *Kvinnovetenskaplig Tidskrift*, No. 1, pp. 33–48.
Birke, L. (1992). Transforming Biology, in Crowley, and Himmelweit (eds.), *Knowing Women: Feminism and Knowledge*, pp. 66–77, Open University, Cambridge/Oxford.
Burell, G. (1984). Sex and Organizational Analysis. *Organization Studies*, vol. 5, no. 2, pp. 97–118.
Burell, G., and Hearn, J. (1989). The Sexuality of Organizations, in Hearn, J., Sheppard, D., Tancred-Sheriff, P., and Burell, G. (eds.), *The Sexuality of Organizations*, pp. 1–28, Sage, London.
Butler, J. (1997). *Excitable Speech*. Routledge, New York.
Calàs, M., and Smircich, L. (1992). Voicing the Seduction to Silenced Leadership. *Organization Studies*, vol. 12, no. 4, pp. 567–602.
Cockburn, C. (1991). *In The Way of Women*. Macmillan, London.

Collinson, D., and Hearn, J. (1996). *Men as Managers, Managers as Men.* Sage, London.

Connell, R. W. (1995). *Masculinities.* University of California Press, Berkeley.

Dworkin, A. (1981). *Pornography: Men Possessing Women.* The Women's Press, London.

Edin, P-O., and Richardson, K. (1997). Lönepolitik, lönespridning och löneskillnader mellan män och kvinnor, in Persson, I., and Wadensjö, E. (eds.), *Kvinnor och mäns löner – varför så olika?* (SOU 1997:136), pp. 87–103, Fritzes, Stockholm.

Ferree, M. M. (1993). Beyond Separate Spheres: Feminism and Family Research, in Richardson, L., and Taylor, V. (eds.), *Feminist Frontiers III.* McGraw-Hill, pp. 237–57, New York.

Franzén, C. (1994). Mäns och kvinnors skilda föreställningar, in *Mäns föreställningar om kvinnor och chefskap* (SOU 1994:3), pp. 57–91, Fritzes, Stockholm.

Franzén, C., Linghag, S., and Zander, S. (1998). *Arbetsglädje i livet – om ledarskap på 2000-talet.* Näringslivets Ledarskapsakademi, Stockholm.

Glennon, L. (1983). Synthesism. A case of feminist methodology, in Morgan, G. (ed.), *Beyond Method*, pp. 260–71, Sage, London.

Gutek, B. (1989). Sexuality in the Workplace: Key Issues in Social Research and Organizational Practice, in Hearn, J., Sheppard, D., Tancred-Sheriff, P., and Burell, G. (eds.), *The Sexuality of Organizations*, pp. 56–70, Sage, London.

Hays, S. (1996). *The Cultural Contradiction of Motherhood.* Yale University Press, New Haven.

Hearn, J., and Parkin, W. (1987). *'Sex' at 'Work'.* Wheatsheaf Books, London.

Hirdman, Y. (1988). Genussystemet – reflexioner kring kvinnors sociala underordning. *Kvinnovetenskaplig tidskrift*, vol. 9, no. 3, pp. 49–63.

Holgersson, C. (1998a). *Styrelseordförandes utsagor om vd-rekrytering.* EFI, Stockholm.

Holgersson, C. (1998b). Den nödvändiga periferin, in Wahl, A., Holgersson, C., and Höök, P., *Ironi och Sexualitet – om ledarskap och kön*, pp. 49–65, Carlssons, Stockholm.

Hollway, W. (1984). Gender Difference and the Production of Subjectivity, in Henriques, C. et al. (eds.), *Changing the Subject.* Methuen, London.

Höök, P. (1994). Kvinnor på toppen – en undersökning av svenskt näringsliv, in *Mäns föreställningar om kvinnor och chefskap* (SOU 1994:3), pp. 37–56, Fritzes, Stockholm.

Hopkins, P. (1992). Gender Treachery: Homophobia, Masculinity, and Threatened Identities, in May, L. and Strikwerda, R. (eds.), *Rethinking Masculinity – Philosophical explorations in light of feminism*, pp. 111–34, Littlefield Adams Quality Paperbacks, New York.

Hunt, J., and Hunt. L. (1982). Male Resistance to Role Symmetry in Dual-earner Households, in Gerstel, N., and Engel Gross, H. (eds.), *Families and Work.* Temple University Press, Philadelphia.

Jackson, S., and Scott, S. (1996). *Feminism and Sexuality – a Reader.* Colombia University Press, New York.

Johnsson, C. (1992). *Manliga och kvinnliga yrkesofficerare. En jämförande studie.* Arbetsmiljöfonden (KOM-programmet) i samarbete med Försvarsstaben, Stockholm.

Kanter, R. M. (1977). *Men and Women of the Corporation*. Basic Books, New York.

Keller, E. F. (1987). The Gender/Science System: Or is Sex to Gender as Nature is to Science, *Hypatia*, vol. 2, no. 3, pp. 37–49.

Lipman-Blumen, J. (1976). Towards a Homosocial Theory of Sex Roles: an Explanation of the Sex Segregation of Social Institutions. *Signs*, vol. 1. no. 3.

MacKinnon, C. (1979). *Sexual Harassment of Working Women: A Case of Sex Discrimination*. Yale University Press, New Haven, Conn.

Martin, J. (1990). Deconstructing Organizational Taboos: The Suppression of Gender Conflict in Organizations. *Organization Science*, vol. 1, no. 4, pp. 339–59.

Pringle, R. (1988). *Secretaries Talk – Sexuality, Power and Work*. Verso, London.

Rich, A. (1983). Compulsory Heterosexuality and Lesbian Existence, in Snitow, A. et al. (eds.), *Powers of Desire, the Politics of Sexuality*, pp. 177–205, Monthly Review Press, New York.

Roper, M. (1996). Seduction and Succession; Circuits of Homosocial Desire in Management, in Collinson, D., and Hearn, J. (eds.), *Men as Managers, Managers as Men*, pp. 210–26, Sage, London.

Rubin, G. (1975). The Traffic in Women: Notes on the 'Political Economy' of Sex. In Rayna Reiter (ed.), *Toward an Anthropology of Women*, pp. 157–209, Monthly Review Press, New York.

Sedgewick, K. E. (1985). *Between Men: English Literature and Male Homosexual Desire*. Colombia University Press, New York.

Segal, L. (1990). Slow Motion: *Changing Masculinities, Changing Men*. Rutgers University Press, New Brunswick, N. J.

SOU (1994). *Mäns föreställningar om kvinnor och chefskap* (SOU 1994:3). Fritzes, Stockholm.

Wahl, A. (1992). *Könstrukturer i Organisationer*. EFI, Stockholm.

Wahl, A. (1998). Könsordning, ledarskap och sexualitet i organisationer, in Wahl, A., Holgersson, C., and Höök, P., *Ironi och sexualitet – om ledarskap och kön*, pp. 19–48, Carlssons, Stockholm.

Wahl, A., Holgersson, C., and Höök, P. (1998). *Ironi och sexualitet – om ledarskap och kön*. Carlssons Förlag, Stockholm.

Weeks, J. (1986). *Sexuality*. Tavistock, London.

Wendt Höjer, M., and Åse, C. (1996). *Politikens Paradoxer, en introduktion till feministisk politisk teori*. Academia Adacta, Stockholm.

Zita, J. (1990). Feministisk forskning om sexualitet – i dag och i framtiden. *Kvinnovetenskaplig Tidskrift*, no. 4, pp. 4–17.

CHAPTER NINE

Educational rhetoric or leadership practice?

Jörgen Sandberg

Introduction

In this chapter I will explore ways in which leadership is socially constructed at the *Institiutet för Företagsledning* (The Swedish Institute for Management, hereafter referred to by the initials of its Swedish name, IFL).[1] It is particularly important to understand these constructions because of IFL's leading role as a management institute in Sweden. More than 30 000 managers have participated in various IFL leadership programmes since the Institute was established in 1969. In view of its dominant role, it seems a reasonable assumption that the constructions of managerial leadership produced by IFL may act as *meta*-constructions of managerial leadership in many Swedish companies.

In investigating the ways in which leadership is socially constructed at IFL, a social phenomenological approach has been adopted closely related to that described in Chapter 2 above. Here this approach involves investigating the forms of leadership construction that the members of IFL express in their activities, and how these constructions are institutionalized and maintained. I begin by identifying the specific forms of managerial leadership that are constructed in the individual IFL leadership programmes, and then explores those constructions in a historical perspective. Finally, I discuss the extent to which the constructions produced by IFL have affected the way in which leadership is practised in Swedish companies and organizations.

In the first step, I use phenomenography to investigate the specific forms of managerial leadership that are socially constructed at IFL. Phenomenography is an interpretative approach aimed at capturing the variety of ways in which a particular group constructs a specific aspect of reality (Marton, 1981; Sandberg, 1994, 2000). To ensure that the variety of managerial leadership at IFL was captured, 13 programme directors were selected to be interviewed for the study.

The following criteria were used in the selection in order to maximize the diversity: programme type, work experience outside IFL, formal education and gender (although only two programme directors were women). The interviews with the selected programme directors lasted between two and three hours, and the following three principal questions were asked: What do you do in your leadership programme? What is the purpose of the programme? What kind of managerial leadership are you trying to develop in your programme? The aim of the first two questions was to get a detailed description of the kind of managerial leadership that each programme director produced in the relevant programme by identifying its specific content, structure, activities and purpose. The aim of the third question was to enable the programme directors to consider more explicitly what they understand by managerial leadership.

These principal questions were elaborated and substantiated by follow-up questions, such as: What do you mean by that? Can you explain that further? Can you give an example? These were asked to encourage the programme directors to elaborate and to demonstrate what their statements about leadership meant in practice. To increase the likelihood of capturing 'knowledge in action' rather than what Argyris and Schön (1978) called 'espoused theories', pragmatic validation (Kvale, 1989; Sandberg, 1994, 2000) was used in the interviews. Pragmatic validation involves testing the knowledge produced in action.

Pragmatic validation was obtained in the interviews by the specific design of the interviews and the particular questions asked; by asking a number of follow-up questions requiring the programme directors to elaborate, exemplify and specify more exactly what their statements about managerial leadership meant in practice; and by observing the reactions of the programme directors to particular interpretations of their statements. The interviews were tape-recorded and transcribed word for word. The aim of the subsequent analysis was to identify how the programme directors constructed managerial leadership, and how they made explicit the basic meaning of these constructions. (For a more detailed description of a phenomenographic analysis, see Sandberg (1994, 2000).)

Constructions of managerial leadership at IFL

IFL was founded as an independent, national, non-profit management institute. It offers a range of leadership programmes open to all kinds of organization and a range of partnership programmes aimed at particular organizations and tailored to their specific needs. In addition to its management programmes, IFL runs two large conference centres where most of their programmes are conducted. Apart from its more international orientation today, IFL's mission remains largely as originally established.

> 'IFL is devoted to working for the development of a society where the management of organizations and the leadership of people vouch for the development of competitive business, the quality of working life and positive collaboration across different sectors of society as well as across countries.'
>
> (p. 8, EQUIS)

Given this mission, what kind of managerial leadership does IFL promote? In my interpretation, three different constructions of managerial leadership are produced at IFL. Seven of the programme directors viewed managerial leadership in terms roughly coinciding with construction 1 below, while four seemed to come closer to construction 2 and two of them to construction 3.

1. Managerial leadership as business development by enabling organization members to grow and develop.

2. Managerial leadership as *long-term* business development by enabling organization members to grow and develop.

3. Managerial leadership as long-term business development by enabling organization members to grow and develop by encouraging *self-understanding* among managers.

Although differing from each other in qualitative terms, all the constructions contain three basic elements, namely businessmanship and personal leadership framed in a humanistic orientation towards managerial leadership. In a general way businessmanship means mastering a set of business techniques for analysing and understanding central aspects of the company such as market, production, finance and organization. Personal leadership refers to the ability to relate to the people working in the company. Framing these two elements in a humanistic orientation means respecting and having regard for people as part of managerial leadership. Depending on how managerial leadership is constructed, however, these elements assume different meanings, and thus produce three qualitatively different managerial leadership styles.

Managerial leadership as business development by enabling organization members to grow and develop

In this construction managerial leadership means, in general terms, the development of a specific company by enabling the employees of the company to grow and develop themselves. Looking more specifically at our three elements, we can say that primarily the humanistic orientation means showing respect for your fellow workers and treating them as unique individuals with the same right to think and act as yourself. Given this humanistic orientation, personal leadership means being able to manage the resources of your fellow workers in such a way as to enable them to develop themselves, freeing their creative ability and thus producing desirable results. Businessmanship is understood as the ability to master a set of specific techniques with a view to analysing a company's specific situation. Without having a clear understanding of your company yourself, you will not be able to inform your fellow workers about its direction and the goals they should be seeking to achieve. The following quotations from programme director A1's interview illustrate the basic meaning of this construction:

> 'I try to get the participants to feel and see that this is a very people-oriented leadership, a humanistic leadership. One based on the feeling, the insight about, well – I've had many leaders who have said "Do unto others as you would they should do unto you". This includes a number of things such as showing respect for others, acknowledging that other people are creative, that others want to work, and that your most important role as a leader is to prepare the ground for those who you work for, those who work for you, so they can release their creative ability and in that way achieve results. Not being the one who always steps forward and wants recognition for things. Daring to take the blame when something goes wrong, even if you know it's your fellow workers who are responsible [for what went wrong]. This is, in the deepest sense, a humanistic leadership.'

> 'The aim of the A-programme [...] is to get people, themselves, to learn what managerial leadership is all about, and it's not only (personal) leadership but also managerial leadership in its widest sense. I like to say that it's about learning to understand the different steering wheels to turn, the levers to open and close, the tools you have to work with and how to use them. You have to have a helicopter perspective in order to really understand and see the whole picture. The wholeness in the complex work of managerial leadership. It's not only a question of being skilful at leadership, not

only a question of being a number cruncher, that is, skilful at financial issues, but they (leaders) must also know about market strategies, all of this, and then you have to manage the resources all in all, together, make explicit where you are going and why you are going in that direction.'

Managerial leadership as long-term business development by enabling organization members to grow and develop

In this construction businessmanship, personal leadership and the humanistic orientation in which these are framed yield another meaning compared with the previous construction, since the focus of this construction is on *long-term* business development as the basis of managerial leadership. Here, the humanistic orientation and the specific type of personal leadership mean not only acknowledging the uniqueness of every individual working in a company, but also considering their development and growth in a long-term business perspective. The same applies to businessmanship, which is now seen not primarily as the ability to understand the company's situation as such, but more importantly, to understand its long-term development. The following quotations illustrate this construction:

> 'We have discussed this about broad perspectives, longer perspectives [...]. We may not believe in maximizing results in the next quarter, but we do believe that business development is a long-term process and that the people in the company are important, we can't just send them off to get on with it. It doesn't work. As a leader you have to work from a core of the whole, which makes it possible for you to work in the long-term with the people you're working with.'

> 'Thus, we need a leadership that is trustworthy, and part of the trust comes from this longer perspective and working according to it, that is, you have to show those you're leading that you're not only governed by the latest (financial) figures, but that you also have an idea about what you want to do with this company and the ambition to do it in the longer term [...]. This is perhaps one of the main things about being able to maintain people's enthusiasm. I think there's an enormous waste of efficiency in companies because people are under-motivated. Usually, they are under-motivated because they don't believe in their leaders, in the pictures they provide. It's hard to believe in these if they're changed from one month to the next. You have to have a core.'

Naturally, you may have to correct your course for some reason or other, but these corrections have to be based on a discussion about a long-term vision [...]. I also believe that leaders must adopt a wholeness perspective with people, that you not only think about your fellow workers as cogs in some kind of machine, but that you also see them as individuals.'

(Programme director B3)

Managerial leadership as long-term business development by enabling organization members to grow and develop by encouraging self-understanding among managers

The programme directors who advocate this construction, regard the leader's *self-understanding as the basis of managerial leadership*. Consequently personal leadership, businessmanship and the humanistic orientation are constructed differently, assigning a different meaning to managerial leadership compared with constructions 1 and 2. As self-understanding is the basis for their managerial leadership, these programme directors emphasize the importance of developing a deeper understanding of what it means to be a human being in organizations and in society at large. This emphasis on self-understanding gives rise to a humanistic orientation that is both broader than and different from that in constructions 1 and 2.

As well as showing respect for your fellow workers, understanding yourself and other people in society is also regarded as important. In this construction, personal leadership thus involves a focus on the leaders' development of themselves and, on this basis, also on enabling their fellow workers and other people in society to develop and grow. Businessmanship yields a similar meaning. As a leader you have to master a set of business techniques in order to understand the long-term development of a company. But more importantly, you have to understand yourself as a person, otherwise you will have difficulty in understanding how your businessmanship affects you, your fellow workers and society in general. The two following quotations illustrate the basic meaning of this construction of leadership:

'One thing is to master the business techniques, but you can put it like this: If you don't understand what filter you have when it comes to taking things in – if you don't know what filter you use – you don't understand why you see the world as you do. That means you won't be good at applying your strategic tools, because they have to be related to both these areas (i.e. other people in the organization, and the environment – local and global in general).'

(Programme director C1)

'I see leadership as consisting to a large extent of a number of paradoxes: you have to be forceful, but at the same time let other people come forward; you also have to be diplomatic, but at the same time be able to make quick decisions; and you should be able to create closeness, but also keep a distance. This is my point of departure I think, that, well, the better I understand myself as an individual, the better I am able to handle the paradoxes and find out what I'm like as a person. Am I closed or am I more open? And try to find out where on the scale I am in different situations. I think this is the most important. So leadership starts inside myself.'

(Programme director C2)

IFL's managerial leadership in a historical perspective

As the results show, three major constructions of managerial leadership are produced in IFL management programmes. But where do these constructions come from? Are they unique to IFL or are they part of certain larger and more general constructions of managerial leadership in society? Let us first consider IFL: it is difficult to see any strong links between the selection criteria in terms of different leadership programmes, work experience outside IFL, formal education and gender on the one hand, and the identified constructions of managerial leadership at IFL on the other. Nor are the identified constructions associated with particular leadership programmes; rather, they are represented across the programmes. Nor are they related to any particular work experience, formal education or gender. One way to find out more about the production of managerial leadership at IFL, and thus to understand it better, is to relate these constructions to the historical development of IFL as an institute.

One way of learning more about IFL is to look back to its possible sources of inspiration. One of these might take us back to the Second World War and the War Production Training Courses offered by the business schools at Harvard and Stanford (Björkegren, 1986). After the war, Harvard developed these courses into Advanced Management Programmes (Andrews, 1966). Another influential event was the 1947 world management organization (CIOS) congress in Sweden (Eliæson, 1997).[2] An important outcome of the congress was a new emphasis on the strong link between practice and the academic in management education. Inspired by the Harvard Business School and the ideas generated by the CIOS world congress, the Swedish Employers Confederation developed and provided the first Swedish management course in 1952. A few years later, the Federation of Swedish Industries also began to offer courses in management, closely followed by the Swedish Association of Economic Graduates.

These three organizations began to discuss the possibility of merging their management education programmes, primarily because to a large extent they were using the same teachers from the Stockholm School of Economics (SSE), and because of the latent threat from the Swedish government of the 1960s to close down the Swedish business schools. As a result, IFL was established in 1968 by four organizations: the Swedish Employers' Confederation, the Federation of Swedish Industries, the Swedish Association of Economic Graduates and the Stockholm School of Economics Association. The Swedish Association of Graduate Engineers joined IFL as a founder a year later than the others. It was intended that the management education provided by IFL should have an academic base, in the sense that it should be oriented toward questioning and critical thinking, while at the same time respecting and drawing upon the experience of its participants.

From 1969 up to the present the content of IFL's courses has remained much the same, namely to provide relevant knowledge, skills and attitudes concerning managerial leadership. However, according to its second CEO, Anders Aspling, the overall focus of the courses has experienced three periods of gradual change due to shifting demands on the part of the market. Between 1970 and 1985 the predominant need from that quarter was for general knowledge in such aspects of management as accountancy, finance, marketing and organization. The main reason for this demand was that the leaders of many organizations at that time had received far less basic education in management than is the case today. In order to tackle this problem, IFL provided courses that concentrated on basic academic knowledge about management. For instance, according to Björkegren (1986) IFL's biggest programme consisted of 95 pre cent basic academic knowledge about business techniques such as accountancy and finance.

Between 1985 and 93 IFL gradually redesigned the content of its courses. Participants were now supposed to learn not only how to apply the various business techniques such as performing a strategic analysis or closing the books, but they were also supposed to consider such things in a wider leadership perspective, that is, how companies should actually be managed effectively. These changes were due primarily to the better education now provided for managers. They had already acquired the essentials of management knowledge from their formal education. Consequently, they now wanted more of the applied knowledge and leadership skills that would enable them to make better use of the business techniques in their overall work of managing a company. To meet this demand IFL gradually began to increase the 'leadership component' in their programmes. For example, a completely new programme entitled *Leadership and Personal Development* was introduced. Further, the *Integrated Leadership* programme that by tradition contained the biggest personal leadership component relative to other aspects of managerial leadership, was now offered twice a year instead of once. The leadership component was also increased gradually in the *General Management Programme*, which was, and still is, the largest programme at IFL.

Since 1993, companies have been calling for more strategic competence to cope with the rapid ongoing changes in their environment. As a result, IFL has begun to assume the role of a strategic partner for their customers. This has implied a shift away from facilitating the managers' individual development and towards the promotion of a shared understanding among managers about their company's strategic development. The changes in the content of the courses over the years have also clearly left their mark on IFL's product mix. To start with, the institute only offered programmes open to managers from any companies. Nowadays, programmes tailored to specific companies comprise almost half (47 per cent) of the total product mix.

The historical development of IFL indicates that the constructions identified above are not unique to IFL but are also part of more general constructions of managerial leadership in society. First, the elements of businessmanship and personal leadership in the IFL leadership constructions can be traced back to the Stockholm School of Economics (SSE) in general and to business administration as an academic discipline in particular. The majority of those who took active part in the establishment of IFL came from SSE. The first director of IFL, Per-Jonas Eliæson, was a teacher and researcher in business administration at SSE. Eliæson was also appointed as President of the Stockholm School of Economics in 1970 as a step toward strengthening the collaboration between IFL and SSE. Professors responsible for the different areas of business administration at SSE, such as accounting, finance, marketing and organization, were actively involved in establishing IFL as a management institute through their participation as programme directors and teachers.

Second, the humanistic orientation in the IFL constructions of managerial leadership also appears to have been greatly influenced by SSE. The main source of IFL's humanistic orientation can be traced back to SSE and specifically to its academic ideal, namely to act as an independent force in society, responsible for generating and passing on the knowledge necessary to a broad and rich managerial education rather than simply teaching the ability to solve problems in the ordinary practice of every day. This academic ideal expresses two humanist core values, namely that our primary goal as human beings is to constantly renew and develop ourselves, and that as human beings we have a unique value that should not be violated.

IFL was established at the end of 1960, and it is not unlikely that the prevalent debate at that time about corporate democracy (see e.g. Aspling, 1986) may also have influenced the development of a humanistic approach to leadership at IFL. Hence, although IFL's constructions of managerial leadership are in some respect unique to the Institute, they appear to be at the same time a reproduction of a more general construction of managerial leadership stemming mainly from the academic world.

Reality strikes back?

Thus far, I have discussed the social construction of managerial leadership at IFL and how this can be related to IFL's particular historical context. Given that IFL is the leading management institute in Sweden and that more than 30 000 persons have participated in its courses since its start in 1969, an interesting question concerns the extent to which IFL's constructions of managerial leadership have had an impact on managerial leadership in Swedish companies.

As a first step in addressing this question, it is necessary to describe the dominant construction of leadership in Swedish companies. Since the number of studies about leadership in Swedish companies is limited, the following identification builds primarily on a review of research literature about leadership in the economy of the western world. As Swedish companies belong to that economy, it is reasonable to assume that the dominant construction of leadership in Swedish companies is similar, apart from certain cultural features, to the prevalent construction of leadership within other companies in the western world economy.

As described in Chapters 1 and 2 above, the most fundamental feature of the dominant construction is that managerial leadership is regarded as a phenomenon relating to the *individual*. In Yukl's (1994) extensive review of the literature on leadership, for example, managerial leadership is primarily perceived in this way, i.e. in terms of individuals who possess some inherent qualities such as knowledge, skills and personal traits that are used in their leadership. In their overview of management, Hosking and Morley (1991) described the prevalent individualistic view of leadership as an entity-related view of leadership. According to these authors, most theories of leadership are entity-related in that they treat the person (i.e. the leader) and the organization as separate entities that can be '. . . theorized as independent of each other' (p. 60). The dominant construction of leadership as a phenomenon relating to the individual has also been described by other researchers such as Hosking, Daschler and Gergen (1995), Alvesson and Willmott (1996) and Sandberg and Targama (1998).

Another central feature is the equating of managerial leadership with men and masculinity. The dominant construction of leadership is male-dominated, in terms of both number and the predominance of masculine images (Kanter, 1977; Cockburn, 1991; Wahl, 1992; Höök, 1995; Collinson and Hearn, 1996). More than 90 per cent of leadership positions at the executive level are occupied by men in the US, in Europe (Collinson and Hearn, 1996) and – within Europe – also in Sweden (Höök, 1995). The most salient masculine images within the dominant construction of leadership are toughness and fighting (see also Chapter 3 above). For example, Collinson and Hearn (1996) found in their overview that most theories of leadership are saturated with masculine images '. . . emphasizing qualities of struggle and battle, a willingness to be ruthless and brutal, a rebellious nature and aggressive, rugged individualism' (p. 3), and that biographies and autobiographies of famous corporate leaders often refer to an '. . . evangelical, personal and lifelong preoccupation with military-like efficiency, ruthless practice and autocratic control' (pp. 2–3). The way in which the dominant construction of leadership is saturated with masculine images is also discussed in the present book, particularly by Karlsson Stider (Ch. 5), Holgersson (Ch. 6), Wahl (Ch. 7) and Höök (Ch. 8).

The male image of toughness is not only one of the most vivid but also one of the most firmly historically rooted and persistent features of leadership. For example, Henderson (1896, cf. Bendix, 1956) described leadership in the following way:

'It would be strange if the "captain of the industry" did not sometimes manifest a militant spirit, for he has risen from the ranks largely because he was a better fighter than most of us. Competitive commercial life is not a flowery bed of ease, but a battlefield where "the struggle for existence" is defining the industrially "fittest to survive".'

(Bendix, 1956, p. 256)

Although the language has changed over the years, the idea that toughness is crucial in leadership has not. This becomes particularly evident in the Total Quality Management (TQM) and Business Processes Re-engineering (BRP) movement in industry. For example, in Grint and Case (1998) the leader as a tough fighter is a prominent figure in an overview of the BRP movement.

'Dramatic improvement has to be paid for in some way, and the coinage is usually denominated by its units of suffering [. . .] it is necessary to deal with them (resisters) gently but by pointing out the gap in their understanding and the errors of their ways. By means of repeated communication and clarification they can be brought to the straight and narrow [. . .]. However, those who are deliberately trying to obstruct the reengineering effort [. . .] need the back of the hand.'

(Hammer and Stanton, 1995, pp. 174 and 183;
quoted from Grint and Case, 1998, p. 562)

The findings reported by Kallifatides in Chapter 3 about how the *chosen ones* develop to become managers, also suggests that toughness is one of the most basic and vivid characteristics of the dominant leadership construction.

Another crucial feature in the dominant construction with a long history is leadership as rational expertise. With the introduction of *Scientific Management* in Taylor (1911), the leader became a scientist, a rational expert. Leadership in terms of rational expertise can be described as an expression of 'technical rationality' (Alvesson and Willmott, 1996; Sjöstrand, 1997). Technical rationality refers to leadership used as a technical or functional means to achieve more or less unquestioned ends, such as profitability and continuous growth. As these business techniques are regarded as scientifically founded, they also acquire an objective and neutral status.

According to Sjöstrand (1997) most literature on management and organization is characterized by a strong belief in technical rationality '. . . as being if not the only, then at least the dominating force in the practice of management' (p. 36). The domination of technical rationality in management is clearly illustrated in a description (Engwall, 1992) of the historical development of business administration in Sweden in terms of strong normative and instrumental managerial tools such as accounting, finance, marketing and organization. These sub-fields are all seen as technical means used for achieving a number of more or less unquestioned goals such as profitability and growth.

A comparison of IFL's constructions of managerial leadership with the dominant construction reveals a number of similarities. Although leadership is treated at IFL as social interaction between leaders and subordinates, the constructions of managerial leadership produced by IFL treat it primarily as a phenomenon relating to the individual in a way that resembles the dominant construction. Nor do IFL constructions of leadership challenge the male ingredient of the dominant construction of leadership in any substantial way. The majority of the programme directors interviewed never questioned leadership as some particular aspect of maleness.[3] The idea of being able to master a set of business techniques accords nicely with the idea of the dominant construction of the leader as rational expert. Except in construction 3, personal leadership can also be seen in IFL constructions as an aspect of rational expertise within the dominant construction, since personal leadership in IFL's constructions is primarily viewed as a means for achieving certain stated ends.

The only point on which IFL differs from the dominant construction concerns the tough fighter. In the IFL constructions, this character in the dominant construction has been replaced by the humanist. Replacing the tough fighter by the humanist is a crucial deviation, however, since the humanistic approach in IFL constructions frames its other elements of managerial leadership in three specific constructions of humanistic managerial leadership. Is it possible then, to see traces of the development of a more humanistically oriented leadership in Swedish companies?

Although there is a form of humanistic leadership rhetoric among Swedish leaders that invokes such things as co-operation and striving for consensus as described by Beckérus et al. (1988) and Jönsson (1995), it is still not easy to find clear evidence to suggest any growing humanistic managerial leadership in Swedish companies. Rather, the opposite appears to be true. For example, over the last decade we have witnessed a continuously growing demand from the capital and financial markets that companies should increase their profits within a constantly shrinking time frame.

The leadership of Swedish companies seems to have reproduced the dominant construction of leadership by responding with tough rationalizations and comprehensive downsizing, resulting in high unemployment, and a stressed and over-worked workforce. This development is confirmed and is being described in detail in the context of an extensive ongoing cross-disciplinary research programme about working conditions in Swedish companies (*Dagens Nyheter*, 1999).[4] Such findings as have so far appeared show that working conditions have become tougher and have led to a greater uncertainty, fatigue and silence among employees. All the programme directors interviewed confirm this trend in statements such as:

'[. . .] managing on the basis of money alone is foolish, but it is not easy to go against it these days. The current trend is pretty plain.'

'[. . .] today, you could say that the dominating feeling among these individuals (the managers who participate in IFL's programmes) is fear – fear of losing their jobs, fear of not being good enough and fear of not being able to run fast enough.'

How is it possible, then, that the humanistic orientation of the managerial courses arranged by IFL do not seem to have had any evident impact on leadership as performed in Swedish companies? One explanation could be that IFL has failed to convey a humanistic leadership approach in its programmes, despite its ambition to do so. The detailed evaluation of IFL's largest and oldest management programme in Björkegren (1986) provides some evidence of course participants not acquiring a humanistic leadership construction. Ninety-five per cent of the course content of that programme was devoted to business techniques and five per cent to social and psychological aspects of managerial leadership.

Björkegren's study also suggests that the learning philosophy underlying the studied programme may have made it difficult to convey a humanistic leadership orientation, as it did not encourage any questioning of the participants' existing views of managerial leadership. According to Björkegren, the studied programme could be characterized as a 'single-loop system of learning' (p. 209). Single-loop learning means primarily that existing views are re-affirmed and reinforced (Argyris and Schön, 1978), which in this case meant the participants' taken-for-granted assumptions about leadership.

Thus, as Björkegren put it: '[. . .] the studied participants reproduced the same social reality every time the course was run' (p. 210). Since this programme has acted as a model for many other IFL-programmes, it is reasonable to assume that these programmes, too, were saturated with similar ideas and a similar approach to learning. On a basis of Björkegren's results, it seems that due to its strong focus on business techniques and single-loop learning, IFL has not been particularly successful in conveying a humanistic image of leadership to its participants, at any rate not up to 1985.

A closely related explanation could be that the humanistic orientation in IFL's constructions of leadership has remained relatively silent in most management programmes, with the result that very few participants have acquired it. This is particularly likely to be the case of the programmes that produce leadership constructions 1 and 2, because the humanistic orientation is not so clearly articulated there as in construction 3. This interpretation is supported by the fact that up to 1985 the majority of IFL's courses focused primarily on transmitting basic business techniques. It was not until after 1985 that the programme directors began to devote more time to personal leadership in their courses, so it would become more natural then to make the humanistic orientation more explicit.

A further interpretation, related to the previous one, is that the dominant leadership construction is so deeply ingrained in the course participants that they only acquire the business techniques provided, but not the humanistic frame of which the techniques are a part. In a study of managerial thinking about value-based management in Swedish companies, Brytting and Trollestad (1999) provide support for such an interpretation. The results of their study show that a large majority of the managers studied did not perceive humanist values as an overarching framework for managerial leadership. Instead, the humanist values were viewed within a traditional and instrumental framework of managerial leadership and were regarded as a business technique for achieving higher profits.

Another interpretation could be that the exchange of experiences between course participants obstructs the teachers at IFL in their attempts to convey the humanistic orientation. According to most programme directors, participants often claim that the most important learning takes place in their discussions with the other participants. This is also confirmed in Björkegren (1986). Indeed this is a form of learning that has been encouraged actively in IFL since its start in 1969. As the participants frequently interact with each other, they may be reproducing the dominant construction of leadership rather than being challenged by the humanistic alternative provided by their teachers. The risk that the participants reproduce the dominant construction also increases if, as Björkegren claims, IFL adopts a style of learning in the programmes that does not encourage any questioning of the dominant construction.

A somewhat more optimistic conclusion, however, is that it takes a long time for the humanistic leadership construction to become established as a viable alternative. The humanistic language used by leaders concerning co-operation, striving toward consensus and so on reported by Beckérus et al. (1988), Jönsson (1995) and Åkerblom (1999), can be interpreted as a sign of a slow change in the social construction of leadership in Swedish companies. This interpretation is further supported by cross-cultural studies such as those reported in Hofstede (1980) and Zander (1997). The results of these studies suggest that the kind of managerial leadership practised in Swedish companies is more humanistically oriented compared with most other countries in the western world. At the same time, this support is undermined by the explanation usually given for differences in leadership styles, namely that these are related primarily to differences in national cultures. That IFL's management programme should have significantly influenced Swedish culture hardly seems realistic.

Further, the humanistic language could also be interpreted as mere rhetoric, used by corporate leaders to attract the necessary support and valuable resources for their companies. In a similar vein, Sjöstrand (1997) has argued that it is common for corporate leaders to use language as mere rhetoric to achieve legitimacy for their action and intentions. For example, as Michael Treschow, the CEO of Electrolux, put it:

> 'When you are going to motivate a strategic decision to your board of directors, you avoid the kind of language that includes words like intuition. You have to pick the right words, those which are not loaded with the wrong connotations.'
>
> (Sjöstrand, 1997, p. 166)

Perhaps the most likely interpretation is that IFL course participants have acquired a form of humanistic leadership construction, but back in their companies this construction is regarded as unrealistic in comparison to the dominant construction embedded in practice. If the humanistic leadership constructions are seen as unrealistic, they will not be given a chance to develop in practice. Instead, they will be dismissed by remarks such as: 'Well, well, I hear you've been on a course again, ha, ha, ha ... but now you're back in the real world.'

But why does it seem to be so difficult to introduce alternative leadership constructions, without the dominant construction 'striking back' by marginalizing the alternative constructions?

Dachler (1998) argued along the same lines when asking:

> '... why all these well meant and constructively intended appeals by business, economics, politics and government, not to speak of churches and humanistic ethics, freedom and social institutions,

have such little effect and are given such little credence in the everyday world.' (p. 2)

In an answer to his own question, Dachler (ibid.) goes on to explain that the basic problem:

'... lies in continually doing the same by increasing our efforts and urgency to convince ourselves and others about the necessity to be more tolerant, more understanding, fair, and mutually respecting, when in fact structures and social processes are left as taken-for-granted which make sensible, normal and natural exactly those views and social actions that fundamentally contradict those appeals.' (pp. 2–3)

Hence, according to Dachler (ibid.), the main reason why humanistic appeals have had such a slight impact is that most attempts to provide a humanistic alternative have taken for granted the social structures and processes that are counter-productive to those very attempts. Perhaps the most deeply rooted assumption that undermines alternative constructions of leadership, is the idea of the individual as the original source and possessor of knowledge about reality. So long as we regard leadership as a phenomenon relating to the individual, our attempt to provide an alternative style of leadership will be reduced to grafting certain specific features onto our managers. IFL's leadership programmes are an example of an attempt to create a more humanistic type of leadership by changing the attributes of individual people.

However, simply introducing humanistic leadership at the level of the individual means disregarding specific social processes and economic structures in society that produce, and reproduce, the dominant construction of managerial leadership in Swedish companies. More specifically, by disregarding the social nature of managerial leadership, that is to say its social construction, we are preserving the dominant construction of managerial leadership. And preserving the dominant construction entails the risk that IFL marginalizes as unrealistic the humanistic leadership constructions produced in its own leadership programmes. Thus, so long as we locate managerial leadership at the level of the individual, we are ignoring the ways in which individuals and groups are embedded in networks of social relationships, where they reproduce specific social constructions of managerial leadership.

One important step in an attempt to break this deadlock is to shift our perspective, and to stop looking at managerial leadership as a bunch of qualities possessed by an individual, and to regard it instead as a social construction. With this view it becomes possible at least to begin to understand how the dominant construction of managerial leadership is produced and reproduced in companies and in society at large. Such an understanding is essential if we are to be able not only to question the dominant construction of managerial leadership, but even to challenge the social processes and economic structures that produce and reproduce it.

The latest change at IFL, whereby the institute acts as a strategic partner for specific companies with a view to promoting collective rather than individual learning, could represent a possible step away from treating leadership as a phenomenon at the individual level and toward seeing it as a social process. As the strategic partnership programmes are conducted within the bounds of the customer's organization, IFL's production of leadership becomes integrated with that of its customer. Such integration, and the increased focus on the collective level, may make it more likely that IFL constructions will have a stronger impact in the future on the dominant construction of leadership. On the other hand, it could also be argued that this kind of integration may reduce the possibilities even more for the participants to distance themselves from the dominant construction, thus giving them even less opportunities to acquire the more humanistic constructions provided by IFL. Further, IFL's ability to promote a humanistic leadership style may be undermined by the fact that the client is commissioning and paying IFL to deliver a particular type of leadership. IFL cannot stray too far from its brief without losing credibility.

Furthermore, should IFL question the social processes and economic structures that reproduce the dominant construction of leadership and thus create an obstacle to humanistic leadership, then the institute may also be calling in question its own existence as an active part of the Swedish capitalist economy.

This last is due to the fact that the dominant construction of the managerial leader, as a male individual who is a tough fighter and a rational expert, has not been constructed in a vacuum. Rather, it has been produced and reproduced as an integral part of the Swedish capitalist economy in the western world. Referring to Hales (1993), Alvesson and Willmott (1996) argued that in the capitalist economies management can be regarded as '... the guardians of private capital and the growth of the modern state' (p. 10).

A central question is then, how far is it possible to provide a humanistic alternative to the dominant construction of leadership, which is an integral and active part of the current capitalist system, without also fundamentally changing the social construction of the capitalist system itself in a fundamental way? For instance, is it possible for corporate leaders to survive on the market unless they are tough and prepared to fight off competitors? And is it possible for corporate leaders to achieve the basic goals of capitalism necessary to the generation of a desired return on invested capital, while at the same time achieving basic humanist goals such as treating human beings with respect and consideration? Perhaps the establishment of the Swedish model in the late 1930s can be seen as one successful attempt to attend to business needs such as profit and growth as well as humanistic needs such as care and respect. Gould (1993), for example, argued that the Swedish model can be regarded as a good example of a capitalistic welfare state, since it:

> '... had achieved an impressive balance between the needs of the business community to respond to changing conditions of private markets, thereby generating profits and demands for employees for security and good standard of living.' (p. 136)
> (quoted in Berglund and Löwstedt 1996, p. 218)

However, according to Berglund and Löwstedt (1996), the Swedish model has gradually lost its ability to hold the balance over the last three decades, with the advantage going to the business community. To a large extent the model has been replaced by the '... corporate machine – Sweden Inc' (p. 224). Nevertheless, since the main justification for IFL's existence has always been to ensure Swedish corporate owners of a supply of qualified managers, and not to question the current capitalist system in itself, these questions are fundamental. If IFL began to question the Swedish capitalist system itself, the owners of the capital might well consider replacing IFL by another provider of 'competent' managers for their companies.

Notes

1 The results reported in this chapter are part of a larger study about what constitutes competence development in organizations.
2 Interview with Eliaeson, the first CEO of IFL.
3 An exception is the leadership programme *Manager and Woman*, which has a different framework compared with the prevalent male framework of managerial leadership.
4 According to the article in an important Swedish daily, *Dagens Nyheter*, the cross-disciplinary project started in 1995, and is being carried out by more than twenty researchers from different disciplines.

References

Åkerblom, S. (1999). *Delade meningar om ledarskap? En enkätstudie av mellanchefers föreställningar om framstående ledarskap.* EFI, Stockholm.

Alvesson, M., and Willmott, H. (1996). *Making sense of management. A critical introduction*. Sage, London.

Andrews, K. (1966). *The effectiveness of university management development programmes*. Wiley, Boston.

Argyris, C., and Schön, D. (1978). *Organizational learning*. Addison-Wesley, Reading, Mass.

Aspling, A. (1986). *Företagsdemokratin och MBL. En empirisk och organisationsteoretisk utvärdering av en arbetsrättsreform*. EFI, Stockholm.

Beckérus, Å., Edström, A., Edlund, C., Ekvall, G., Forslin, J., and Rendahl, J-E. (1988). *Doktrinskiftet. Nya ideal i svenskt ledarskap*. Svenska Dagbladet, Stockholm.

Bendix, R. (1956). *Work and authority in industry*. UC Press, LA.

Berglund, J., and Löwstedt, J. (1996). Sweden: the fate of human resource management in a 'folkish' society, in Clark, T., *European human resource management*, pp. 215–44, Blackwell, Cambridge.

Björkegren, D. (1986). *Företagsledarutbildning – en fallstudie*. EFI, Stockholm.

Brytting, T., and Trollestad, C. (1999). *Managerial thinking on value-based management*. EFI Working paper, Stockholm.

Cockburn, C. (1991). *In the way of women*. Macmillan, London.

Collinson, D. L., and Hearn, J. (1996). *Men as managers, managers as men*. Sage, London.

Dachler, P. (1998). Threats to the potential of global leadership, in Mobley, W., (ed.), *Advances in global leadership*. JAI Press, pp. 68–85, Greenwich, Conn.

Dagens Nyheter, (1999). Arbetslivet har hårdnat, 5 May, p. 13.

Engwall, L. (1992). *Mercury meets Minerva. Business studies and higher education. The Swedish case*. Pergamon Press, Oxford.

EQUIS. (1999). IFL, Stockholm.

Gergen, K. (1994). *Realities and relationships. Soundings in social construction*. Harvard University Press, Cambridge.

Gould, A. (1993). *Capitalist welfare systems: a comparison of Japan, Britain and Sweden*. Longman, London.

Grint, K., and Case, P. (1998). The violent rhetoric of re-engineering: Management consultancy on the offensive. *Journal of Management Studies*, vol. 5, s. 557–77.

Hales, C. (1993). *Managing through organization*. Routledge, London.

Hammer, M., and Stanton, S. A. (1995). *The reengineering revolution: a handbook*. Harper Business, New York.

Hofstede, G. (1980). *Culture's consequences*. Sage, Beverly Hills.

Höök, P. (1995). Woman at the top. A survey of Swedish industry, in Wahl, A. (ed.), *Men's perceptions of women and management*. Ministry of Health and Social Affairs, Stockholm.

Hosking, D-M., and Morley, I. E. (1991). *A social psychology of organizing*. Harvester Wheatsheaf, New York.

Hosking, D-M., Dachler, P. H., and Gergen, K. J. (1995). *Management and organization: Relational alternatives to individualism*. Avebury, Aldershot.

Jönsson, S. (1995). *Goda utsikter. Svenskt management i perspektiv*. Nerenius & Santérus, Stockholm.

Kanter, R. M. (1977). *Men and women of the corporation*. Basic Books, New York.

Kvale, S. (1989). To validate is to question, in Kvale, S. (ed.), *Issues of validity in qualitative research*, pp. 73–92, Studentlitteratur, Lund.

Marton, F. (1981). Phenomenography: Describing conceptions of the world around us. *Instructional Science*, vol. 10, pp. 177–200.

Sandberg, J. (1994). *Human competence at work: An interpretative approach*. Bas, Göteborg.

Sandberg, J. (2000). Understanding human competence at work. An interpretative approach. *Academy of Management Journal*, vol. 43, pp. 9–25.

Sandberg, J., and Targama, A. (1998). *Ledning och förståelse. Ett kompetensperspektiv på organisationer*. Studentlitteratur, Lund.

Sjöstrand, S-E. (1997). *The two faces of management. The Janus factor*. Thomson, London.

Taylor, F. W. (1911). *The principles of scientific management*. Harper, New York.

Wahl, A. (1992). *Könsstrukturer i organisationer*. EFI, Stockholm.

Yukl, G. (1994). *Leadership in organizations*. Prentice Hall, Englewood Cliffs.

Zander, L. (1997). *The licence to lead – An 18 country study of the relationship between employees' preferences regarding interpersonal leadership and national culture*. IIB, Stockholm.

CHAPTER TEN

Creative leaders – or prisoners of the past?

Daniel Ericsson

The concept of creative leadership has recently acquired buzz-word status in the managerial discourse in Sweden. The number of articles written on the subject published in business papers has more than doubled[1] since 1993; an increasing number of seminars on creative leadership are held in executive programmes and at trade fairs;[2] text-books used in MBA programmes deal explicitly with the phenomenon;[3] recruitment ads for managerial positions give elaborate job descriptions stressing the necessity for creativity; and, perhaps most importantly, managers have begun to describe themselves as 'creative' leaders.

This obsession with creative leadership knows no national boundaries. Following in the wake of the neo-conservatism of the 1980s leaders are 'in' (cf. Czarniawska-Joerges and Wolff, 1991), and so is creativity. As modernism's striving for rationality and efficiency has been if not replaced, then at least played down in favour of a plea for new ideas, for flexibility and change, creativity has become one of the hottest issues in the discourses of the 1980s and 1990s (cf. Bloom, 1987; Joas, 1996). Altogether, creative leadership has become one of the main topics on the managerial agenda (cf. Ford and Gioia, 1995; see also *The Economist*, 17 August 1996).

Despite the many voices calling for creative leaders, creative leadership has not established itself either as a distinct area for empirical research, or as a clear-cut theoretical concept in the leadership literature. The theoretical meaning of creative leadership is therefore rather elusive. For instance it is wrapped in obscurity, whether it is the creativity of the leader or the creativity resulting from the leadership that is being referred to. The term is used explicitly in the *traitist* approach, where creative skills have been distinguished as one of the conceptual skills that differentiate between leaders and non-leaders (cf. Stogdill, 1974). This line of research draws upon and joins forces with a major strand in creativity research, whose primary objective has been – as in the works of J. P. Guilford (e.g. 1950, 1956, 1957) – to identify the personal, psychological and cognitive traits or attributes that either facilitate or constrain creative individual action.

Structurally oriented researchers, on the other hand, stress the importance of leadership for organizational creativity (e.g. Vedin, 1985; Cyert, 1985; Ekvall, 1988; Ford and Gioia, 1995). Following the review of creativity literature on leadership in Ford and Gioia (1995, p. 34), it could be argued that in many aspects creative leadership resembles, and is thereby covered by, theories on transforming leadership (cf. Burns, 1978), transformational leadership (cf. Bass, 1985; Bennis and Nanus, 1985), cultural leadership (cf. Trice and Beyer, 1991), charismatic leadership (cf. Conger and Kanungo, 1987; Conger, 1989), and change-oriented leadership (cf. Connor 1995; Kotter 1996).

Thus, in most theoretical writings on creative leadership the only consequence of creative leadership is creativity itself – either the leader's or the followers'. Theorists have focused one-sidedly upon the creative leader as the indisputable 'causer', either neglecting the causes and consequences of this leadership completely by taking them for granted, or pre-defining them theoretically in terms, for instance, of behavioural or psychological attributes. Either way, descriptions of creative leadership, albeit indirectly, are in many cases produced independently of the actor's purposes and definitions of the situation, thus in a way merely reproducing the researcher's own theoretical understanding of leadership and creativity. With reference to Silverman (1970), I bring forward the idea that these descriptions and explanations could be of a teleological kind, that is, implying that the causes of creative leadership are to be found in its consequences, or vice versa.

Underlying this vicious circle of superficiality are processes of reification, that is, a deeply ingrained cultural mystification and objectification of leadership (cf. Gemmill and Oakley, 1992). To break this circle a shift in scientific approach is required, towards a perspective that can overcome the dichotomy of subject and object. Here, this will be done following the tradition of Berger and Luckmann (1966) and Silverman (1970), that is to say by adopting the stance that has come to be known as social constructionism (cf. Gergen 1985), whereby reality is understood as an ongoing dialectical process of externalization, objectivation and internalization. Creative leadership, as well as creativity and leadership, is thus seen as socially constructed and not as a trait attaching to the individual.

In this chapter an enquiry is made into the causes and consequences of creative leadership. At focus is the construction of the creative leader, as externalized and objectivated within the managerial discourse. Questions at issue are what does it mean to be a creative leader, and what does it not mean?

To exemplify the managerial discourse on creative leadership, two interviews with leaders in the newspaper industry have been selected from a larger study of the way in which creativity is constructed in organizations. The Chief Editor was chosen to be part of the study partly because of his editorial role, and partly because the financial paper he represents has published many articles on the subject of creative leadership. The Chairman of the Board was chosen because he has become known as a creative leader, and also because he has expressed strong, explicit opinions in public about the nature of creative leadership. As will be shown, these two accounts are found, in a Weberian (cf. Weber, 1962, 1968) sense, to be ideal-types of creative leadership.

In examining the accounts of the two leaders, a radical humanist perspective on leadership has been adopted, incorporating a deconstructionist approach (cf. Parker and Shotter, 1990; Gemmill and Oakley, 1992). In this way hidden assumptions and repressed meanings of the managerial discourse on creative leadership can be uncovered. As attention is drawn to these assumptions and to the unintended consequences of creative leadership, the notion of the creative leader as causer of creativity will be challenged.

The chief editor

Just before Christmas 1989, the chief editor-to-be of the recently started Swedish daily business paper *Finanstidningen* was contacted by its founder. The two men had been fellow students at the Stockholm School of Economics, and the founder – remembering that his friend had worked for the school paper – now offered him a job as a financial reporter. The chief editor-to-be had long been interested in the media industry, but had given up the idea of becoming a journalist early on, since he knew no one in the business. After completing his degree he had gone to work as an accountant at a small computer firm instead, and had disliked it almost from the beginning, citing its 'total lack of creativity' as the reason. Needless to say, he jumped at the opportunity that was given him and began his climb up to the position of chief editor, which he reached in 1994.

'I'm ultimately responsible for the product. My main duty is of course to develop the paper. To make it better, to [...] ensure that we meet the demands of the readers, and [. . .] to develop the product so that we also attract new readers. It is my responsibility that we have a staff in here that can deliver what we want to see in the paper. And of course, I'm the one who handles the contact with the readers. I'm the one who fronts the paper.' (A1)[4]

'I'm fairly involved in the paper operatively. I sit in on the morning meetings, try to come up with ideas, listen to what ideas others come up with, etc., and generally play around with good ideas. [. . .] "This is a good angle, but the heading should have read more like this [. . .]". That is, I try to explain how I want the paper done. I'm the news editor [. . .]. I'm the one who decides the news priorities, and heads the production of the paper. What's up first? [. . .] Have all relevant aspects been covered? [. . .] That kind of thing. And I allocate the resources. I say "OK, this is what we'll do, we need five men to cover it."' (A2)

Conquering the mind

'In assessing the news we work according to what we call the "top-of-the-mind" model. We assume that people have approximately three things at the top of their mind. I think [. . .] we got this from some psychology professor somewhere. You have three things in your head, you know, that you're thinking about, that is "top of the mind", right? And these subjects could be of current interest. And then you have three seasonal subjects at the top of your mind. The subjects [. . .] of current interest are often aspects of these seasonal subjects.' (A3)

'Ultimately, the best thing to do is to find a completely new subject that establishes itself at the top of your mind. Then you set the agenda. You sort of steer the chatter at the lunch table [. . .]. Then you have your scoop. The second best thing [. . .] is to have an item from a top-of-the-mind subject already established, or a new angle. [. . .] You present something from the top of the mind that was previously unknown, something that moves the discussion on [. . .]. The third best thing, we call "journal of record". You cover what's top of the mind, but you don't know more than the others. So, starting from the seasonal and current issues [. . .], I . . . eh, you . . . make your news assessment.' (A4)

The art of asking the right question

'The best stories come from tips. Someone phones in, "Hey, you ought to look into this, it smells fishy", and then it is just a matter of getting the story validated by reliable sources. But tips are rare. Most news is the result of your own thinking and of asking the right question. You've discovered that "*Astra* said a year ago that they were going to save x million in a rationalization programme. What's happened?" You give them a call, [...], and they say the programme has been dropped, [...] they aren't going to save any money. Here you have [...] done some thinking on your own, asked the right question, obtained an interesting answer, [...], and gotten a piece of news that is really good. You were the first to think and ask the right questions.' (A5)

'It's all about either ingenuity or routine. The best thing is if you have both. [...] If you have ingenuity, then you can become a good reporter almost immediately. Or you can acquire experience and gradually, after a couple of years, learn where to look for "top-of-the-mind" news. Some people never learn. Some figure it out gradually. Some just seem to have it from the beginning.' (A6)

'Normally, the editor is more experienced. So, it's often the editor who comes up with the good ideas and gets the reporters to check them out. I mean, I sit in on the morning meetings because I am pretty experienced and so I can contribute lots of ideas and angles.' (A7)

The morning meetings

The question of what is top-of-the-mind is raised daily at the morning staff meeting. There are two kinds, micro and macro. The former refers to issues related to business and the latter to political and foreign issues. When opinions differ among the reporters about what is top-of-the-mind, the discussions can sometimes get out of hand. Generally, though, there is no doubt about what is top-of-the-mind.

'Then it doesn't make sense to do anything else. If there's a crisis in Asia, the Hong Kong stock exchange falls and everybody's worried about their savings, the only thing they want to read about is Asia.' (A8)

The morning papers are gone through at the meetings, to see what the main competitors have come up with. If they have covered something that's seen as new or interesting, a follow-up is discussed.

'We have to add something. We have to do our bit. Especially, if some paper has established a new top-of-the-mind subject. Well, then we have to accept this new state of mind and add some new information on the subject tomorrow.' (A9)

'An article you read often provokes a lot of questions. [...] There are things that haven't been answered. [...] An excellent reporter reads [...] an article, and sees what's *not* written. And that's what goes into tomorrow's paper. The news of tomorrow is what wasn't there yesterday.' (A10)

'The editor leads the discussion in the morning, but the reporters are expected to have read all the other papers. And then you usually have your own area to cover. [...] The more experienced and ingenious the reporter, the more likely he is to come up with an idea of his own, a follow-up. If not, then the editor says something like: "OK. This is top-of-the-mind now. [...] What do we want to know? [...] What do people want to read about tomorrow?" And then you talk about what the relevant aspects are. It's the editor, then, who makes the final decision about the questions that should be answered.' (A11)

What about creativity?

To the chief editor creativity is a matter of producing lead stories. And, as he sees it, some reporters are simply better at this than others.

'Yes, definitely. You could measure it by counting the number of times a given reporter has written the lead story of the day. [...] Some are simply better than others. And this is something we acknowledge every year at our anniversary celebration, when we reward the reporter who has produced the most lead stories that year. There are some who never write any top articles. It doesn't mean that they're useless to the paper. They may do excellent work. First of all, they may be analytical. That's also something we appreciate. Above all, we need these people who do the "bread and butter" jobs on the paper.' (A12)

'When you're discussing what top-of-the-mind articles you're going to write for the next day, you obviously try to give the assignment to someone who's up for the task, the one who's *most* suited to the task. [...] It depends very much on what subject you're dealing with, but you could say that the creative individuals get chosen for assignments more often.' (A13)

'You tend to know that if you send these people out, the chances are pretty good that they'll come back with a great article that you can actually have as lead story that day.' (A14)

However, it is not only the ability to ask the right people the right questions that counts. A good reporter also has to ask the questions in an open manner. By asking questions starting with: Who? What? When? Where? and How?, the reporter gets people to talk, instead of the other way round. This kind of creative ability is not easily recognized, but the chief editor usually tries to separate the good from the bad at the recruitment stage.

'I have three kinds of question. [. . .] There are the personal questions: Who are you? What have you done? etc.; the questions that have to do with competence; and there are the creativity questions – the latter are of course the hardest. They are often, you know, like if I were to ask you to write an article right now, what would it be about? And, how would you go about it? [. . .] It's really hard to know before-hand if the person you hire is creative or not, but they often come up with ideas for articles that you would like to write, questions you would like to have answered, things that you find interesting.' (A15)

'Quite a few who come direct from school [. . .], don't have the answers to the creativity questions worked out.' (A16)

'School' here refers primarily to the universities offering MBA programmes. With an annual staff turnover of approximately 15–20 per cent, some years as high as 50 per cent, the paper's recruitment policy has been to hire recent economics graduates. Here, training in creativity is seen as crucial, and the chief editor conducts two seminars a year on the subject of how to ask the right questions.

'I try to point out good examples. [. . .] And then I try to give feedback. [. . .] I believe in giving proper feedback. By confronting each and every one of the reporters and asking, you know: [. . .] "What did he say when you asked him this?" "Well, but I didn't ask him that." "Well, you should have." And by discussing what they've actually done. Or just giving someone a pat on the back when they've done something really good.' (A17)

'It's very hard to get people to develop their creativity if you're not concrete. You have to show them what you want, what it is that you're after. I think it's really hard just to walk into a room and say: "Hey, let's all be creative." [...] That way people may get stuck. This is why I believe in having an instrument to channel creativity.' (A18)

'I believe a lot of creativity arises in the meeting room where we hold our morning sessions. Lots of people are there together, you have a discussion and people give input direct to one another. You come up with these different ideas and get instant feedback. [...] It's a very stimulating environment and I think that the setting and all the discussions encourage people's creativity.' (A19)

'It's important to have an editor who leads the discussion, who listens to what the reporters have to say, and then decides if it's good enough. Or brings up some dimension that no one has thought of. [...] And then puts an end to the discussion when he thinks the subject is exhausted. Under weak editors I think discussion tends to drag on. They hold on to a subject too long, and then the creativity dries up. [...] So the point is, you have to stick to your agenda to maintain the level of the discussion, this creative dialogue that the morning meeting is all about. The quality of the morning meeting has great impact on the next day's paper. [...] Actually, I can take a paper, look at it, and tell whether we had a good or a bad meeting the day before.' (A20)

'To me, creative leadership means giving people room to use their creativity. It's not so much the leaders' own creativity that I'm talking about, but the use that's made of the creative potential of the staff. To make them work to their fullest potential. To make them discover new sides to themselves. To make them realize that they have the ability to make associations. To train people who don't have it in themselves, to become better at it.' (A21)

The Chairman of the Board

The chairman has come to be recognized as a charismatic and successful leader, both in the eyes of the public and in the industry. As chief editor of a big Swedish daily evening paper *(Aftonbladet)* in the 1980s, he set out on what was seen by many as a mission impossible: to challenge the mighty *Expressen*'s 40-year-long position as the leading evening paper in Scandinavia. It took him nearly ten years, but eventually he managed to recapture the number one position that *Aftonbladet* had lost 50 years earlier to *Expressen.*

> 'When I was 17 and started a school paper, I was influenced by the Stockholm papers. I was especially influenced by the founder of *Expressen,* and how his paper was able to explain complicated matters without over-simplifying the issue. [...] Another thing was the idealism of the Anglo-Saxon tradition. "Publish and be damned." What you wrote made a difference. I remember that I wrote a piece in the school paper on a teacher who was hated by everyone. The day after it was published he gave me *two* bad grades. [...] This made me, sort of, a hero. People saw that I'd had the courage to write the article, and they saw that I'd been punished for it. I felt this was rather amusing – being confirmed as a rebel in my own right. A romantic version perhaps, but anyway. [...] For most journalists this is what it's all about.' (B1)

The chairman started his career as a reporter on *Aftonbladet* in the late 1960s. In a climate greatly affected by the strong radical leftist movement, his route to the top was straight as an arrow, but it didn't come easily. A strong union and an organizational culture that stressed democracy of ideas made managerial decision-making illusory.

> 'Practically every decision was questioned by the journalists' union. They had more power than management, and in reality it was they who appointed lower management. [...] Everybody gathered at the central office, someone made a speech, and then a statement was issued often against management. Somehow it all came naturally.' (B2)

Abandoning the romantic myth

The chairman describes these mass meetings as verbal fights, from which the most rhetorically and politically inclined journalists came away victorious. These 'entertainers', however, were seldom elected to editorial positions.

> 'No, you see, it was much harder to take the responsibility that went with the statements. This was a time when competition between journalists was much tougher. We had a larger editorial staff than now, but above all the papers were very thin. And managing people with big egos who can't appear on the stage because of the limited

room, so to speak, is a problem. When the next day you may have to ask the reporter who was refused yesterday to write another piece. Then, of course, it's really hard to be the boss. Especially if you're not appointed by the employer, but by your colleagues. I was appointed editor-in-chief in 1981 and then we abolished the practice of mandates. I think I was the last one to be appointed at a mass meeting.' (B3)

The chairman became chief editor in 1987, and vice president in 1991. To be both chief editor and vice president was an important step for him. It gave him the opportunity to exert influence on issues concerning the paper as a whole and not just editorial matters.

'There is this romantic myth in journalism, I mean, that you ought to keep words and figures apart.' (B4)

'When I joined the management team in 1982, a news agency published a piece on how I, the editor-in-chief, was hobnobbing with the CEO. [...] At that time, something that was done solely for the benefit of the paper, was seen as an intrusion on journalistic integrity. Now, it's the other way round. [...] Integrity has nothing to do with money, on the contrary, it's the foundation of our operations.' (B5)

A balancing act

The chairman sees leadership in the newspaper industry as a question of striking a balance between commercial interests and serious journalism. In this sense, a paper like *Aftonbladet* is something of a 'tight-rope walker'.

'You have to be commercial, but you can't only be commercial, because then the effect may recoil on you and no one wants to work for the paper. You have to be serious too.' (B6)

As chief editor, the Chairman managed this balancing act by working strategically on the paper's image. This included the internal and the external image, because – as he points out – whether you're a reader or an employee you must be able to take pride in your paper. Thus, as well as working with marketing and branding issues, he tried to encourage serious and well-known journalists.

'Big egos choose a big audience. I think this is the root of the balancing act. But it's not enough to attract a big audience. It's always those with the biggest egos that leave the paper when circulation drops. They have high market value. Of course, this makes the working environment very fragile. It's like a psychological game about being on the right stage, so to speak. And I think this is one thing you have to think about, [...], that is, getting hold of the soloists. Because it spreads: "Oh! Is *he* working for *that* paper?" That's why we've been contracting top columnists from TV lately.' (B7)

'If you collect famous names like X, Y and Z, it makes the people in your organization feel proud. [...] Indirectly they're receiving confirmation of themselves.' (B8)

The big ego of the star journalist

Fame and ego tend to go hand in hand. Not all journalists get big egos, but to work on a paper as a journalist does mean visibility. You get read. You have an impact. And you make a difference. For the chairman this lies at the very foundations of the journalistic credo.

'I think a lot of the incentive to become a journalist is that you want a stage, because you think you have something to say.' (B9)

'There is, of course, a struggle for this kind of magnifying situation. [...] But you mustn't become unbearable as you grow. You have to be able to cope with your privileges.' (B10)

The chairman's view is that the extreme egos are used to having a whole crowd of people looking after them, doing their research, etc. – something that can create problems.

'It would be impossible to have Y (a famous journalist and writer) working on the paper. That you can understand. [...] He couldn't possibly be a member of an organization. And no one could possibly stand watching X (well-known journalist) showing off all the time. Actually, he used to work on the paper, so I know what I'm talking about. People get aggressive. It's simply not possible to bear these extreme egos, with their need to hold forth in front of a crowd of people. Z (well-known journalist) was like that. He was editor-in-chief once and it was a total disaster. He held court. He made speeches and told people what to do. And it simply doesn't work that way. People don't want to shrink, you have to let people grow in these [...] organizations.' (B11)

'You can keep these types at a distance, however, and just collect their pieces. Then it's up to the chief editor to work with them, because somebody has to pamper them. But they shouldn't be part of your organization.' (B12)

And the fragile ego of the leader

So it's not an easy task to work with big-ego journalists, or to be in a position of managing them. The chairman is rather cynical about this.

'A former colleague of mine became head of the City Opera. I asked him what the difference was between running an opera house and a paper. He said: "They sing at one place, and scream at the other." He was, you know, almost driven to despair by these big egos.' (B13)

'I've seen so many strong, creative people lose their confidence. And it easily happens in an environment like this. The people around you have really got to see that you know what you're doing. You must know the job by heart. If you move from a paper to the opera, [...] it's basically the same, but you'll be tested. [...] And that's why "courage and patience" has always been my motto.' (B14)

'I think the hardest part of creative processes is that they can't be measured. If you're making nails then you know that 4" is 4", but if you write an article or you're a stage artist [...], nobody can say exactly how it should be done. And that's why [...] an inner sense of security is critical. [...] You don't have it from the beginning. You have to acquire it. And [...] as a creative leader [...] you must be extremely careful about protecting middle management. Because harassment occurs as soon as people notice that a manager is not completely confident [...].' (B15)

The firm and benevolent leader

Experience is the key word for the chairman: the longer you've been a creative leader, the better you are at being one.

'To get the big artists to perform in front of the big audience you have to have an orchestra that works, and in that orchestra you have to have lesser egos, like editors and managers. To be a manager and to have a big ego – that makes for huge conflict. You can't go around thinking you're somebody. Or if you think you are, you can't act like it. If you use your paper to market yourself, there's a risk [...] that everything will go to hell, because then you don't give a damn about any of the others. So, to work with the big egos, it seems to me that you have to give them plenty of room. You have to pamper them. [...] As chief editor, you work more with the big artists than with the team. But I think you have to be fair. You have to be attentive to the others as well. In my view that's the most important aspect of creative leadership, perhaps of all leadership: feedback – to provide recognition both negative and positive, to react, and to act. To be a sort of father. [...] You can see how people grow when you tell them they've done something good. But it's not as simple as that, because they also want to know "what" they did that was good. I can't simply tell Y that he's written a nice column, he wants to know why it was nice.' (B16)

'Compared to 10 or 15 years ago, there's much more supervision in the editorial office of a paper today. There's more hierarchy. It's more top-down. The boss rules. Do an article, because .... [...] And if, as a reporter, you don't have specialist knowledge, then it's the editor-in-chief that decides who'll get the assignment.' (B17)

'In all creative organizations the need for leadership is paramount. You know that thing about not needing authority? That's bullshit. If there's one thing you do need, it's someone to show approval – someone to say: "You're brilliant." But also someone to say: "You're not doing your best. Why didn't you make two more phone calls?"' (B18)

The credo of the creative leader

In the accounts of the chief editor and the chairman of the board, creative leadership is referred to as 'giving room' (see quotations A21 and B16, above). This 'giving room' could be interpreted literally, but it could also be read metaphorically. What, then, does it mean to 'give room'? Who – or what – is given room? And what room is given?

Meetings and seminars for ideas and discovery

As the chief editor sees it, 'giving room' is concerned with the use and development of creative potential (A21). And use of creative potential boils down to coming up with good ideas (A2), and the development of potential is intrinsically a matter of discovering good ideas (A17–19). 'Giving room' could thus be interpreted as 'giving room for good ideas' and as 'giving room for discoveries to be made.'

Good ideas are primarily given room at the morning meetings (A19). Here, the chief editor acts as leader of the creative dialogue (A11, A19–20) and plays around with good ideas (A2) by being concrete (A18) in accordance with the top-of-the-mind model (A3–4). As it is felt to be necessary that the meetings be structured, giving room could thus be interpreted as 'structuring the morning meetings to promote good ideas'. However, as the chief editor has the prerogative to interpret what a good idea is (A4, A7, A11, A17, A20), this interpretation becomes somewhat misleading. Instead, a more appropriate interpretation would be 'structuring the morning meetings for ideas that the chief editor thinks are good'.

The possibility of discovery is primarily given room at the twice yearly training seminars. Here, the chief editor shows what it is that he's after. This is leadership by being concrete (A18). However, once again, the room 'given' is strictly limited by the chief editor and oriented towards his own notion of creativity. 'Giving room for discovery' could therefore be interpreted as 'holding training seminars twice a year to discover what the chief editor thinks is creative'.

Stages for the big egos

The chairman perceives journalists as having something to say (B9). To be given room could thus be understood as being 'given room to speak' or 'given room in the paper to write in'. However, the chairman uses another metaphor as well, to clarify the meaning of giving room, as he suggests that creative leadership is about giving the journalists a 'stage' (B9 and B13).

The main stage is of course the paper itself, where the journalists get to be read and make an impact (B9–10). But not just any stage will do, it has to be the right one. And the main 'right' stage is a paper for the big egos, that is, a paper that attracts a big audience (B7). Creative leadership is thus a matter of providing the right stage by striking a strategic balance between the commercial and the serious (B6), but it is also a matter of casting (B7–8, B17) and conducting (B16).

Daily life on the paper could also be seen as a stage, an internal stage, where the big-ego journalists get their positions confirmed by playing psychological games (B7), holding court (B11), singing and screaming (B13) and, at least traditionally, entertaining each other with political agitation (B2). These performances are part of the big-ego dilemma: you can't live with them, but you can't live without them. The chairman solves the dilemma by keeping the extreme egos outside the organization (B12) and pampering them at a distance, or by paying special attention to the big egos within the organization (B16) and consciously restraining his own ego (B16).

The metaphor of giving room could thus be interpreted as 'giving the big-ego journalists an external stage before a big audience, and an internal stage before their colleagues and the chief editor'. In the case of the really extreme egos, however, it is a matter of keeping them *off* the internal stage.

The 'stage' metaphor is rich in meaning. While it still carries the meaning of 'give room to speak', associated with the sphere of artistry, drama and performance, it also encompasses the meaning of interpretation, expression and explanation (cf. Palmer, 1969). In the study reported here, there is evidence in favour of the interpretation that for the chairman giving room means that creative leadership is primarily about 'giving room for expression' (B7, B11). It seems as though the 'room for explanation' (B1) that he found so attractive in the early days of his career, has been exhausted.

Bringing these two interpretations together, creative leadership could be interpreted as 'giving the big-ego journalists a stage for expression'. But what is being expressed? I would like to suggest that yet another specification can be made, namely that to give room means to 'give the big-ego journalists an external stage upon which to express themselves publicly before a big audience, and an internal stage to express themselves before their colleagues and the chief editor'.

The social construction of creative leadership

In a social constructionist perspective (cf. Berger and Luckmann, 1966), the accounts of the chief editor and the chairman of the board could be seen as externalizations of the meaning of creative leadership as it is objectivated in the managerial discourse on creative leadership, and of their own subjective meanings of creative leadership. To take the second of these first, we could say that these meanings reflect the leaders' internalization of the institutionalized actions that are conveyed in the everyday life of their papers and in the newspaper business in general.

The basis for the leaders' construction of creative leadership as 'giving room' is the reciprocal typification of habitualized actions by types of actors into roles. For instance, the construction of the creative leader as a 'giver' presupposes the existence of a construction of the followers as 'takers'. In the accounts above, the role of 'takers' is played by creative, big-ego journalists and ordinary reporters, and the distinction between 'givers' and 'takers' is reaffirmed on an ongoing basis in the actors' interactions with each other at the paper. By attending morning meetings for creative ideas and seminars for the discovery of creative ideas, for instance, the different actors learn what it means to be a creative leader, a big-ego journalist or a reporter who does the bread-and-butter jobs on the paper. And, as they externalize their beings into these arenas for social interaction, they simultaneously internalize one another as being part of an objective reality.

The processes of socialization into creativity in these arenas entail the moulding of creative identities. Through identification with creative leaders as significant others, aspiring creative leaders learn to ask creative questions, get promoted to creative positions, appear on the right creative stages, and are finally appointed as chief editors or board chairmen. At this stage, they experience a sense of belonging; they know that they have something in common with creative leaders and that they are somehow different from other leaders. In short, they know that they are creative leaders. The 'room' given by the creative leadership is thus not only produced by creative leadership; it also constitutes the arenas for the social (re)production of the construction of creative leadership as 'giving room'.

Once crystallized, the identity of the creative leader is maintained, modified or reshaped by the social structure at the paper. But as all the stages, all the arenas that constitute the transition from journalist to creative leader are structured by creative leaders, creative leadership can be interpreted as the 'explainer' or 'justifier' of the institutionalized order inherent to the social structure. The creative leaders thus (re)produce creative leadership and thereby themselves.

Thus, in the dialectic between creative arenas and creative actors, creative leadership is simultaneously both product and producer. But, who are the actors and what are the arenas that are being (re)produced by this creative leadership? Let me once again examine the accounts of the chief editor and the board chairman. But before that, I would like to position the material in an institutional, or rather an ideo-historical, frame of reference. The purpose of this is twofold: it provides a language that 'gives room' (sic!) for interpretations and, as will become apparent, it throws some light on certain processes of internalization of objectivated knowledge in the social construction of creative leadership.

Metaphors of creativity

In working towards a new theory of action based on creative action, Joas (1996) proffers a typology characterizing the most important forms in which ideas of creativity surface and are influential in society. He does this by examining and deconstructing works of some of the most influential philosophers of our time: Dewey, Schopenhauer, Marx, and Habermas among others. From the period 1750–1850 he singles out three conceptions of creativity, or metaphors as he calls them, as being of the utmost importance.

'The idea of *expression* circumscribes creativity primarily in relation to the subjective world of the actor. The idea of *production* relates creativity to the objective world, the world of material objects that are the conditions and means of action. And finally, the idea of *revolution* assumes that there is a potential of human creativity relative to the social world, namely that we can fundamentally reorganize the social institutions that govern human co-existence.'

(Joas, 1996, p. 71)

Creativity as expression is related to the romanticism of *Sturm und Drang* that, according to Joas, succeeded the works of Herder; creativity as production and creativity as revolution emerged mainly from the works of Marx. Each and every one of these metaphors anchors creativity as a way of relating to the world.

These different meanings of creativity, with their accompanying ways of relating to the world, are all inherent in the social stock of knowledge. They are historically objectified constructions of creativity, embedded in culture, and existing side by side. However, in as much as knowledge is socially distributed, so too are the meanings of creativity distributed among different institutional sub-worlds and different types of actor.

Now, there is reason to believe that the managerial discourse on creative leadership transcends these different institutional sub-worlds, such that when creative leadership is spoken of, a variety of institution-alized meanings of creativity are made present. From an interactionist perspective (cf. Crozier and Friedberg, 1980; Sjöstrand, 1985, 1997; Weick, 1995) it could be argued that the managerial discourse on creative leadership is both a product and a (re)producer of these institutionalized notions of creativity.

However, since externalizations of this discourse are grounded in the identity constructions of creative leaders, the (re)production of the institutionalized notions of creativity follows the stratification of the institutional sub-worlds. This means that, due to their past moments of socialization and present moments of experience, creative leaders in their actions, in different arenas, (re)produce different notions of creativity.

Creationalists and creomantics

Starting from this idea of stratification in this interpretation of the actors and arenas being (re)produced by the creative leadership, I have also used Joas' metaphors of creativity have also been used to generate differentiating theoretical concepts that are not only empirically possible, but also highly probable. From the accounts of the chief editor and the chairman I have constructed a typology by intensifying some of the aspects of creative leadership that the two leaders found meaningful. The chief editor is found mainly to be (re)producing the notion of creativity as production; the chairman is found mainly to be (re)producing the notion of creativity as expression and revolution. The first of these externalizations of creative leadership is called *Creationalist*, and the second *Creomantic*.

Although the following portraits of the Creationalist and the Creomantic leaders are rather roughly sketched, it can be claimed that in a Weberian sense the two constructs represent ideal types of creative leadership (cf. Weber, 1962, 1968). As ideal types, creationalist and creomantic leadership should be seen as a heuristic instrument for descriptive classification that mediates direct empirical understandings of reality, and not as corresponding to real phenomena.

A creationalist tale

The chief editor sees the morning meetings as an important instrument (A18). From his account we might conclude that it is also the most important instrument for creativity. Thus his use of the word instrument pretty much sums up the kind of arenas that are being constructed at *Finanstidningen*, namely, rationalistic ones. Or, as I have dubbed them in order to emphasize their creative features, creationalist arenas. The top-of-the-mind model stands as the very symbol of these.

First of all, the top-of-the-mind model ties the desired end result – creative ideas – to the specific means – creative dialogues, etc. From the chief editor's point of view, the structuring of the morning meeting could be interpreted as a clear-cut example of instrumental rationality (cf. Sjöstrand, 1997), but the chosen means, that is to say the top-of-the-mind model, makes it more of a procedural kind. However, it is nevertheless rationalistic in the sense that it is assumed that the reporters are guided by the creative goals that have been set.

Secondly, the overarching goal of the model, as well as of the editorial role, is the maximization of the value of the paper to its readers. In this regard, the model is an instrument for news evaluation, and it is assumed that the value of a news item is objectively given (A8), and that it is possible to order news in terms of value (A4). It is also assumed that creativity can be objectively measured by counting the number of lead stories that a reporter has produced (A12). These are all aspects that are reckoned to be characteristic of the notion of economic man (cf. Sjöstrand, 1985, 1993). The assumptions of *homo oeconomicus* inherent in the model is further confirmed by its psychological and cognitive foundation (A3, A5).

Considering that it is the account of the chief editor of a financial paper that is being scrutinized, and that the majority of the reporters have degrees in economics (A16), the interpretation of the arena as rationalistic is almost trivial, as is the handy interpretation that the reporters internalize and externalize themselves as economic men. For instance, it is symptomatic that the reporters refer to each other as belonging to either the 'micro' or the 'macro', terms taken from neo-classical economics. However, relating these interpretations to the metaphors of creativity in Joas (1996) and to the issue of identity construction, gives rise to a more complicated picture.

Returning to the purpose of the top-of-the-mind model, this could be rephrased in terms of 'bringing forth a dimension that no one has thought of' (A20). Together with the model's rationalistic assumptions of economic man, this corresponds very well with the meaning that Karl Marx attributed to labour as 'pro-duction', that is, '... the bringing forth of something new in the world' (Joas, 1996, p. 91). And, in turn, this Marxist metaphor corresponds well with the way in which the creative identities are being constructed at the paper.

When the chief editor portrays himself as head of production (A2), he is simultaneously placing himself in opposition to the reporters, that is to say to the 'producers' or the 'labourers'. And, compared to them, he is in another position. First of all, in light of his right of interpretation regarding creativity, he is the only one to be in a position that enables him to fully recognize himself in what has been created. Secondly, it is he who fronts the paper (A1) and gets credit for its successes – as well as its failures. Thus, in terms of a Marxist frame of reference, expression and appropriation go hand in hand. For the reporters, however, the situation could be alienating. They are only 'given room' for a highly structured and controlled pro-duction, and the surplus-value that they generate is appropriated by the readers of the paper, that is, the capitalists of the financial markets (A1).

However, promotion as a result of being creative offers an escape from alienation. Promotion, though, is something that is exclusively for the chosen ones, in other words for those who either possess the creative trait from the beginning (A6) or those who manage to learn to ask the questions that the chief editor regards as right. These creative reporters are given the assignments that lead out of alienation, leaving their uncreative colleagues to do the 'bread-and-butter jobs on the paper' (A12).

A creomantic tale

Creative leadership as the (re)production of a creative élite is perhaps even more apparent in the case of the chairman of the board, as he consciously acknowledges the status and privileges being given to the big-ego journalists and the creative leader (B10, B16). From a Marxist perspective, his part in constructing big-ego journalists could be seen as an act of ennoblement of the creative bourgeoisie, and his part in the construction of the creative arenas as a means of upholding his privileged position.

However, in directing attention towards the problems that accompany this ennoblement, the chairman does not talk for the most part in accordance with the metaphor of creativity as production. Rather, as he describes life at the paper in terms of competition (B3), struggle (B10), aggressiveness (B11) and harassment (B15), his accounts fall back on a revolutionary vocabulary. And life at the paper could indeed be interpreted as an arena for struggle between the classes of big egos and small egos, with the fair-minded leader (B16) steering things to avoid the worst clashes (B11–12) by being concrete (B16). To use Marx's words, this could be seen as materialistic leadership. But, in the Marxist sense of the reorganization of social institutions, the struggle is not revolutionary. It may once have had that meaning (B1), but this has now come to an end (B3–B5). Instead, it is now a struggle for the right to express identity. And the identities being expressed are those of the artist (B16), the hero (B1), the rebel (B1), and the father (B16).

It can thus be argued that, despite the chairman's description of the abandoning of the romantic myth, life at *Aftonbladet* is grounded upon a conception of creativity as (revolutionary) expression. Given the romantic connotation that goes with Herder's expressionism, creative leadership in this setting could be described as creomantic.

The unintended consequences of creative leadership

In this chapter I have tried to throw some light on the managerial discourse on creative leadership by examining the accounts of two creative leaders in a social constructionist perspective. I have indicated how creative leadership is constructed in processes of social interaction and the internalization of culturally embedded notions of creativity. As Berger and Luckmann (1966, p. 152) would have put it, creative leadership entails the dialectic between objectively assigned and subjectively appropriated identities.

I have also tried to show that creative leadership is not objective in the sense that it is 'out there' or 'in there', as theorists in the field of creativity have so often assumed. Creative leaders were not born creative leaders, they have *become* creative leaders. And, by using their positions to ennoble their underlings by raising them to creative positions, they play an active part in the (re)production of their own creative identities. To adopt a concept often used by Bourdieu (1988, 1998), creative becoming is an act of (self) consecration. And to continue along the same line of reasoning, the outcome of this consecration is an identity that not only differentiates creative leaders from other leaders, but also gives them a social capital of legitimacy (Bourdieu, 1984, 1988, 1998) that allows them to define creativity.

However, the use of this capital seems to generate consequences that contradict the leaders' intentions. Instead of bringing forth new ideas and discoveries into the world, the creationalist leader produces the alienating notion of economic man; instead of giving the journalists a stage for expressing identities, the creomantic leader gives artists, heroes, and rebels an arena that is a battleground for conflict.

The beneficiaries of these unintended consequences are those who conform to the objectivated notions of creativity. In the creationalist setting, it is the reporter who asks the right questions who leaves the field victorious; in the world of creomantics, the winner is the humble artist with the biggest ego. It is only those who present themselves and their actions in relation to the creationalist and the creomantic ideal who will be perceived, judged and labelled as creative. The rest are excluded from the creative arena.[5]

Thus, it becomes apparent what creative leadership is *not* about. It is not about being egalitarian (cf. McCall, 1980). It is not about impartially providing people with equal opportunities. It is not about 'giving room' for anybody. Rather, creative leadership is about making distinctions.

This 'hidden' aspect of creative leadership is a very important one, since it turns creative leadership into a question of opening and closing arenas and opportunities, a question of choice and rejection, and a question of those who get in without applying and those who will never get in.

Creative leaders or prisoners of the past?

The discourse on creative leadership is thus undermined by the very philosophy on which it is based. Instead of 'giving room' for creativity, creative leadership (re)produces institutionalized conceptions of creativity that are deeply rooted in socio-historical structures. Taken to extremes, the managerial discourse on creative leadership can be seen as a social hoax aimed at maintaining the status quo (cf. Bennis, 1989).

In a social constructionist perspective the notion of the creative leader as causer of creativity is thus a myth. Although, as a myth, it makes perfect sense: it explains, it expresses, and it provides a narrative, a ready-made recipe that carries past and present into the future. But, seductive in style and logically consistent as it is, it obscures the fact that the sense it does make is one of many, and thus it obscures its own foundations, that is to say that it is created within a social discourse, as too are its consequences – the (re)production of the status quo.

The notion of the creative leader as a causer of creativity, and indeed the whole managerial discourse on creative leadership, could thus be seen as a psychic prison, an iron cage of creativity, in which managers have become trapped by their own conception of creativity as a trait attaching to the individual. In idealizing the creative leader, they run the risk of cutting themselves off from the capacity for critical thinking, from visions, inspirations, and emotions (cf. Gemmill and Oakley, 1992) – and, most importantly, they run the risk of failing in their ambition to 'give room' for creativity. However, if the objectivist trait perspective on leadership and creativity is abandoned in favour of a social constructionist stance, a creative liberation of managerial leaders comes closer.

Notes

1 Based on the number of hits on *kreativ* (i.e. creative) and *ledar* (i.e. leader) in the electronic database *Affärsdata* containing articles from the main Swedish business papers and journals. In 1993, 88 hits were found; in 1994, 106; in 1995, 114; in 1996, 161; in 1997, 182; and in 1998, 210.

2 For example *Komptensgruppen* and *Kompetensmässan, Lustra* (Management Development and Strategy) at *Chalmer Innovation, Psykosyntes Akademien,* and *Swedish Institute of Management.*

3 For example Swedish translation of Bolman and Deal's (1991) *Reframing Organizations: Artistry, Choice, and Leadership,* San Francisco: Jossey-Bass *(in Swedish Nya perspektiv på organisationer: Kreativitet, val och ledarskap)* in use, for example, at the Stockholm School of Economics and at the universities of Gothenburg and Umeå.

4 To facilitate interpretation of the two accounts, quotations from the Chief Editor have been labelled A1 to A21, and the quotations from the Chairman of the Board B1 to B18.

5 It is important to note here that creative action, from religious beliefs, via Joas' metaphors of creativity, to the creationalist and the creomantic tales, is gender-typed. Creative action *is* male action, and, as such, women are *a priori* seen as 'the Other', inferior and different from the norm of male creativity and the male creative leader.

References

Bass, B. M. (1985). *Leadership and Performance Beyond Expectations.* Free Press, New York.

Bennis, W. G. (1989). *Why Leaders Can't Lead: The Unconscious Conspiracy Continues.* Jossey-Bass, San Francisco.

Bennis, W. G., and Nanus, B. (1985). *Leaders: The Strategies for Taking Charge.* Harper & Row, New York.

Berger, P. L., and Luckmann, T. (1966). *The Social Construction of Reality.* Anchor Books, London.

Bloom, A. (1987). *The Closing of the American Mind.* Simon & Schuster, New York.

Bourdieu, P. (1984). *Distinction: A Social Critique of the Judgement of Taste.* Routledge, London.

Bourdieu, P. (1988). *Homo Academicus.* Polity Press, Cambridge.

Bourdieu, P. (1998). *On Television.* New Press, New York.

Burns, J. M. (1978). *Leadership.* Harper & Row, New York.

Conger, J. A. (1989). *The Charismatic Leader: Behind the Mystique of Exceptional Leadership.* Jossey-Bass, San Francisco.

Conger, J. A., and Kanungo, R. (1987). Toward a Behavioral Theory of Charismatic Leadership in Organizational Settings. *Academy of Management Review,* vol. 12, pp. 637–47.

Connor, D. R. (1995). *Managing at the Speed of Change: How Resilient Managers Succeed and Prosper Where Others Fail.* Villard Books, New York.

Crozier, M., and Friedberg, E. (1980). *Actors and Systems.* The University of Chicago Press, Chicago.

Cyert, R. M. (1985). The Design of a Creative Academic Organization. In: Kuhn, R.L. (ed.) *Frontiers in Creative and Innovative Management.* Ballinger, Cambridge.

Czarniawska-Joerges, B., and Wolff, R. (1991). Leaders, Managers, Entrepreneurs On and Off the Organizational Stage. *Organization Studies,* vol. 12, no. 4, pp. 529–46.

Ekvall, G. (1988). *Förnyelse och Friktion. Om organisation, kreativitet och innovation.* Natur och Kultur, Borås.

Ford, C., and Gioia, D. (1995). *Creative Actions in Organizations*. Sage, London.

Gemmill, G., and Oakley, J. (1992). Leadership: An Alienating Social Myth? *Human Relations*, vol. 45, no. 2, pp. 113–29.

Gergen, K. J. (1985). The Social Constructionist Movement in Modern Psychology. *American Psychologist*, vol. 40, pp. 266–75.

Guilford, J. P. (1950). Creativity. *American Psychologist*, vol. 5, pp. 444–54.

Guilford, J. P. (1956). The Structure of Intellect. *Psychological Bulletin*, vol. 53, pp. 267–93.

Guilford, J. P. (1957). Creative Abilities in the Arts. *Psychological Review*, vol. 64, no. 2, pp. 110–18.

Joas, H. (1996). *The Creativity of Action*. Polity Press, Cambridge.

Kotter, J. P. (1996). *Leading Change*. Harvard Business School Press, Boston.

McCall, M. W. (1980). Conjecturing About Creative Leaders. *Journal of Creative Behavior*, vol. 14, pp. 225–42.

Palmer, R. (1969). *Hermeneutics*. Northwestern University Press, Evanston.

Parker, I., and Shotter, J. (1990). *Deconstructing Social Psychology*. Routledge, New York.

Silverman, D. (1970). *The Theory of Organisations*. Heinemann, London.

Sjöstrand, S-E. (1985). *Samhällsorganisation*. Doxa, Lund.

Sjöstrand, S-E. (1993). Towards a Theory of Institutional Change, in Groenewegen, J., Pitelis, C., and Sjöstrand, S-E. (eds.), *On Economic Institutions – Theory and Applications*. Edward Elgar, London.

Sjöstrand, S-E. (1997). *The Two Faces of Management. The Janus Factor*. Thomson, London.

Stogdill, R. M. (1974). *Handbook of Leadership: A Survey of the Literature*. Free Press, New York.

Trice, H. M., and Beyer, J. M. (1991). Cultural Leadership in Organizations. *Organization Science*, vol. 2, pp. 149–69.

Vedin, B.-A. (1985). *Corporate Culture and Creativity Management*. Studentlitteratur, Lund.

Weber, M. (1962). *Basic Concepts in Sociology*. Secaucus, New Jersey.

Weber, M. (1968). *Economy and Society: An Outline of Interpretive Sociology*. Bedminster, New York.

Weick, K. (1995). *Sensemaking in Organization*. Sage, Thousand Oaks.

CHAPTER ELEVEN

Professional norms and managerial leadership

Johan Stein

Introduction

This chapter focuses on the professionalization of work and how it relates to the construction of leadership. In particular it will be argued that the specialization of knowledge in society is affecting the role of leaders in various ways. An empirical study of how top managers in insurance firms try to lead their organizations will be used to illustrate this influence. The study will reveal the importance of 'professional fields' as the domains of interaction, in which certain beliefs and identities are produced and reproduced. It appears that these professional fields create a communication distance between individuals from various fields, which in turn leads to further professionalization and an even greater communication distance.

The empirical study is based on in-depth case studies, which are used here to enhance our understanding of the way strategies, as patterns in streams of action, are shaped over time. Particular attention was paid in the study to the challenges that had faced managers in their efforts to pursue strategic change. In this context, the question of professionalization came up in the interviews. Data was collected for the study as whole from taped interviews with 78 top-level managers in 16 insurance firms in the Stockholm area. Secondary sources, such as internal documentation and annual reports, provided further data.

A primary unit of analysis was the role of leaders in the formation of strategies. The patterns initially traced in the data were consistently compared with further data as it accumulated. This interplay between the data and the emerging patterns continued throughout the analysis. This chapter focuses on the most common themes only, which means that there is a certain amount of latent variation that is not represented in the themes presented in the chapter.

Professionalization as a phenomenon

The division of labour, as Adam Smith and Emile Durkheim among others have observed, is a central fact of industrialized societies. Groups of individuals are organized into roles that centre around specialized knowledge areas. This often leads to individuals building their working lives around roles that enhance specialized knowledge. Vygotsky (1962) argues that people belong to 'communities of practice', where they share beliefs that are both a 'signature' of their belonging to a particular community and a major source of the reproduction of beliefs and identities in this community.

In order to develop their professional knowledge, individuals tend to interact with others in the same professional area (Galaskiewicz, 1985). Naturally, there can be other reasons too for such *intra*disciplinary interaction. By trying to monopolize the supply of knowledge, people can obtain a good deal of power over others in the competition for the economic rents created. Further, this collectivization around knowledge areas may also stem from tradition or from people's individual efforts to legitimize themselves in relation to others (Larson, 1977; Freidson, 1986). Control of group members is often used to create the reliability and accountability needed to acquire status in society.

Several of the managers interviewed in the study of the Swedish life insurance firms noted the problems they had encountered in managing personnel in specialized knowledge areas. Obviously, this appeared to be particularly troublesome for managers who lacked knowledge in a given area. The interviews revealed that the specialization of knowledge today is making it difficult for managers to keep up with developments in several knowledge areas, which means that they are unlikely to acquire any deeper understanding of what is happening in such areas. A CEO for one of the insurance firms describes the problem as follows:

'I sometimes visit the investment office in order to sit in on their morning meetings. They (those active in the investment operations) use a terminology and a way of approaching problems that makes me feel like an outsider. I'm standing there, trying to look as if I understand something. I'm glad they don't ask me for advice.'

In his statement, the manager confesses that he doesn't understand one of the lines of business that he is responsible for. At the same time, he tries to hide this problem from the organization, so as not to lose status and power. Obviously, he becomes very dependent upon the information provided by others. A manager for the actuarial operations in another firm illustrates how much power he acquires as a result of professionalization.

> 'An actuary has a special competence that provides him with a certain status. This means that ... if I express my opinion as a professional actuary there are very few questions about it internally in a company like this, since there's no one who has the competence to see through it. There are a lot of bright people who don't have the actuarial knowledge, but who do have the experience or general ability to acquaint themselves with what the actuarial issues really are. These people can question certain conclusions; others have to accept them.'

Apparently, the actuaries, as a group, have acquired an autonomy that makes it difficult for 'outsiders', including managers, to question the job they are doing. Although the actuaries don't have a special union, they have organizations where they discuss mainly technical issues.

Hence, the manifold nature and the complexity of the interdependencies among people with the same functional role in society in terms of knowledge, can obviously affect beliefs and identities at the individual and at the group levels (cf. Larson, 1977; Galaskiewicz, 1985).

It became clear from the interviews that the division of labour in society most certainly affects management and organizations. Although organizations may involve groups possessing different knowledge and occupying different functional roles, there are often one or more particular areas of knowledge that form the basis for an organization's existence (Hannan and Freeman, 1989). It is not only a question of technological knowledge, but also of knowledge about customer demands, norms and values in society, etc. Such knowledge in an organization is also something that the organizational members try to communicate to the business environment in order to create a legitimate and powerful role for themselves and the organization (ibid.).

DiMaggio and Powell (1991, p. 70) observe that members of an occupation engage in a struggle to '... define the conditions and methods of their work, to control the production of producers, and to establish a cognitive base and legitimization for their occupational autonomy'. In making this claim, the authors emphasize the role of education and professional networks in the development of beliefs and identities. In addition, they suggest that the selection of individuals is an important mechanism in the course of professionalization (DiMaggio and Powell, 1991). They give examples of the way this selection can be reflected in organizations in the norms and values internalized by way of recruitment, training, promotion and control mechanisms. Individuals thus become socialized into a frame of beliefs that include norms, values and expectations. Such socialization processes can of course vary in strength, but generally it appears that socialization is a necessary requirement for individuals to become members of a professional collective.

The taken-for-granted manner whereby internalized beliefs influence the role of managers and managerial leadership has been captured in several studies. Murray (1985), for instance, compared 1425 managers in two industries (food and petroleum), and found that the executives there had on average 20 years' experience not only in their particular industry, but also in a particular firm. He also reported that during this period managers were exposed to a learning process that led to a sharing of beliefs. In a case study of 15 general managers, Kotter (1982) concluded that the studied managers were not generalists, but that they possessed specialized knowledge, an 'agenda', about their respective firms and industries, which included knowledge about whom they should contact for various purposes. This study shows how important it is for managers to be part of the core knowledge area in a firm.

The question of managers' industry-related knowledge was also addressed by Spender (1989) in a study of three industries in the UK, which emphasized the mutual professional proximity of managers within inter-organizational settings. Spender shows how the studied managers shared certain beliefs, or 'business recipes', about how to run a firm in a particular industry. Hence, as a group, top managers can be socialized into a set of beliefs, which then guides their interpretations and actions. The case of the insurance sector described above illustrates how the domains of interaction pivot around professional areas. The chief executives have their associations, while the actuaries, investors and marketing people all have theirs. These associations often have a long history. For example, the Swedish Life Insurance Companies' Association of Management Directors (*Svenska Livförsäkringsbolagens Direktörsförening*) was founded in 1906 (replaced in 1948 by the Swedish Life Insurance Companies Association). Other associations include the Actuarial Committee of Swedish Life Insurance Companies and the Insurance Companies' Marketing Committee.

Pfeffer (1981) and Kanter (1977) have also documented something resembling a managerial order of succession that applies to certain professions within organizations and sectors. There is evidence that interorganizational professionalization is fostered by the flow of individuals between organizations (e.g. Galaskiewicz, 1985, 1991; DiMaggio, 1991).

The construction of professional beliefs

'The interplay between the individual and collective levels is crucial for the understanding of how professional beliefs are produced and reproduced.'

(Berger and Luckmann, 1966, p. 21)

In cognitive terms, individuals develop beliefs about the way things are and the way things should be done, in the form of cognitive schemes and scripts (Anderson, 1985). Together with emotions, these cognitions are used to create meaning out of the contextual stimuli that continuously confront the individual. Two principles are involved here: reduction and extrapolation (Reed, 1988). Reduction means that the amount of information is reduced in order to create meaning, while extrapolation refers to the recovery of information from the long-term memory to add information to the sensory input.

The creation of meaning can become automatic as it proceeds without intention and without giving rise to conscious awareness (Posner, 1989). Very distinct signals from the social context may be needed to raise the awareness of individuals (ibid.). Berger and Luckmann (1966, p. 78) note that individuals even possess the ability to externalize themselves from their internalizations – and that man '... is capable of producing a world that he then experiences as something other than a human product'. According to cognitive theory, people are forced to take certain things for granted, due to their limited information-processing capacity (Simon, 1989). Other scholars have observed that individual people's emotions consciously or unconsciously influence the extent to which individuals acquire and change their beliefs (hence, learn) (LeDoux, 1996).

The interviews with the top executives in the life insurance firms revealed how the managers had been trying to create emotional ties between the company and its employees, not least due to their fear that the employees might leave and go to work for their competitors. However, several of the interviewed managers mention how difficult it is to change people's values.

'We are very dependent upon (the employees') values and their way of thinking. We cannot change this easily. Instead, we have to take account of how they think and function when we want to make a change. [...] There are professional groups in these firms as in every other industry.'

According to managers working with specific professional groups, many specialists have closer emotional ties with their professional colleagues than with their company. In addition they often feel emotional links with their particular knowledge area, and consequently identify themselves with it and seek to legitimate their actions among other professionals in the same field. Their status among their fellow professionals is more important to them than any other kind. A manager's ability to judge the performance of different specialists appears to be crucial to winning their trust and thus being able to lead them.

Domains of interaction and the formation of identities

The concentration of social interaction to certain domains affects the identities of both groups and individuals. Various forms of identity can be uncovered here. The view that individual people have of themselves, within the frame of their own beliefs, can be referred to as an internal identity. People's internal identities then give rise to certain expectations about them and others. The shared beliefs that are entertained about any individual in their own environment can be defined as that individual's external identity.

The external identity represents an important influence on the development of the internal identity, since the beliefs about individual people are shared among those in their environment, where the beliefs function as cognitive preconceptions. An individual does not need to share these preconceptions, in order to perceive the expectations generated by the external identity. However, it has been claimed that it is more or less impossible for individual people to understand these expectations if they do not also share the preconceptions (Schutz, 1964).

Following Scheler and Mannheim, Schutz (1964) distinguishes between 'in-groups' and 'out-groups', basing the distinction on the sharing of beliefs. The members of an in-group have a 'collective self-interpretation' or inside view of their own social embeddedness (Schutz, 1964). He suggests that the members of these in-groups have 'we-relations' with one another, and that within this circle their experiences are 'genuinely understood' (Schutz, 1970). In his own words (1970, p. 166): 'The participants in an ongoing we-relation apprehend this relation only in the shared experiences which refer, by necessity, to the specific partner confronting them.' In 'they-relations', the experiences are not shared, but participants 'know of their co-existence' (Schutz, 1964).

On a basis of the arguments presented by Schutz and others (e.g. Goffman, 1959; Berger and Luckmann, 1966), we can say that an individual's beliefs and identity are influenced primarily by the expectations of those whom – because of shared beliefs and joint participation in a we-relationship – that individual understands best. It is their own perception of the social expectations about themselves that influence individual people's behaviour. These expectations are likely to be accepted if they are congruent with the individual's own experiences (cf. Goffman, 1959).

Since the internal identities of individuals or groups are affected by changes in their beliefs, any development in their beliefs (i.e. learning) will affect their internal identities. Furthermore, part of each individual's external identity is related to their functional role or roles in society. Changes in an individual's or a group's external identity may stem from changes in knowledge areas in society as a whole. The internal identity of group members may change as a result of changes in the knowledge possessed by others either inside or outside the group.

Moreover, new experiences may be overly distorted to fit the beliefs that dominate in an interaction domain, such that details or discriminative differences are ignored and stereotypes are likely to flourish (Galaskiewicz, 1985).

The empirical study of the insurance sector makes a strong case for a particular effect of professionalization, namely that it leads to homogenization of strategies as patterns in streams of action. This relation emerges most clearly in the case of investment and actuarial operations.

> 'I cannot distinguish any kind of ideational considerations between the companies in their investment function. Everyone has been forced to conform to a certain line of business, and to provide themselves with the competence necessary to act accordingly.'

The professionalization of the investment function is described as very strong in its effects. It seems to be more or less impossible for individual firms not to comply with the general development of knowledge in this area.

> 'Given the development of the financial markets, we have been forced to apply more advanced techniques and methods, and to be more professional.'

It is evident that many firms try to position themselves as unique in relation to different customer groups in various types of advertising. However, several managers observe that the homogenization of firms that is provoked by professionalization, is problematic in that it limits the freedom of the individual firm to act independently. The role of the leader as a person who chooses among strategic alternatives thus also becomes more restricted. The institutionalization of certain practices is so strong that it appears to be difficult for individual managers not to comply with it.

Collective identities

A collective identity can also be divided into internal and external subtypes. The first of these, the internal collective identity, can thus be seen as the view that collective members have of their own collective. The external identity of a collective corresponds to the beliefs about the collective held by those who don't have a we-relationship with it. Within an organization there may be several collectives that share different beliefs and, as a result, probably different internal identities too. In a review of the literature, Meyerson and Martin (1987) observe that organizations seldom have a coherent identity. The empirical study of the insurance sector (see above) clearly supports this conclusion. Several managers apparently regard the heterogenization that follows professionalization as a problem, since they are anxious to emphasize the importance of trying to create organizational identities to include all the employees.

From a cognitive viewpoint it seems difficult to argue that an organization could ever have a coherent internal identity, since its members do not share the same beliefs. However, even if the members only share a limited range of beliefs, this can still be an important building block in an organizational identity. Since one individual can share beliefs with more than one collective (Friedland and Alford, 1991), it is possible that the identities formed in one collective may be transferred to other collectives via individuals. Due, for instance, to its size and/or status, a group within an organization can thus influence other groups to adopt its identity and the identity of the organization as a whole (see the case described below). Sometimes, of course, only certain aspects of an identity are adopted, so that the various collectives retain a certain uniqueness in their respective identities. There often appears to be an inclination among groups to maintain a certain degree of autonomy regarding their identities vis-à-vis an organization as a whole. This uniqueness is noted as something that holds a group together and reduces the uncertainty of individuals (cf. Weber, 1947; Wuthnow, 1987). The various kinds of group identity that appear in organizations seem to be related to such factors as professional skills, hierarchical positions and/or ethnic background (cf. Goffman, 1959; Geertz, 1973).

The beliefs shared within an organization need to be adaptive to the broader socio-cultural context in order to survive (Hannan and Freeman, 1989). Population ecologists note that knowledge of the norms and values that define what actions are legitimate in the environment are crucial for survival (Hannan and Freeman, 1989). Hence, an organization can have several identities that are all regarded as legitimate. From a leadership perspective, it seems that the ability to handle the variety of demands associated with the various interest groups in the environment must be an important skill (Scott and Meyer, 1991). Consequently, organizations need individuals – information managers and chief executive officers, for instance – who know how to handle the environmental demands. Hence, there is still a need for the knowledge commanded by generalists even in firms that are highly specialized in certain areas of knowledge.

However, the interviews indicate that generalists may run into trouble if they try to manage specialized areas. For instance, in several of the studied firms, it is apparent that top managers often misjudge the possibilities of some new technology. This problem is most obvious in the case of information technology. A CEO of one of the companies confessed that the requirements he has set with regard to new information systems are too high. Therefore, it takes a very long time to develop the systems.

> 'The implementation of strategies is imbued with a substantial degree of inertia. It only takes me a couple of weeks to formulate a product that seems good, but it can then take two years to implement the product into technical systems.'

Sometimes the professional groups complicate matters. One of the managers interviewed argued that this could be very troublesome, if some change is necessary.

> 'The change process is very weak in many companies, and this is due to the actuaries who want insurance products with excessively intricate technical ingredients. They complicate rather than simplify the products.'

If the professional group gains too much autonomy in relation to other parts of the organization or the environment, it can obviously take a long time for managers who lack the relevant expertise to see this, and to act. In the interviews several managers argued that the move towards greater specialization generates a demand for managers who are both specialists and generalists. They need the knowledge, status and legitimacy to lead groups of specialists, but they also need to handle the variety of requirements that face the different groups.

Concluding remarks

The discussion presented in this chapter reflects the link between the role of leadership and the professionalization that accompanies increasing specialization. This means that the construction of the leadership role is affected by growing professionalization.

It seems that professionalization can cause various problems for managers who lack knowledge of the relevant specialized areas. Hence, the specialization of knowledge areas appears to be creating a demand for managers who are also area specialists. This development stems from several factors. To be part of the group identity, to have – in Schutz's words – a we-relationship, is important if a manager is to win the trust necessary for leadership. To take an active part in the specialized language games seems to be necessary in order to understand what is going on. Managers who are unable to take part in the specialized language games are likely to face various problems associated with the communication distance – i.e. to understand and to be understood.

Consequently, professional groups may thus acquire considerable autonomy in relation to top management, to other parts of the organization and to the environment. This autonomy can thereafter increase the 'distance' to these groups – a distance that is related not only to the specialization of knowledge, but also to norms, values, interests, emotions, etc. As individuals begin to identify themselves as a group, which is a process that can stem from increasing specialization, in-group socialization is also likely to be fostered. Managers working in areas of specialized knowledge therefore need to be able to handle the various kinds of distance relative to other groups.

Generalists, who are not part of the group identity, will have to rely on the knowledge possessed by others. The generalists interviewed in our study have tried to solve this problem in a number of ways. Creating emotional ties with the organization is one common strategy. For instance, top management may emphasize an organizational identity that includes various professional identities. It is noticeable that none of the interviewed generalists has attempted to outmanoeuvre the various professional groups.

Generalists are obviously needed in order to coordinate various activities within firms, and to handle relationships with a variety of interests in the environment. Specialists may face problems here, since they are likely to be infused with the norms, values, languages, etc., associated with their active 'membership' of a group of specialists. The leaders of such groups face a dual challenge, since they need the trust of the specialists and of the members of other groups. The construction of leadership is consequently influenced by this duality.

References

Anderson, J. R. (1985). *Cognitive Psychology and Its Implications*. Freeman & Company, New York.

Berger, P., and Luckmann, T. (1966). *The Social Construction of Reality: A Treatise in the Sociology of Knowledge*. Penguin Books, London.

DiMaggio, P. J. (1991). Constructing an organizational field as a professional project: U.S. art museums, 1920–1940. In Powell, W. W., and DiMaggio, P. J. (eds.), *The New Institutionalism in Organizational Analysis*, pp. 267–92. University of Chicago Press, Chicago.

DiMaggio, P. J., and Powell, W. W. (1991). The iron cage revisited: Institutional isomorphism and collective rationality in organizational fields. In Powell, W. W., and DiMaggio, P. J. (eds.), *The New Institutionalism in Organizational Analysis*, pp. 63–82. University of Chicago Press, Chicago.

Friedland, R., and Alford, R. R. (1991). Bringing society back in: Symbols, practices, and institutional contradictions. In Powell, W. W., and DiMaggio, P. J. (eds.), *The New Institutionalism in Organizational Analysis*, pp. 232–66. University of Chicago Press, Chicago.

Freidson, E. (1986). *Professional Powers: A study of the institutionalization of formal knowledge*. University of Chicago Press, Chicago.

Galaskiewicz, J. (1985). Professional networks and the institutionalization of a single mind set, *American Sociological Review*, vol. 50, pp. 639–58.

Galaskiewicz, J. (1991). Making corporate actors accountable: Institution-building in Minneapolis – St. Paul. In Powell, W. W., and DiMaggio, P. J. (eds.), *The New Institutionalism in Organizational Analysis*, pp. 293–310. University of Chicago Press, Chicago.

Geertz, C. (1973). *The Interpretation of Cultures*. Basic Books, New York.

Goffman, E. (1959). *The Presentation of Self in Everyday Life*. Doubleday Publishing, Garden City, NY.

Hannan, M. T., and Freeman, J. (1989). *Organizational Ecology* Harvard University Press. Cambridge, Mass.

Kanter, R. (1977). *Men and Women of the Corporation*. Basic Books, New York.

Kotter, J. P. (1982). *The General Managers*. The Free Press, New York.

Larson, M. S. (1977). *The Rise of Professionalism: A Sociological Analysis*, University of California Press, Berkeley.

LeDoux, J. (1996). *The Emotional Brain*. Simon and Schuster, New York.

Meyerson, D., and Martin, J. (1987). External change: An integration of three different views, *Journal of Management Studies*, vol. 24, pp. 623–46.

Murray, V. (1985). Taking stock of organizational decline management: Some issues and illustrations from an empirical study, *Journal of Management*, vol. 11, pp. 111–23.

Pfeffer, J. (1981). *Power in Organizations*. Pitman, Marshfield, Mass.

Posner, M. I. (1989). *Foundations of Cognitive Science*. MIT Press, Cambridge, Mass.

Reed, S. K. (1988). *Cognition: Theory and Applications.* Brooks and Cole Publishing, Pacific Grove, CA.

Schutz, A. (1964). *Collected Papers II: Studies in Social Theory.* Martinus Nijhoff, The Hague.

Schutz, A. (1970). *On Phenomenolgy and Social Relations.* University of Chicago Press, Chicago.

Scott, R., and Meyer, J. (1991). The organization of societal sectors: Propositions and early evidence. In Powell, W. W., and DiMaggio, P. J. (eds.), *The New Institutionalism in Organizational Analysis,* pp. 108–40. University of Chicago Press, Chicago.

Simon, H. A. (1989). *Models of Thought, vol. 2.* Yale University Press, New Haven.

Spender, J.-C. (1989). *Industry Recipes: The Nature and Sources of Managerial Judgement.* Basil Blackwell, Oxford.

Vygotsky, L.S. (1962). *Thought and Language.* MIT Press, Cambridge, Mass.

Weber, M. (1964/1947). *The Theory of Social and Economic Organization.* Oxford University Press, New York.

Weick, K. (1979). *The Social Psychology of Organizing.* Addison-Wesley, Belmont.

Wuthnow, R. (1987). *Meaning and Moral Order: Explorations in External Analysis.* University of California Press, Berkeley, California.

CHAPTER TWELVE

Constructing leadership in small talk

Gunnar Ekman

Introduction

This chapter will try to shed some light on the relation between the actions of organization members on the one hand, and the written texts and the managers whose intention it is to direct such actions, on the other. In doing so I will challenge traditional hierarchic thinking and illustrate the dilemma that arises for management when texts produced by one set of actors are expected to play a part in the management of actions produced by another set. We are dealing here with situations in which the interaction between those who produce the texts and those who produce the actions is limited.

The following pages will consider the production of texts as a form of leadership construction, and investigate what happens when there is little or no reasonably close or continuous contact with vertical management (with or without texts). The traditional hierarchic leadership construction in terms of leaders and led is then replaced by a construction of leadership in a horizontal social process, occurring among those who are expected to take action. The argument is made that leadership is produced, reproduced and practised in the form of small talk – an ongoing process between people, in which the written word and verbal directives regarding action are interpreted in 'rational processes of small talk'. Such horizontal small talk processes generate the construction of shared perceptions of actions, and it is these – rather than the hierarchies represented by managers and the official texts – that actually guide the actors 'on the job'.

The following exploration of the relation between text and formal leadership on the one hand, and action on the other, has been based on an earlier study of a Swedish neighbourhood police outfit. There are several reasons for this choice, the first being that the police force is an organization whose organized actions we assume to be governed by texts.

The second is that police actions are carried out at a physical distance from any formal managers. Police officers work almost without exception in teams of two. Another reason is that the work of the police – the meeting between the police and the public – is one that involves a high degree of uncertainty. This uncertainty that the police must cope with, can be the result of not knowing:

- when something is going to happen;

- what it is that will happen;

- whether it will involve physical violence;

- where it will happen; and finally,

- how the situation will be dealt with.

The extreme uncertainty, and thus also the great variety that characterizes police work, is expected to be governed by a large number of texts.

From text to action

People believe in the written word. This is not surprising, considering the vast quantity of texts in the world around us and the role that they play there. Everywhere we turn, there are texts, in the mass media, and in books, information brochures, rulebooks, instruction manuals, etc. The fact that texts convey information is obvious, but we also attribute other qualities to them. We perceive them as possessing the ability to steer actions in organizations. That some individuals are able to create texts that then steer others is a fundamental notion underlying the way organizations in general are managed.

Earlier research into the relation between text and action has often taken its point of departure in the processes whereby texts are created. The analysis of how people relate to texts thus starts from the way these are formulated. In research focusing on action, a common procedure has been to interview managers at different levels in an organization. However, it is difficult to capture the essence of action from interviews. People are not always aware of – or do not always want to tell about – their actions, which means that managers are often unable to describe the actions of others. The difficulty in describing both one's own and other people's actions is a general phenomenon, which Kunda and Barley (1998, p. 6) explain in the following way:

'Interviews, whether with managers or workers, are also inadequate for studying work practices because most managers do not know what their employees do and because most work practices are so contextualized that even people who do the work can not articulate what they do unless they are in the process of doing it.'

In this chapter I investigate the extent to which it is possible to govern actions by means of traditional hierarchical management and the formally written texts pertaining to it. In addressing this issue, I take my point of departure in police work, in an effort to elicit the roles played by formal leadership and text. The following discussion builds on a larger study of neighbourhood police, presented in my doctoral thesis (Ekman, 1999).

Taking police work as a starting point, an empirical study based on observation has been made. From a personal standpoint, this offered a suitable approach since I have had nine years working experience as a police officer. My background in the force helped me to understand the jargon used by the police officers in the study, which in turn made it easier to acquire a wealth of empirical data. It also facilitated access to 'uncensored' data, something which is often difficult to get hold of in studies of police work (see e.g. Fielding, 1988).

For a period of three months in the autumn of 1996, I accompanied and observed members of the neighbourhood police at work. I did not wear uniform, but was in civilian clothes. The observations made during this period were complemented by interviews with approximately 15 police officers. In addition I conducted interviews with the officers' superiors and studied the written texts upon which the police work is supposed to be based. But how are these actions – which are meant to be steered by texts – to be understood?

Action

Traditionally two schools of thought have shaped the way in which most researchers see human actions. One is based on the concept of 'intention', whereby human intentions and judgements about what will happen in the future form the basis for the way a person will act. Where possible alternatives exist, known present (and future) preferences determine the choice between them. The individual is expected to be familiar with the various alternatives available and, above all, to be able to judge the future consequences of the different actions. The alternative that yields the highest value in relation to the known preferences is chosen in a process of calculation. Intentional logic can be briefly described as consisting of a number of questions that people ask themselves, such as: What am I going to like in the future? What alternatives do I have? What are the consequences of the different alternatives? And which of the consequences best suit my future preferences? (Jacobsson and Brunsson, 1998).

Intentional logic is linked to the future, and it is easy to identify a number of disadvantages attaching to it. To begin with, the future is always uncertain. Rarely can the future consequences of actions be predicted with any certainty. It is also unusual for actors to know their preferences (present and/or future) in all situations, or even to be familiar with the alternatives available to them (see Sjöstrand, 1985, 1997). Thus intentional logic alone is not enough to explain human action. Something else is also needed, namely *norms*.

Much of what people do can be explained in terms of norms, in the broad sense of the word. The environments in which people find themselves comprise a number of norms, which they follow to a greater or lesser extent. Norms influence people and help them to cope with the uncertainty that is constantly present, with respect both to other people and to 'nature'.

In the world of norms, we learn that different norms apply to different people and different situations. The actions expected of a police officer at a traffic accident are different from those expected of a doctor or a fireman. According to March and Olsen (1989), when people are confronted with diverging norms, there are three basic questions that they must ask themselves: Who am I? What situation am I in? What actions are expected of a person like me in a situation like this?

But neither intentional nor norm-based logic alone can explain the actions of human beings. Many researchers, among them Elster (1989) and March and Olsen (1998), have attempted to find answers regarding the relation between these two schools of logic. One answer is that some actions can be explained by intentional logic, others by norms. Another explanation has simply been that what people perceive as norm-based action is in fact intentional (rational). In other words, the best thing for individuals is to follow the norms obtaining in their own environment. A third approach has been to define the 'intentional' as a norm governing how individuals should act. It has been argued that such intentional action is characteristic of the western world, and this is used in turn to support the claim that intentional/rational action is in itself a norm (Elster, 1989).

However, it is beyond the scope of this chapter to solve the dilemma of the relation between intentional and norm-based action. For the purposes of the study, this chapter views the relation between the two according to the perspective proposed in March and Olsen (1998). That is, clear logic dominates unclear logic. When preferences and consequences are known but norms are ambiguous, intentional logic dominates norm-based logic. In situations where the reverse is true – where norms and preferences are distinct but consequences are not – norm-based logic dominates intentional logic. In this study it is reasonable to view the actions studied as largely norm-based, since earlier research on police work has shown many norms to be especially strong and commonly held. An examination of norms in greater depth is therefore warranted here.

The world around us is full of norms of various kinds and strengths. They co-ordinate people's actions and facilitate the cooperative efforts of groups. Thus, norms are important to, and in, organizations. Some norms are 'visible', in the sense that they are expressed through formal channels, such as texts for example. Operating plans and laws are expressions of this. Other norms are more 'invisible' and are never committed to paper. These last are often more implicit, and may also sometimes be perceived at a subconscious level only – even by those who are governed by them.

Norms tell people what to do in certain situations by identifying what is suitable or permitted or, conversely, what is unsuitable, forbidden or taboo. Norms generally apply to more than one individual and to more than one situation (e.g. Homan, 1950). They therefore have a controlling function: others will do the same thing in similar situations. Norms can be either abstract or concrete, or can appear in varying combinations of the two. Concrete norms provide direction in specific, well-defined situations while abstract norms guide actions in a more general sense. Norms are based on evaluations of experiences and are linked to the expectation that these conditions will be repeated in the future.

Expectations refer not only to conditions, incidents or events in nature, however, but also to interpersonal relationships. They can be divided into the *predictive* and the *normative*. The former refer to people believing that others will behave in a certain way, while the latter concern the way in which individuals develop preferences in their relations with others about how these others *should* behave (Sjöstrand, 1973).

A set of normative expectations constitutes a norm – i.e. a perception of how something is or should be. In cases where people are unfamiliar with each other, their expectations usually relate to function, status or position. When the relation is more personal, however, it affects the content of the expectations (Sjöstrand, 1973). For example, the behaviour expected of an unknown police officer is often different from that expected of a police officer with whom one has a personal relationship, being decided by position in the first case and person(ality) in the second. Expectations regarding compliance with a norm also vary, depending on the type of relations between the individuals involved. In some cases the origin of such expectations is obvious, in other cases not. Norms expressed as texts often have a more easily identifiable sender compared with other forms of dissemination.

As noted above, norms may be either formal and visible or informal and invisible, and thus can be expressed in many different ways. Routines, myths, rituals, talk, mental structures and texts are examples of this diversity. Norms can be socially agreed upon, such that a collective can share an understanding of how something is or should be. Socially agreed norms can be found on different levels, and some norms are likely to be shared by almost everyone in a society, while others may be specific to different individuals, groups and organizations. Actors in the same profession usually constitute such a norm-sharing collective, and in the present study the police officers represent just such a professional body.

Norms expressed in action are dependent on the approval or disapproval of others. These others indicate the norm that they expect to see followed, which in turn implies sanctions against those who do not act in accordance with it. It is often unnecessary to apply such sanctions, nor need they even be real. The very fact that people perceive sanctions or believe them to exist, and that they may be subject to them, is usually enough to make them behave in accordance with a particular norm (Napier and Gershenfeld, 1993). Some sanctions are so powerful that the norms are interpreted as 'imperative'.

As we have seen, it is often difficult to identify the origin of many norms. But there are also norms whose sources are relatively easy to pin down. Examples of these include norms that have been put in writing or some other explicit form, and that are provided by individuals other than those who are expected to follow them. Such norms are often expressed in texts and will be referred to below as directives (Jacobsson and Brunsson, 1998).

Directives are defined as norms issued by a small number of individuals for making (many) others perform certain actions. Directives are often motivated by claiming that others will benefit from following them. The common motivating factor is often related to some rather vague general value or purpose. A person who can issue directives and expect them to be followed thus commands considerable power – like managers for instance, who issue policies and rules, or politicians who make decisions on legislation.

Action and small talk

A system of directives that is supposed to govern action is usually based on the ideas and intentions formulated by one set of individuals being carried out by another such set. However, these ideas and intentions are not often visible to others (i.e. the readers). What is 'visible' are the texts and the associated talk and actions. Thus, it is through these texts, this talk and these actions that norms are produced and reproduced. This in turn occurs in human interactions, by way of what Gustafsson (1994) describes as 'small talk'.

Gustafsson claims that an individual's environment is made up to a large extent of continuous streams of talk. Naturally there are also other elements in this environment, such as things, actions and perceptions, but the crucial ingredient is *talk* – a constant flow of narratives, chatter and the exchange of opinions. People exist in the midst of a constant and habitual exchange of thoughts, views and values. Largely this small talk is trivial, or is seen as such, and is concerned with things like the weather, a neighbour's new car, and taxes – anything and everything of value and every bit of trivia. Small talk is not only used to convey information; it can also be talk for the sake of talking. Talk that touches upon something other than an individual's thoughts and intentions often leads to more or less clearly formulated statements about what is right or wrong, good or evil, or suitable or unsuitable.

Because of its evaluative content, small talk represents a process whereby human understandings are interpreted and reinterpreted with regard to what is right or wrong and good or bad. Small talk embraces individuals, topics, phenomena and states of being, and much small talk involves what could be called moralizing about what is preferred and, consequently, advocated. And since norms are also concerned with what is right and desirable for different people in different situations over time, this moralizing small talk can be said to have a *norm-reproducing* function.

Small talk can be found in all organizations. It is especially visible within professional groups, however. Some researchers suggest that for the most part professional groups spend their days 'small-talking'. They talk about their colleagues, their clients and others working with them, as well as about work and missions. Svensson (1989) claims that this talk amongst professionals plays an active part in producing common perceptions and understandings.

The relation between written words and actors differs from that between different small-talking actors. Firstly, the relation between text and actor is impersonal and, secondly, it is of a one-way kind. The directive type of text expects that certain norms will be followed by the readers – the former is a norm sender and the latter a norm follower.

Relations

It is possible to distinguish between norm senders and norm followers, as people are interactive social beings. That is, most of a person's actions occur in relation to other people.

One individual may have a number of different relations with other individuals. These relations have several important aspects. Who are the other individuals that this person is related to? Are these other individuals known or unknown to the first one? Are the relations of a co-operative or compulsory nature? Are they voluntary or forced? Are they characterized by closeness or distance? Are the relations temporary or do they last for long periods of time (Sjöstrand, 1985, 1987, 1997)?

One type of relation can be impersonal and temporary. Sjöstrand (1997) explains this as follows: An individual has a limited capacity to relate to others. As society today is so complex and specialized, it has to build to a large extent on impersonal relations. It is not possible for us to be acquainted with, or have a personal relationship with, everybody upon whom we are dependent for survival and wealth. Quite a small number of exchanges with known others has therefore been replaced by an almost uncountable number of impersonal exchanges between more or less organized people. Sjöstrand (ibid.) calls this second type of relation a *calculating* one. The lack of personal involvement and the distance between people make simple calculations necessary and efficient. In such situations, people are 'known' only as positions or functions, and any more personal information about them is not obtainable. Instead, information has to be restricted to very basic, simple visible qualities such as prices, quantities and the like, all associated with the particular exchange at hand.

But often the relation itself also has a value, a meaning, for the interacting individuals. Sjöstrand (ibid.) has described one such type of non-calculating relation as *genuine*, since such a relation involves closeness between individuals who know each other well. Family and friends are examples of this kind of relationship. Such a relation is emotive in character and those involved are not interchangeable. The relationship takes time to build; it is unique and is based on trust and confidence. It is further associated with a history of shared experiences in which the expectations of the people involved have been mutually learned.

In a third type of relation, the exchange is based on *shared ideals*. This kind of relation brings together people who do not know each other but who do share some value or ideal. Sharing ideals makes those who are otherwise unknown to one another move into a closer relationship, and helps to build up (some) degree of trust between them. Such shared ideals are then tied to sanctions of different kinds – sanctions that can be manifested by groups as well as by individuals (ibid.).

A fourth type of relation, finally, has its basis in *violence*. Violence can be manifest or latent, the latter being the more common form in work organizations. Threats and extortion of different kinds are examples of this latent form (ibid.).

The relation between text and action

The relation between the written word and the actor is usually impersonal, and is either calculating or based on ideals (the actor can share the ideals expressed by the text). But it is very seldom genuine, as the writer and the reader seldom have a close relationship. For individuals to act in accordance with a text, they have to be familiar with it and to possess the necessary resources (in the broad sense of the word). They must also understand the text and want to comply with it. If they hesitate, the sanctions for refusing must be such that, considered in relation to other alternatives, the actors decide to comply.

Earlier studies of the relation between text and action, for example Brunsson (1985), have focused on the decisions that have been recorded in texts, that is to say, on how directives are formulated. Brunsson classifies these decision processes as 'rational' or 'irrational'. In a rational decision-making process different alternatives are made visible, compared with one another, and the best alternative is chosen. In irrational decision-making processes, one alternative is chosen beforehand, and all the others are hidden from the actors. Brunsson concludes that rational decision-making processes do not generate collective action because rationality creates uncertainty among the actors. This uncertainty is connected with other alternatives becoming visible and the preferences of the actors becoming activated.

Another way of looking at the relation between text and action is to view texts as *incomplete*, which means they must be interpreted in light of a valid local value system. Texts are always ambiguous, which allows for interpretations about how they are to be understood – an uncertainty that somehow has to be dealt with. It is suggested here that this is handled in the ongoing small talk in arenas such as offices, lunchrooms, corridors, and lifts, etc. This small talk concerns, among other things, how directives should be interpreted. It is in fact a rational process that helps to expose and evaluate all alternatives. Out of this small talk process between actors, decisions crystallize about the alternatives that are best for action. Actors can agree on a certain alternative because, after lots of talk comparing it with other alternatives, it is judged to be the best. Thus, a decision shared by the actors is reproduced, as are ideas about how things are or should be.

This can be illustrated with some examples from the empirical data. The police officers in the study work with what is known as neighbour-hood policing. In short, this means that they fight 'everyday crime' by working to achieve certain goals, and try to do so by following a flexible working plan. The idea is that the police officers plan their work around the type of crime that they have to fight. This has been described in written form in a text produced by the neighbourhood police chief, and it runs as follows: 'Police officers are to plan their work schedule in modules, on a basis of the types of crime upon which the operating plans themselves are based.'

Many officers use this kind of period planning to schedule their work so that it corresponds with the times when they want to work. Some officers prefer long periods of consecutive days off, others choose to work only in the evenings. Small talk serves as an arena where limits can be tested and possible sanctions for exceeding the limits can be evaluated. Decisions about how the text of the directives should be interpreted are made and transmitted to other parts of the police force. Consider, for example, the following passage of small talk, in which the exchanges between the police officers concern another officer's interpretation of the text. The subject of discussion is the possibility of arranging a lot of time off under the period-planning system.

> P1: 'Think about it – Tommy has had five days off, worked for two, and then he was off five days again. Then he took his holiday so he was off for another twelve more days. I don't imagine that's very popular.'

> P2: 'No, I shouldn't think so. But did anyone go for him about it?'

> P1: 'Not that I know of.'

The police officers then concluded that period planning is a good thing and almost anything can be 'fixed'.

This sort of fixing can gain precedence. For example, the *Tommy* story makes the rounds as a concrete example of how the text can (should!?) be interpreted.

The following example of small talk shows how the decision about 'how to fix your own hours to work' spreads through the force. Two police officers are discussing police work (specifically, working hours), when one of them declares:

> 'That's why people want this job. It's great to be able to decide for yourself when you're going to work. If it weren't for this, most of the officers would probably be trying to get out.'

The above decision was not associated with any sanctions that were regarded as 'serious'. And where decisions are associated with tougher sanctions, this is hidden and reproduced in small talk. In the case of police work, legal texts are a good example of this.

Texts can also be 'disqualified' by the actors because they don't give any 'workable' directives. An example could be some all-embracing text on police work dealing with police intervention, although it is supported in the law. The fact that such a text (law!) can be disqualified is reflected in the norm of 'street justice'. In my study, I found that most police officers believe that people who disturb the peace should be dealt with. And they do deal with this, at times without the support of any text in the law, but simply in line with the 'street justice' norm. The following episode is an example of how such a decision (to disregard a text) is made in practice and then spreads through the force distributed in 'hidden' small talk. The police officers conducted a check on a man without the support of the law, and one of the officers describes how he confiscated things from the man without recording it in any report (which policemen are obliged to do):

> P1: 'What've we got here?' (Starting to walk towards someone lying across the pavement.)

The officers approach the man and shake his legs to wake him up.

> P2: 'Have you got your ID?'
>
> X: 'No.'
>
> P1: 'How about emptying your pockets of any sharp objects[1] we might prick ourselves on, and put them right here.'

The man slowly starts doing what he is told, and when he is finished, the police go through his pockets and turn them inside out. They then run an identity check on him from his tattooing,[2] and when they are sure he is not wanted, they ask him to move on. The police officers then continue their patrolling on foot. One of them (P2, above) explains that strictly speaking it was not right to check this man out as there was no 'real suspicion', but added, '... you have to check to see if they have drugs or not'.

Another officer describes how he had run into the same man once before. On that occasion he had taken needles and knives off him, and disposed of them in a waste bin without recording it in any report. 'You have to keep them on a tight rein' [he says with a snigger].

This kind of small talk is kept hidden, that is to say, hidden from those responsible for setting and enforcing sanctions in the department. It only goes on between fellow police officers.

Small talk replaces hierarchy

This type of small talk is a horizontal process that occurs over time in interaction between police officers. The norm-construction process inherent in small talk can on occasion replace the traditional hierarchic leadership constructions provided by texts and managerial talk. In the present case, the construction of small talk has two main ingredients. Firstly, it contains experience from practical work. Secondly, in their conversations the police have substituted themselves for those who are formally their managers. Practical police work then has to build on the 'real' world, a world that only the police officers understand. Consider the following example from small talk between police officers discussing their managers – those formally in charge of them.

> 'The managers are no good, and they're often at the wrong level. They don't understand the reality of the situation. Take Hedström, for instance, he just doesn't understand that we sign out cars because we do need transportation. He's always griping about it, but of course we don't take any notice.'

Thus, formal management is replaced by the police officers' interpretations of reality. Managers are replaced by role models – in this case older police officers, officers with experience from the real world and still working as policemen. In addition, police officers classify themselves according to years of experience, whereby the senior police officers serve as role models for the younger ones. Many years' experience of police work then carries authority, since police work – according to the officers themselves – can only be learned by doing it. Senior officers thus operate as role models and, as such, also as leaders. This 'hierarchy of experience' is further illustrated in the following example, in which several police officers in a bus taking them to the central square are deciding who should work with whom. The decision is made quickly and without argument:

P1: 'How shall we split up for this?'

P2: 'I'll go ... and Mats.'

One of the policemen (P2, above) is able to make this decision because he is the senior person on the bus and thus ranks highest in the hierarchy of experience. It is a hierarchy of which everyone keeps track, and voicing it aloud is not necessary. It is strong and gender-independent, as can be seen in a comment made by one of the women officers interviewed:

'Pia, Rutger and Klas are the ones we listen to.'

These three officers are the ones with the most experience of the neighbourhood precinct in the study.

It is difficult for formal managers to compete with the senior police officers, since it is the latter who make the decisions. This is illustrated below in small talk about senior officers and formal managers (the latter represented here by Hedström, the neighbourhood police chief). It takes place during a bus trip, and the talk turns to the vandalism squad at Söderport, one of the entry points to the city.

'Hedström doesn't dare to touch that lot. The old "fogies" are there, and he wouldn't risk getting across it with them. All the younger ones have left the squad and there's only the old guys left.'

The police officers manage their work themselves, taking senior officers as their role models. They decide what's going to be done, and how and when. The fact that they work like this – independently in relation to the hierarchy and making their own decisions vis-à-vis the civilians they meet on the job – is reflected in the following excerpt from a conversation between two police officers about their work:

'It's really great, in fact. We're pretty free to do what we want, and we can work pretty much when we want.'

Or the following comment by an officer talking about a written directive on traffic in the city at night:

'Söderport is closed to traffic after 11 p.m. and there are a lot of one-way streets. This is something I'm pretty lenient about. It's just not reasonable to write tickets for driving in here; I never do it. It's like a good friend told me: police are here to make up for bad politics. There's a lot of truth in that.'

The fact that police officers manage their work themselves is also something that came up in interviews with the officers in the study. One woman officer with six years' experience, said:

'You regulate your work yourself. If you don't want to see something, you can just walk past – if you prefer to get involved and want to do something about it there's always work to do. It is up to the individual.'

Thus, the autonomy of police officers vis-à-vis the formal hierarchy (both managers and texts) is evident.

Horizontal organizations

The possibility of managing on a basis of the texts is limited. If texts are to be used, they must be interpreted, and since texts are imperfect and can never be all-embracing, they are seldom associated with any sanctions that could be regarded as 'serious'. In small talk between actors, the texts are discussed and different interpretations are negotiated. Limits on the freedom to act are explored, as well as possible sanctions for overstepping these limits. In the process of small talk, directives are complemented and in some cases 'disqualified'.

The decision process revolving round the directives takes place in an arena that is not the one in which the directive texts were created. The decisions are made in an arena, to which those who would enforce any sanctions (or those who produce the texts) do not necessarily have access, namely the arena of the actors' small talk. Small talk takes place between individuals, and in confidence. Trust between individuals is something that is built up over time, and is founded on genuine or ideal-based relations.

In this chapter I have argued that traditional vertical management (with or without written directives) is replaced by management constructions produced in a horizontal process between individuals. This horizontal interaction becomes dominant, and small talk between police officers is the process in which management is constructed and reproduced. The vertical forces, management hierarchies and hence also the written directives associated with these play a less important part. Texts and managers are things one has 'a relation to', not things one identifies with. The actors do not construct leadership together with any managers, nor do they automatically consult the texts to seek guidance. In some instances, they compare their actions with the legal texts or some manager's interpretation. The horizontal hierarchy described is possible in a work environment that varies and is difficult to control, where there is little or no system of reasonably close and continuous vertical management, and the work is directed to a large extent by abstract texts whose sanctions are not considered 'serious'.

It is worth considering how far these results are generally applicable, and whether horizontal small-talk processes may dominate over hierarchies in other organizations and environments as well.

It could be suggested that organized human action – as it has been defined here – is often characterized by its enormous variety and its inaccessibility to control, and by the fact that formal managers often work far away from the action. This is true primarily of certain professions – medicine, dentistry, teaching, to name a few. There is also the element of bureaucracy at the grass roots level, among people working in government sectors and who are exposed to the public in all sorts of situations. Social workers are a good example here.

In addition, we must also recognize that small talk exists everywhere and in all organizations. And virtually all directives, verbal or written, are subject to different interpretations. Small talk plays a part – a part that often presupposes trust between the individuals interacting with one another and one that moulds the understandings of those individuals. It is in the process of small talk that the norms are formed and then used to navigate human actions in environments where many demands collide and converge – regardless of how variable the practice may be and irrespective of the distance between the managers and the practice of everyday.

Notes

1 The reference here is to needles used by drug addicts.
2 That is, in the ISP Registry that allows police to check a person's identity by their tattoos or other known identifying marks. This is a channel used for finding people that are wanted by the police for questioning or for some other reason.

References

Brunsson, N. (1985). *The Irrational Organisation*. Wiley, Chichester.
Ekman, G. (1999). *Från text till batong. Om Poliser, busar och svennar.* Stockholm: EFI.
Elster, J. (1989). *The Cement of Society. A Study of Social Order.* Cambridge University Press, Cambridge.

Fielding, N. (1988). *Joining Forces*. Routledge, New York.

Gustafsson, C. (1994). *Produktion av allvar*. Nerenius & Santerus, Stockholm.

Homan, G. C. (1950). *The Human Group*. Harcourt, Brace, New York.

Jacobsson, B., and Brunsson, N. (1998). *Standardisering*. Nerenius & Santerus, Stockholm.

Kunda, G., and Barley, S. R. (1998). *Bringing Work Back In*. Conference Paper, Scancore Stanford University, 20–22 Sept.

March, J. G., and Olsen, J. P. (1989). *Rediscovering Institutions. The Organizational Basis of Politics*. The Free Press, New York.

March, J. G., and Olsen, J. P. (1998). *The Institutional Dynamics of International Political Orders*. Working Paper, Scancore, Stanford University.

Napier, R. W., and Gershenfeld, M. K. (1993). *Groups, Theory and Experience*. Houghton Mifflin Company, Boston.

Sjöstrand, S-E. (1973). *Företagsorganisation. En taxonomisk ansats*. EFI, Stockholm.

Sjöstrand, S-E. (1985). *Samhällsorganisation*. Doxa, Lund.

Sjöstrand, S-E. (1987). *Organisationsteori*. Studentlitteratur, Lund.

Sjöstrand, S-E. (1997). *The Two Faces of Management. The Janus Factor*. Thomson, London.

Skolnick, H. J. (1994). *Justice Without Trial*. Macmillan College Publishing, New York.

Svensson, L. G. (1989). Teori och praktik i professionellas vardagsarbete, in Selander, S. (ed.) *Kampen om yrkesutövning, status och kunskap*, pp. 183–210, Studentlitteratur, Lund.

■ CHAPTER THIRTEEN ■

Managing positions or people?

Birgitta Södergren and Johan Söderholm

Introduction

Can knowledge-intensive work be managed and evaluated by applying quantitative measures? Can management-by-numbers, originally developed for traditional industrial or service production, be used for managing knowledge-intensive units?

These questions were raised during our research for two empirical studies, about the performance of knowledge-intensive work (Södergren, 2001) and managing-by-objectives in two service organizations (Söderholm, 1998).

This chapter explores, from a constructionist perspective, what happens when the management-by-numbers construction clashes with the specialists' construction of what knowledge-intensive work actually is. First the management-by-numbers construction is discussed, its basic assumptions, and why it has become so popular. It is followed by analysis of how knowledge-intensive work is constructed. Finally, we will look at some of the problems that can arise from the clash between managing-by-numbers and knowledge-intensive work.

Managing-by-numbers – an important part of the management construction

We believe that managerial leadership is a combination of several social constructions (Berger and Luckman, 1966) under constant reproduction both inside and outside the organization. An increasingly important construction is the one known as management-by-numbers, a term coined by Townley (1995) in her study of accounting. The management-by-numbers construction emphasizes the need for measurements in the management of organizations. Two popular and oft-quoted catchphrases are: 'What gets measured gets done' (see Roos et al., 1997) or 'If you can't measure it you can't manage it' (see Edvinsson and Malone, 1997). In short, without measurement there can be no management.

According to the available literature in the field of management, the management-by-numbers construction would appear to have many positive qualities: it co-ordinates work and reduces the risk for suboptimization in work (Drucker, 1954), it has a positive motivating effect, almost regardless of which motivational theory the researchers believe in, and it seems to offer recognition, feedback, self-actualization, monetary rewards, and fair competition (Söderholm, 1998). Contemporary literature on management-by-numbers focuses on the ability of the system to improve customer value, strategic competence, and the ability to innovate, and to increase organizational learning and the potential for predicting the future (Kaplan and Norton, 1996; Edvinsson and Malone, 1997).

Westerlund and Sjöstrand (1979/1975) argue that the need to provide some measure of efficiency is perhaps driven mainly by people's need to be identified as being good or bad at doing some particular thing. Another motivating factor is that measurements help to reduce managerial uncertainty: managers may feel they are doing their managerial job well, when they implement this seemingly efficient management control system.

Measures also offer information that is easy to grasp, that can be presented to the managers, to the superiors, to the boards or to outside groups who want to know more about how the business is doing. The ability to provide these numbers then projects an image of management as being up-to-date and in control of the situation. In short, management-by-numbers increases co-ordination, learning, motivation, control and legitimacy, and it is sometimes believed that each individual measure in itself can actually provide all these positive benefits (Söderholm, 1998).

Managing-by-numbers has a long tradition

Managers have long been engaged in monitoring and measuring organizational outcomes. Profitability, sales and market share have commonly been used as measures. As early as 1954, Drucker describes the advantages of management-by-objectives, which relies heavily on measurement as a key element. Many researchers found that when firms decentralized their operations, they often created centralized management control systems based on financial measures. This has been criticized for promoting short-sightedness and analytic detachment (Hayes and Abernathy, 1980). After all, the financial side of a business is only one of many important aspects.

A common response to this has been to introduce the measurement of non-financial aspects. Although non-financial measures, too, have a long history, they seem to have exploded in numbers in recent years. The measurement of quality has expanded into a comprehensive management philosophy – *Total Quality Management*. Simple customer surveys have developed into elaborate indexes for customer service and/or corporate image. Some companies produce and distribute an annual environmental report of all their environmental measures.

More recently, there has also been an increasing focus on measuring the company's workforce and the knowledge the workers represent. A growing number of personnel surveys have been used to measure leadership quality and attitudes (e.g. Gröjer and Stark, 1974; Cascio, 1986; Gröjer and Johansson, 1992). The search for ways to measure knowledge has led to the introduction of concepts and methods such as Intellectual Capital (Stewart, 1997; Edvinsson and Malone, 1997). This method can result in about a hundred new measures. Another similar method, Knowledge Management, formalizes and structures knowledge by using IT systems.

Some management philosophies attempt to integrate financial and new non-financial measures into a single model. The Balanced Scorecard (Kaplan and Norton, 1996) and the Diagnostic Control System (Simons, 1995) are two such models. By integrating several measures, linking each measure to an overall strategy and discussing future events, it is hoped that these models will avoid earlier criticism of shortsightedness, analytic detachment and too much focus on the past. Advocates of management-by-numbers are constantly looking for new ways to cope with knowledge-intensive and rapidly changing organizations.

Management-by-numbers as a language

From our constructivist perspective it is interesting to note the claim made by many authors of such integrated models that the models do not create efficiency in themselves, but they do create an arena or common language between management and local units. This can be interpreted in different ways. One interpretation is that management tries to increase its control over the business by creating its own form of language. Another interpretation is that the search for a shared view of the different aspects of a business in numerical form, gives a sense of safety and security – mainly to the managers (see Westerlund and Sjöstrand, 1979/1975). A third interpretation is that with the help of these measurements, management can create an arena for a more focused dialogue with important people in the operating core and thus increase organizational learning (see Olve et al., 1997). But what, more exactly, is management-by-numbers?

Managing-by-numbers as a social construction

As with all social constructions the definition of management-by-numbers varies according to who is doing the defining. However, the differences are small and many authors even use the same metaphor, namely the thermostat, to describe the principles of management-by-numbers. The construction can be seen as a rational step-by-step model of how to manage an organization. It specifies the actions managers should perform to become good managers. The manager should:

■   Define the objective or objectives of the organizational unit.

■   Develop ways of measuring this objective.

■   Commit themselves and/or their subordinates to obtaining a certain level in terms of this measurement. Here, subordinates should feel as if they have promised to achieve this level.

■   Evaluate how subordinate managers/units perform in relation to this goal.

■   Take corrective actions if the goal cannot be achieved. Since managers so often focus on exceptionally good or bad performances, Simons (1995) calls this 'management-by-exception'.

■   Reward subordinate, when the goal is achieved. This final step has been contested both in the academic literature and among practitioners, and is not always a part of the model.

So far, we have discussed the management-by-numbers construction without mentioning its basic assumptions, of which there are several:

■   It is possible to develop a pre-set goal. All work in a company should aim towards fulfilling a pre-set goal. Work that does not fulfil the goal should be minimized.

- The aspects of work can be measured in numbers. Otherwise, it is impossible to set measurable goals.

- Managers should control their employees' performance.

- It is possible to define boundaries between units and/or work roles. Otherwise, it is not possible to see who is responsible for the measured results.

- The manager should take corrective actions if goals are not achieved. One corrective action may be to remove any of the subordinates concerned from their posts.

These assumptions, with minor variations, are commonly held by several researchers (see e.g. Westerlund and Sjöstrand, 1979/1975; Merchant, 1985; Johansson and Östman, 1992; Simons, 1995).

As will be shown, the measures themselves are not much of a problem. The basic assumptions behind management-by-numbers, however, do seem to be problematic when it comes to managing knowledge-intensive units.

The empirical basis

The discussion in this chapter is based on empirical findings from our research on knowledge-intensive workers (KIWs) and staff specialists in large organizations. One study deals with the working conditions of specialists in high-tech companies (Södergren, 2001). In this study, 32 specialists were interviewed about their knowledge-intensive work, and about how they and their work were managed. The specialists/KIWs in this study (engineers, lawyers, chemists, IT experts, physicists, etc.) all held some kind of specialist position. They were all employed in large organizations, i.e. they did not work as freelance consultants or as managers (with the exception of temporary assignments as project leaders). The other study focused on the management-by-objectives system in business units and staff units in two service firms (Söderholm, 1998). The majority of the interviews, more than 40 in all, concerned managerial work, but some concerned specialist work. The interviews focused on how the respondents experienced measurements and other management tools.

The managers interviewed seldom expressed any clash or contradiction between management-by-numbers and knowledge-intensive work. We have no examples of any experts actively resisting any measurement system. On the other hand, our studies consistently show that the two constructions have few similarities. When knowledge-intensive workers discuss their managers, they focus on aspects other than measurements. They regard measurements as a marginal and sometimes useless management tool. When the managers (and the management literature) discussed management, they stressed measurements as an important part of managing. Some were even rather emotional about it.

It seems that the knowledge-intensive workers, with their knowledge construction, find it difficult to talk to the managers with their management-by-numbers construction.

Why is this strongly held management construction so weak in knowledge-intensive units? This puzzling issue will be analysed after providing a description of what knowledge-intensive work actually means.

What is knowledge-intensive work?

Knowledge-intensive work can be described in different ways. Earlier literature on the subject focuses on:

- Work in knowledge-intensive units, where the focus is on KIWs or intellectual work (Starbuck, 1992).

- Research into what is special about work in professional organizations (cf. Freidson, 1986; Selander, 1989; Granberg, 1996).

- Literature on specialists in high technology organizations (cf. Kunda, 1992; Pelz and Andrews, 1966).

Knowledge-intensive, professional and specialist work can be defined in several ways, and it is difficult to draw a clear line between these and other forms of work. It is sometimes argued, for instance, that all kinds of work are knowledge-intensive, and that it is only a matter of how we define 'knowledge'.

However, several researchers claim that professionals/specialists/KIWs represent a special category of employees: not blue-collar workers and not managers, but rather a 'third kind' in the working world (Freidson, 1986). Freidson also points out that studies of traditional industrial work have little analytic value in the professional employees' understanding of the situation.

Professionals and specialists are sometimes, though not always, authorized by way of some kind of system of credentials (e.g. occupational licence, certificate, or specialized education). Sometimes a professional trade of sorts evolves, characterized by common professional ethics, fraternities, etc. (i.e. a strong social construction is developed around the professional category).

It would be beyond the purpose of this chapter to elaborate too much on the question of defining knowledge-intensive work. However, the US National Labor Relations Board states in its formal definition of 'professional employees', that such employees are engaged in work:

- that is predominantly intellectual and varied in character;

- that involves the consistent exercise of discretion and judgement in its performance;

- that is of such a character that the result accomplished cannot be standardized in relation to a given period of time;

- that requires knowledge of an advanced type in a field of science or learning customarily acquired by a prolonged course of specialized intellectual instruction or study in an institution of higher learning (Freidson, 1986).

The work of the specialists/KIWs in our studies is generally characterized by great complexity, and the expected quality or success of their output is often hard to judge in advance (and sometimes even in retrospect). More often than not they work 'on the verge of the unknown', and accordingly have vague job descriptions. Their work depends to a substantial degree on personal judgement and personal intuition. Their work is primarily immaterial, assuming the form of analyses, problem-solving, etc. The output of their work is not only physical, such as the number of jobs done, problems solved, projects completed, but is also and above all knowledge. A knowledge-intensive unit is constantly adding to the intellectual capital of the firm.

To put it another way, managing a knowledge-intensive unit means developing and increasing the amount of knowledge that can be used in future business. In organizations that deliver knowledge-intensive goods or services, quality is very closely related to the capacity to learn and reproduce knowledge (Stein, 1996). It is therefore interesting to discuss how management control systems affect learning and knowledge creation.

Management and knowledge workers seem to speak different languages

We have found that management and knowledge-intensive workers frequently use different languages. The following quotations from a computer engineer are typical of the knowledge-intensive workers.

> 'How do you work with a new problem? There are lots of questions that pop up and need to be solved. You don't know how to start, but piece by piece the puzzle eventually fits together. You have to read a lot. It's a mixture of public knowledge and knowledge that supposedly doesn't exist. You have to call people and figure out why things are the way they are. It's a dialogue and you're a part in developing this new knowledge.
>
> [...] By the time you can formalize the knowledge, teach courses and write it down, it's almost too late – the knowledge has reached maturity. On the other hand, that's important too. One problem for both management and us is that we seldom take the time to document it when we're finished.'

Compare the above quotation with the following one from the literature of management-by-numbers.

> 'The use of measurements as a language helps translate complex and frequently nebulous concepts into more precise ideas, that align and mobilize all individuals into actions directed at attaining organizational objectives.'
>
> (Kaplan and Norton, 1996, p. 270)

From a social constructionist perspective we appear to be dealing with two separate constructions, which are not in accord with each other. Knowledge-intensive workers argue that management control systems are of limited importance, or sometimes even disturbing. Management, in turn, sees it as a problem when knowledge-intensive workers do not take part in management information and discussions. The KIWs hold the same view as management, but they put it the other way round:

> 'You can't help feeling sorry for the management. They've lost the ability to take part in the most strategically important dialogue – the one that occurs at the organizational core.'

The lack of dialogue between management and knowledge-intensive workers may be due to the above-mentioned fact, trivial as it may seem, that knowledge-intensive workers produce knowledge. We believe there are several possible explanations of the phenomena that emerge from the analysis of the basic assumptions of the two constructions. Three aspects of this will be discussed in this chapter.

Firstly, knowledge work is loaded with tacit knowledge, which is hard to measure. Secondly, knowledge work requires constant redefinition, as well as interaction between individuals and a network that crosses many organizational borders. It is consequently difficult to establish clear boundaries between units. Thirdly, knowledge-intensive work often requires constant and informal learning, while management control systems are based, as their name would suggest, on a controlling logic. As we shall soon see, knowledge-intensive work challenges the basic assumptions of the management-by-numbers construction regarding measurability, clear boundaries and controllability.

Knowledge-intensive work is loaded with tacit knowledge

Our study of knowledge-intensive work shows that it is based to a high degree on tacit knowledge. Tacit knowledge, following Polanyi's classical work (1967), is defined as the knowing we cannot explicitly tell. Tacit knowledge has a specific from-to direction. The individual's attention is directed *from* formal facts, details, etc. and *to* the underlying meaning, the practical implications and thus to a deeper understanding of the field (see also Sandberg and Targama, 1998). Polanyi (1967) illustrates this with a male concert pianist who might become 'paralysed' if he pays too much attention to the finger settings, but creates great art if he dwells on the musical experience. The pianist's attention is directed *from* the technical details *to* the result, the music. Likewise, skilled doctors are better able to make their diagnoses by looking beyond the separate facts at hand, in other words if they shift their attention away *from* formal knowledge such as symptoms, test results, etc. and *to* the patient as an individual.

Polanyi also argues that a scientist or technician uses tacit knowledge to identify problems that a layman cannot even perceive. Tacit knowledge also helps the specialist to recognize a good solution and become convinced that it will have fruitful implications in the future. Tacit knowledge has many roots, and according to Polanyi its important ingredients include empathy, insight and experience.

Polanyi argues that theories and facts are indeed important aspects of knowledge creation, and that by learning more facts and theory you create a basis for tacit knowledge (just as pianists must do their scales), but also that it is not until you are able to incorporate or internalize these theories that you are able to make new discoveries. That is to say, innovation is achieved when you no longer see the theories as theories, but start to use them to create meaning of a higher order.

The experts and specialists in our studies frequently spoke of the importance of tacit knowledge in their work, albeit without using those very words. Since the term 'tacit knowledge' is hardly widespread in the corporate world, it is also rarely used. Instead, the phenomenon is referred to as *fingerspitzgefühl*, business intuition, experience, educated guesses, beliefs, suspicions, inklings and hints. 'We can't explain why we had to follow this track – we just knew we had to', said one respondent, smiling rather sheepishly.

This embarrassment may be a sign that tacit knowledge is not really accepted as 'true' knowledge. Polanyi notes this as well, but concludes that it is a widespread misbelief that details should be more true just because they are more tangible. It is rather empathy with other people or problems that creates full knowledge.

Thus the use of traditional social engineering techniques to focus on specific parts or details of complex knowledge may 'destroy' some of the tacit dimension, instead of producing greater clarity (see also Hansson, 1998). As Polanyi (1967) puts it:

'We can see now how an unbridled lucidity can destroy our understanding of complex matters. Scrutinize closely the particulars of a comprehensive entity and their meaning is effaced, our conception of the entity is destroyed [...]. Meticulous detailing may obscure beyond recall a subject [...].' (pp. 18–19)

One of the communication experts in our study expressed similar concern about the focus on measurements:

'I'm a bit concerned that we may be giving our higher managers and our board a sense of false security.'

Bohm (1980) argues that fragmentation is one of the greatest dangers to the creation of knowledge. Specialization is necessary, but must be linked to a whole, and the whole must not be allowed to be hidden behind details. He also warns that (numerical or fragmented) measurements may make it difficult to affect change.

'To suppose that measures exist prior to man and independently of him leads, as has been seen, to the "objectification" of man's insight, so that it becomes rigidified and unable to change,

eventually bringing about fragmentation and general confusion.'
(ibid., p. 23)

Another staff manager interviewed also expressed concern about how difficult it was to establish a good dialogue between managers.

'It's not possible today to have a constructive dialogue with the profit area managers, like "don't raise this fee because it will hurt the company as a whole". How can you argue against them, when they have concrete economic goals that are regarded as the "truth" that decisions should be based on?'

Role expansion is important for knowledge-intensive work

As noted above, a basic assumption in the managing-by-numbers construction concerns the possibility of clearly defining knowledge work roles, or knowledge units, in order to be able to measure the work done. This assumption does not seem to fit very well with our findings, or with those of other researchers.

An important reason for this is that, since knowledge-intensive work is complex and linked to several other fields of knowledge, knowledge is not created within the individual or even within the unit. Instead, the 'true' contribution of immaterial knowledge-creation lies in the links, for example between specialists and their environments. This view also accords with a social constructionist perspective on knowledge-creation. As Sandberg has said in Chapter 2 of this volume:

'[...] the social interactions between individuals, rather than the individual mind, is the primary vehicle for developing knowledge.'

Regarding the individual (or specialist unit) as the single bearer of knowledge is thus misleading.

As Freidson (1986) points out, professional knowledge cannot be analysed by way of formal texts about a topic or other indicators, but must be analysed by way of the human interaction that creates the knowledge and transforms it in the course of using it in a practical enterprise. Formal knowledge is transformed and modified every day by the activities of those participating in its application.

Knowledge is therefore created more often by transferring knowledge between, rather than within, individuals or units. To regard the individual specialist as the only source of knowledge is therefore also misleading.

The empirical data from this study supports this view. The knowledge-intensive workers interviewed seemed very conscious of this interactive aspect of the nature of knowledge, arguing that their team – rather than they themselves – was the most important base for their personal knowledge. Such teams also seem to be very flexible groups that can be restructured according to the prevailing needs. The group seldom consists of people from the same unit or within the same organizational boundaries, as is illustrated by the following comment from one of our interviewees:

'You get people together, with complementary – and even overlapping – knowledge. The team should reflect knowledge relevant to the project. When the demand for knowledge within the project changes, the project teams must also change.'

(Technical engineer)

The interviewees also say that their contribution to a product or an application is often of a very indirect kind. They may attract knowledge or spread their own knowledge to another unit, thereby contributing to the whole or to the redefining of the problem. The two following excerpts from the interview material illustrate this point.

'One of my work assignments is what we call the x-project [...]. They've drawn an empty box on a chart and said, there is your place. And that's it. They call it the "system object", to have a name for it, and nothing more. You're then supposed to fill this box with whatever's necessary. So I gather people around me and try to grasp what the problems are, and what should be done. And I create a technology meeting, and decision processes. I identify technological problems and take part in the meetings to review the technology. This is how you work. The assignment descriptions are rather vague.'

(IT specialist)

'My job is to create a web of the specialized knowledge that exists in the organization, so that this knowledge can be retrieved or used when it is needed. It's very difficult to foresee when and where this demand will occur [...]. This is sometimes a problem with the managers. They don't see that it's sometimes important to go direct to key people rather than going via the managers themselves.'

(Biopharmacologist)

Working in flexible teams and sometimes 'invisible' networks seems to be a common element in the knowledge-intensive work. Knowledge-intensive workers seem to make their biggest contribution when they are spreading their knowledge, not when they are gathering it. In other words, the biggest contributions made to the creation of knowledge by these workers are also the most difficult to trace. Their knowledge has become an integrated part of the tacit knowledge of the recipient.

Another reason why it can be difficult to establish clear boundaries or roles for knowledge work is that the role of the knowledge-intensive worker seems to be constantly changing.

Because of the variety of tasks and problems that they encounter during their work, and because they have to work on the verge of the unknown, specialized professionals or knowledge-intensive workers tend to draw on a mixture of professional work roles. That is, they play different roles in different work contexts. In one case they may be the leading expert and in another just a marginal contributor. In some cases they may act as a project leader, in others they are a member of the team. At times, they need to engage in hands-on production or implementation activities. Their role vis-à-vis the customer may also vary. In one case they may collaborate very closely with customers or clients, working almost like an employee, while in other cases their role is more that of a negotiation partner.

Similarly, the question of who they actually represent may not be altogether clear. It is not unusual for them to act on behalf of top management, and even to exercise formal authority vis-à-vis other members of the organization. It is also common that people with specialized knowledge serve as consultants to line managers or local units. Sometimes it may also be unclear whether their professional identity or their organizational identity should guide their behaviour, perhaps because their individual interpretation of the ethical principles of their profession collides with the strategic decisions of top management. It was striking to hear how informally and seemingly without friction the interviewed specialists would take on quite different work roles, often without even reflecting upon it. They tend to move quite freely, and without any great loss of prestige, between the roles of manager and consultant, and between customer-oriented and expert/professional thinking.

They are thus continually engaged in what might be called role redefinition and role expansion (Södergren, 1998), and this data indicates that such redesigning of work roles may in fact be essential to the development and use of knowledge in an organization. It did also happen, however, that the interviewed specialists reported feelings of frustration due to their conflicting roles, especially when they were expected to act as consultant and authority at one and the same time.

Why, then, should there be a problem with numerical evaluation, just because an individual's work role varies over time? The problem is not the existence of such measurements in themselves. They may be useful in many situations. The risk is rather that these measurements may stifle the flexibility of the work roles. Measurement is usually based on a single role and attempts to establish a strict definition of the employee's work role, which in turn tends to restrict that person's ability to act and react freely to the various contexts and problems he or she may encounter. If there is too much focus on formal measures, then too much attention may turn on achieving greater numbers and higher goals, and on ensuring that the results of these efforts are made visible. There is therefore a risk that specialists will be less inclined to work towards the good of the organization as a whole, and will concentrate instead on proving themselves to be competent specialists. This may destroy the invisible networks or webs that are so essential to knowledge-creation.

Measuring systems require role conformity, while a 'competence logic' demands the expansion or redefinition of roles. The conflicting foci may hinder the creation of a learning organization as well as inhibiting a constructive dialogue between management and specialists.

Learning vs. control

The following are some of the typical responses of the knowledge-intensive workers when they were asked about the type of leadership they needed:

'A knowledge leader [...] who inspires continuous learning.'

'Someone you can talk to.'

'Managers who ask more than they declaim.'

'A processor or catalyst in a dialogue.'

'A *primus inter pares* – first among equals.'

These answers suggest a type of leadership that could be labelled the 'leadership of learning' (see also Södergren and Fredriksson, 1998).

Surprisingly, perhaps, the KIWs seem to prefer rich and intensive leadership. They accept the managers' superior position and want their leadership to be based on dialogue and personal interaction. This accords well with the discussion above about the nature of knowledge production.

Another surprising point is the rarity of any suggestion that managers should state clear goals and visions. It seems as though the knowledge-intensive workers have already grasped these things for themselves. And whenever visions are mentioned, it is often with an infusion of social and human values.

Although the new philosophies of management-by-numbers often speak about the need for dialogue, they seldom encourage the kind of dialogue that knowledge-intensive workers long for. While management-by-numbers methods seem to be successful in creating a functional dialogue between top managers and non-specialist managers (Söderholm, 1998), they fail to achieve a similar dialogue between top managers and specialists. Information gained from formal measurements are often not enough to base knowledge-developing decisions on. Perhaps the language created by these measurement systems just does not seem relevant to the knowledge-intensive workers. Perhaps such formal management systems simply serve as an excuse for management not to engage in a discussion that they do not fully comprehend (Sjöstrand, 1997). Instead of creating a common language, the evaluative methods used in management-by-numbers make the separation of the two languages even more marked.

The problem may lie in the basic assumption underlying such management systems – namely, that managers should be able to control and evaluate important aspects of the organization. We have found that these management tools can produce a sense of control that reinforces the hierarchical relation between professionals and managers, thereby creating a defensive climate rather than opening up opportunities for an unbiased dialogue. This in turn seems to cramp any learning dialogue more than the information gained from the measurements enhances it.

> 'The positive thing about this company is its recent reorientation towards the markets. But at the same time management must be more open to signals from within the organization. We have a number of really great products that started as "hidden work" in our basement, and they've become winners. A changing situation can suddenly provide an opportunity to do something new and exciting. This is where I really miss a true dialogue.'
>
> (Technical engineer)

Conclusion

This chapter has looked at some of the reasons why numerical evaluation systems are something of a problem in knowledge-intensive areas of organizations. In such areas, tacit knowledge plays an important part, and we have argued that the development and application of tacit knowledge may even be harmed by excessively sophisticated numerical measurement systems. To rephrase the well-known dictum quoted at the beginning of this chapter, the suggestion is that *what gets measured may not get done.*

It has been argued that the interactive nature of knowledge-creation can make it difficult to measure this process. In measuring the results of knowledge-creation, it is not possible to establish clear boundaries between people or units. It is also argued that the reverse also applies: when such measurement systems are used, they can hinder the really effective knowledge-creating processes.

It has been suggested that the kind of leadership based on learning that the specialists prefer does not accord with a leadership based on extensive control and evaluation.

We are certainly not against numerical evaluations in knowledge organizations. On the contrary, a few basic measurements such as measures of costs and revenues or simple measures of volume or productivity, are likely to be both useful and widely accepted, and certainly give top management a basic tool for monitoring organizational efficiency. Nor do we advocate that 'clever people' should be left alone out of sight to do whatever they think is right, without being subject to any kind of evaluation.

Instead, our concern is about the tendency to let numerical evaluation systems become increasingly complex and, in many cases, to let them replace other forms of personal contact. Since professional and knowledge-intensive work is based to a high degree on tacit knowledge, there is a risk of energy being redirected away from the intricate development of qualitative, professional skills and towards the measurement and evaluation of formal, explicit and measurable action. And we are convinced that in the long run top managers are the losers, since they tend to be decoupled from the essence of the knowledge base that they are actually supposed to be managing.

Many decisions made by organizational specialists are in reality extremely important to the strategy of the firm, since their decisions often have a considerable impact on the core business. This means that what they need is a dialogue based on mutual respect and some degree of guidance about what action to take, but not voluminous data reports. As we see it, there is an obvious need in many organizations to make more room for learning, dialogue and the development of the tacit dimension.

Or, as David Bohm (1980) put it:

'[...] when measuring is identified with the very essence of reality, *this* is illusion'. (p. 23)

References

Alvesson, M. (1995). *Management of Knowledge-intensive Companies*. De Gruyter, Berlin.

Berger, P. and Luckmann, T. (1966). *The Social Construction of Reality*. Anchor Books, New York.

Bohm, D. (1980). *Wholeness and the Implicate Order*. Routledge, London.

Bohm, D. (1996). *On Dialogue*. Routledge, London.

Cascio, W. (1982). *Costing Human Resources: The Financial Impact of Behavior in Organizations*. Kent, Boston.

Drucker, P. (1954). *The Practice of Management*. Harper & Row, New York.

Edvinsson, L. and Malone, M. S. (1997). *Intellectual Capital – The Proven Way to Establish your Company's True Value by Finding its Hidden Brainpower*. Currency Doubleday, New York.

Ekman, G. (1999). *Från text till batong*. EFI, Stockholm.

Freidson, E. (1986). *Professional Powers*. University of Chicago Press, Chicago.

Granberg, O. (1996). *Lärande i organisationer*. Stockholms Universitet, Stockholm.

Gröjer J. E., and Johansson, U. (1992). *Personalekonomisk Redovisning och Kalkylering*. Arbetarskyddsnämnden, Stockholm.

Gröjer, J. E., and Stark, A. (1974). *The State of Social Accounting*. Stockholms Universitet, Stockholm.

Gustavsson, C. (1994). *Produktion av allvar*. Nerénius & Santerus, Stockholm.

Hansson, J. (1998). *Intellectual Capital – The Latest Trick to Make Management Scientific?* Cepro, Stockholm. Web-publication, see www.cepro.se

Hayes, R. and Abernathy, W. (1980). Managing our way to economic decline. *Harvard Business Review*, July–August, pp. 67–77.

Johansson, S-E., and Östman, L. (1992). *Lönsamhetskrav – redovisningsmått – styrning*. Studentlitteratur, Lund.

Kaplan, R., and Norton, D. (1996). *The Balanced Scorecard*. Harvard Business School Press, Boston.

Kunda, G. (1992). *Engineering Culture – Control and Commitment in a High-Tech Corporation*. Temple University Press, Philadelphia.

Merchant, K. (1985). *Control in Business Organizations*. Pitman, Marchfield, Massachusetts, USA.

Olve, N-G., Roy, J., and Wetter, M. (1997). *Balanced Scorecard i svensk praktik*. Liber ekonomi, Stockholm.

Östman, L. (1977). *Styrning med redovisningsmått*. EFI, Stockholm.

Pelz, D. and Andrews, F. (1996). *Scientists in Organizations*. John Wiley & Sons, New York.

Polanyi, M. (1967). *The Tacit Dimension*. Routledge, London.

Rombach, B. (1991). *Det går inte att styra med mål*. Studentlitteratur, Lund.

Roos, J. et al. (1997). *Intellectual Capital. Navigating in the Business Landscape*. Macmillan Business, London.

Sandberg, J. and Targama, A. (1998). *Ledning och förståelse – Ett kompetensperspektiv på organisationer*. Studentlitteratur, Lund.

Selander, S. (ed.) (1989). *Kampen om yrkesutövning, status och kunskap – Professionaliseringens sociala grund*. Studentlitteratur, Lund.

Simons, R. (1995) *Levers of Control – How Managers Use Innovative Control Systems to Drive Strategic Renewal*. Harvard Business School Press, Boston.

Sjöstrand, S-E. (1997). *The Two Faces of Management – The Janus Factor*. Thomson, London.

Södergren, B. (1998). *På väg mot en horisontell organisation*. EFI, Stockholm.

Södergren, B., and Fredriksson, L. (1998). *Ledarskap i en lärande organisation – lärdomar och idéer*. Arbetsgivarverket, Stockholm.

Södergren, B. (2001). *Kunskapsarbetaren – om villkoren för specialister i arbetslivet*.

Söderholm, J. (1998). *Målstyrning av decentraliserade organisationer – Styrning mot finansiella och icke-finansiella mål*. EFI, Stockholm.

Starbuck, W. (1992). *Learning by Knowledge-intensive Firms*, Conference paper presented at Knowledge Workers in Contemporary Organisations. Lancaster, 2–4 Sept.

Stewart, T. (1997). *Intellectual Capital. The New Wealth of Organizations*. Currency Doubleday, New York.

Stein, J. (1996). *Lärande inom och mellan organisationer*. Studentlitteratur, Lund.

Townley, B. (1995). Managing by Numbers: Accounting, personnel management and the creation of a mathesis, *Critical Perspectives on Accounting*, vol. 6, pp. 555–75.

Westerlund, G., and Sjöstrand, S-E. (1979/1975). *Organizational Myths*. Harper & Row, London.

Subject index